Tongan Saints
LEGACY OF FAITH

Books of Related Interest from
The Institute for Polynesian Studies

Moramona: The Mormons in Hawaii
R. Lanier Britsch

Mormons in the Pacific: A Bibliography
Russell T. Clement

Southern Cross Saints: The Mormons in Australia
Marjorie Newton

Intensive Course in Tongan
revised edition
Eric B. Shumway

Tongan Saints
LEGACY OF FAITH

TRANSLATED AND EDITED BY
ERIC B. SHUMWAY

Published by
The Institute for Polynesian Studies
Laie, Hawaii

In association with the
Polynesian Cultural Center
Brigham Young University–Hawaii

PUBLISHED AND DISTRIBUTED BY
THE INSTITUTE FOR POLYNESIAN STUDIES
BRIGHAM YOUNG UNIVERSITY–HAWAII
LAIE, HI 96762

© 1991 Eric B. Shumway
All Rights Reserved
Manufactured in the United States of America

First Paperback Edition 1998

LIBRARY OF CONGRESS CATALOGING-IN-PUBLICATION DATA

Shumway, Eric B.,
    Tongan saints: legacy of faith / by Eric B. Shumway.
      p.   cm.
    Includes bibliographical references.
    1. Church of Jesus Christ of Latter-day Saints–Tonga–Biography
2. Mormons–Tonga–Biography. 3. Tonga–Biography. 4. Tonga–Church history–Sources.   I. Title.
BX8693.S57   1991
289.3'092'29612–dc20   91-7947
[B]   CIP
ISBN 0–939154–52–8
ISBN 0–939154–64–1 (pbk)

∞ This book is printed on acid-free paper and meets
the guidelines for permanence and durability
of the Council on Library Resources

Design by Connie Disney
Cover painting by A. L. Garside

Contents

An Apostolic Blessing upon King Taufa'ahau Tupou IV	xi
Chronology of Church Events in Tonga	xiii
Acknowledgements	xxxiii
Preface	xxxv
Introduction	1

PART I
BEGINNINGS, 1891–1926
THE SEEDS OF FAITH

1. John Alexander Nelson, Jr.
   The Gifts of the Holy Spirit — 43

2. Frank Winn
   "Laying the Foundation of a Great Work" — 48

3. Tēvita Pita Pauni
   "The Pestilence That Walketh in Darkness" — 51

4. Talitaufa Vaha Uasila'ā
   "Death, Where Is Thy Sting?" — 55

5. Pī Feleti Maile
   The Faith of My Father — 57

6. 'Elenoa Mē Mataele
   "The Lord Gave and the Lord Hath Taken Away" — 60

PART II
MAKEKE, 1926–47
THE GROWING TREE

7. Ada Layne Cahoon
   "With God Nothing Shall Be Impossible" — 73

8. Sālesi Vānisi
   A Legacy of Prayer — 79

9. 'Iohani and Sālote Wolfgramm
   "And I Will Give You Power to Heal All Manner of Sickness" — 82

10. Filipe Kioa
    One Heart and One Faith — 90

11. Albin ('Alipini) Johannson
    "The Lord Is Good to All" — 93

12. Charles (Siale) 'Ataongo Wolfgramm
    The Work of the Carpenter — 95

13. Ermel J. Morton
    The Gift and Power of Translation — 101

14. Tēvita Muli Kinikini
    Whatsoever I Shall Command Thee Thou Shalt Speak" — 106

15. 'Epalahame and Lilevai Tua'one
    No Greater Cause — 113

16. Solomone and Sālome 'Ulu'ave
    Seeds of Faith and Fruits of Courage — 118

17. Sēmisi Nukumovaha'i Tonga
    "A Refiner's Fire" — 124

PART III
LIAHONA, 1948–59
ABUNDANT GOSPEL FRUIT

18. Lu'isa Palauni Kongaika
    "Speaking the Truth in Love" — 141

19. Joan Winegar Coombs
    "His Spirit and His Breath" — 145

Contents

20.	'Isileli Lolo Tuiaki *"He Shall Prepare a Way for Them"*	147
21.	Manase Nau *"Whether by Mine Own Voice, or the Voice of My Servants"*	150
22.	John H. Groberg *"There Is the Light"*	155
23.	'Isileli Kongaika *Caring for the Servants of God*	158
24.	Taukolo Langi *God Honors Those Who Honor His Servants*	160
25.	Taukolo Langi *"There Shall Not an Hair of Your Head Perish"*	162
26.	Lela Jesperson Dalton *"In Vision . . . a Temple in These Islands"*	165
27.	Mosese Lui Muti *"Faithful . . . over Many Things"*	167
28.	Charles ("Chuck") J. Woodworth *Fighting for Salvation* by R. Lanier Britsch	173
29.	Enoch LaVell Manwaring *The Savior's Bleeding Hands*	178
30.	'Uiha and Senivia Tu'ikolovatu *"Receive Your Blessing"*	181
31.	Mosese Naeata *Richness in Poverty*	184
32.	Tēvita Folau Mahu'inga *Promptings, Promises, and Priesthood Blessings*	192

PART IV
STAKEHOOD, 1960–73
DEEP ROOTS, WIDE-SPREADING BRANCHES

33.	Tonga Toutai Pāletu'a *"These I Will Make My Rulers"*	209

34. Sifa and Sela Tāfisi
   "Though I Walk Through the Valley of the Shadow of Death" — 216

35. Vaikalafi Lutui and Mele Tafuna Lutui
   "Out of Our Wilderness" — 221

36. Tonga Pōteki Mālohifoʻou and ʻAna Toki Mālohifoʻou
   "He Arose, and Rebuked the Winds" — 226

37. Sela Feinga
   "Throw the Baby!" — 229

38. Saia Paongo
   "Take No Thought for Your Life" — 233

39. Samuela ʻIloa
   "And Hath Compassion on Thee" — 235

40. Irene Clare Holmes Tukuafu
   "And Sent His Servant" — 237

41. Tonu Naeata
   "Fled from the Presence of the Lord" — 240

42. Sione Moala Fineanganofo
   "The Fast That I Have Chosen" — 243

PART V
TEMPLE, 1974–91
GRACING THE LORD'S GARDEN

43. Leni Tuʻihalangingie
   "The Trial of Your Faith" — 259

44. Sione Tuʻalau Lātū
   "I Go to Do His Bidding" — 264

45. Sālesi Falefoʻou Havili
   "Ask in Faith, Nothing Wavering" — 267

46. Mōleni Tanginoa Fonua
   Returning Good for Evil — 270

47. Tēvita Kaʻili
   When the Spirit Moves — 272

Contents

48.	Pita Foliaki Hopoate *"I Will Be on Your Right Hand and on Your Left"*	274
49.	Tēvita Pōmeʻe *Brought Forth by Prayer and Fasting*	282
50.	Muli Lisala *"Behold Your Little Ones"*	286
51.	Melino Kinikini *Out of the Mouths of Little Children*	290
52.	Sione ʻOleli Piutau Tupou *"The Heart of the Children"*	292
53.	Tēvita Taimani *He Will Protect His Servants*	294
54.	Sifa ʻAuka Lātū and Feleti Kusitafu Havea *"Cry unto Him over the Crops of Your Fields"*	296
55.	Viliami Fisiʻiahi *"The Prayer That Is Made in This Place"*	298
56.	ʻAlofanga Moli *"He Ran to Meet Him and Embraced Him"*	301

Appendix
Early Priesthood Leaders in Tonga 305

Index 315

Maps 334

His Royal Majesty Taufa'ahau Tupou IV, King of Tonga, and Queen Halaevalu Mata'aho, 1990, at the Royal Palace in Nuku'alofa. (Courtesy Rainbow Studio, Nuku'alofa)

An Apostolic Blessing upon King Taufa'ahau Tupou IV

The following apostolic blessing was bestowed by Elder James E. Faust of the Council of Twelve Apostles of The Church of Jesus Christ of Latter-day Saints, upon His Royal Majesty King Taufa'ahau Tupou IV, at a special Sunday Family Home Evening with His Majesty and the Saints of the Nuku'alofa Tonga South Stake in the Haveluloto Stake Center, June 19, 1988.

Members of the Royal House of Tonga and distinguished guests, you do us a great honor by coming to these services.

Your Royal Majesty, we extend to you our congratulations and best wishes on your seventieth birthday. We should like to be with you a week next Tuesday when members of the Church in these islands will gather at the Royal Palace to pay you honor and President Eric Shumway will deliver to you a written message of congratulations from our prophet and his counselors in Salt Lake City. And then on the 4th of July, our entire country has declared a holiday and we will be remembering you in our household.

I do not believe that Your Royal Majesty has more loyal subjects than the members of this Church. I should like to read the Twelfth Article of Faith: "We believe in being subject to kings, presidents, rulers, and magistrates, in obeying, honoring, and sustaining the law." And these children have been taught and can recite these Articles of Faith.

Because of the lateness of the hour, Your Royal Majesty, I shall not like to speak longer; but I should like, as a humble servant of the Lord, to bear my witness to Your Royal Majesty that Jesus is the Christ, our Redeemer, our Savior, who has atoned for the sins of all mankind.

And as an apostle of the Lord Jesus Christ, I should like to invoke an apostolic blessing upon Your Royal Majesty and pray that the Spirit of our Heavenly Father will be on your right hand and be on your left hand, that his Spirit shall be in your heart and his angels round about you.

I invoke a blessing upon Her Majesty the Queen, and upon your family, and upon all your subjects of these great and blessed islands.

We are grateful for noble kings and queens in these islands who have permitted their subjects to worship God according to the dictates of their conscience.

And I bear you this humble witness and invoke these blessings upon you, and do so in the name of Jesus Christ, Amen.

Chronology of Church Events in Tonga

1891 **July 15:** First LDS missionaries, Alva Butler and Brigham Smoot, arrive in Nukuʻalofa, Tonga, from Samoa, opening the Tonga District of the Samoan Mission.

July 16: Visit King George Tupou I.

1892 **May 15:** Mission House dedicated at Muʻa, Tongatapu.

August 22: First LDS day school established at Muʻa.

September 11: First Tongan convert, ʻAlipate, baptized.

Olonzo Merrill succeeds Smoot as presiding elder.

1893 **February 18:** King George Tupou I dies.

May: Elders James Kinghorn and William P. Hunter preach in Haʻapai.

Two missionary couples arrive, Thomas and Luella Adams and Alfred and Margaret Durham.

1894 **September 29:** First Tongan, Tevisi Lutui from Nomuka, ordained to the Aaronic Priesthood.

September: Merrill and Durham preach in ʻEua.

1895 First LDS school opened in Pangai, Haʻapai.

May 12: First death of a member, Sione Paula.

September 8: First LDS meeting held in Vavaʻu.

September 9: Vava'u dedicated to the preaching of the restored gospel.

1896 **October:** Elders James R. Welker and Robert Smith preach in Niuatoputapu and Niuafo'ou.

1897 **April:** Missionaries return to Samoa, closing the Tonga District.

1907 **June 13:** At the invitation of 'Iki Tupou Fulivai, Elders Heber J. McKay and W. O. Facer arrive in Neiafu, Vava'u; they establish a branch and a small school in Neiafu.

1908 Branch and school established in Mataika, Vava'u.

1909 At the invitation of Sē Saulala, Mormon missionaries establish branch and school in Ha'alaufuli.

1911 Mormon missionaries establish school in the home of Siosaia Mataele in Fo'ui, Tongatapu.

Branch of the Church established in Koloa, Vava'u.

July 15: King George Tupou II attends a Mormon baptism at Fanga'uta.

LDS schools established in Nukunuku and Ma'ufanga.

Branches maintained in Fo'ui, Nukunuku, Houma, and Ma'ufanga on Tongatapu.

Among the Caucasian missionaries are Elders Frank Winn, George Seely, and three identified only by surnames: Ormond, Olson, and Wright.

1912 Ha'akame Branch organized (first president, Elder Evon Huntsman).

Chapel in Ha'alaufuli and school house in Nukunuku dedicated.

LDS school starts anew at Mu'a.

Two Samoan sister missionaries, Malia and Lillie Josephs, organize Relief Society and Primary. They were the first full-time sister missionaries in Tonga after the return of the Church.

1916 Tongan Mission established.

Chronology

	May 11: President Willard L. Smith, accompanied by wife, Jenny, and family arrives.
	First Tongans ordained to the Melchizedek Priesthood.
1917	Missionaries begin work anew in Haʻapai.
1918	**April 5:** King George Tupou II dies.
	October 9: His daughter, Queen Sālote Mafileʻo Pilolevu (reigned 1918–65), succeeds him.
	November: First mission-wide conference held in Nukuʻalofa.
	Influenza kills hundreds, including an Elder Langston from the United States.
	Mission home in Matavaimoʻui completed.
	Convert baptisms recorded for the year: 118.
1920	Church well established in Vavaʻu, Haʻapai, and Tongatapu.
	August 9: M. Vernon Coombs, accompanied by wife, LaVera Wilcox Coombs, and two children, arrives to replace President Smith.
1921	**June 11–July 4:** Apostle David O. McKay visits mission.
	Foreign missionaries number twelve: Reuben R. Wiberg, Clermont A. Oborn, Stirling Ivie May, Reuben Clark, Harvey Sorenson, Althen Rasmussen, George W. Robinson, Walter J. Phillips, Clarence Henderson, Lewis B. Parkin, O. Wilford Olsen, and Emile C. Dunn.
1922	Total LDS membership exceeds a thousand.
	Elder Oborn dies of typhoid fever in Pangai.
	Effective June 29, the Passport Act forbids the entry of any foreign LDS missionary.
1923	**July 4:** Elder Rasmussen dies of typhoid fever.
	President Coombs and Saints fast, pray, and circulate petitions for the repeal of the Mormon exclusion law.
1924	**July 3:** Sections of Passport Act excluding Mormon missionaries repealed. At that point, only a handful of Tongan missionaries and five Caucasian missionaries were serving. Six new mis-

sionaries from Canada and the United States would arrive the following year, in addition to Jay A. Cahoon and Ada Layne Cahoon: Alden Glines, Orrin Fisher, DaCosta Clark, Maurice Jensen, and Austin A. Carter.

President Coombs acquires lease for seventy-five acres at Makeke.

1925 Makeke school under construction.

Herman Wolfgramm, a German convert and the first local brother, called to preside over Vavaʻu District.

Eleven branches thriving: Nukuʻalofa, Foʻui, Nukunuku, Fāhefa, Houma, Haʻakame, Fuaʻamotu, and Muʻa (Tongatapu); Lifuka, Haʻano, ʻUiha (Haʻapai); Neiafu, Haʻalaufuli, Mataika, Koloa, Tefisi, and ʻOtea (Vavaʻu).

Tongan missionaries distinguishing themselves as leaders are: Lisiate Talanoa Maile, Tēvita Pita Pauni, Misitana Vea, Sione Fine Valahulu, Sione Taufa, Lolohea Pupungatoa Faʻanunu, and Siosaia Fatani.

1926 First classes at Makeke begin, with Elders Samuela V. Fakatou and Maurice Jensen as teachers, Filisone Manisela as chaperone and work supervisor.

Missionary Jay A. Cahoon assigned to succeed President Coombs.

1927 Makeke School becomes a "drawing card" for Tongan Mission.

Saints donate labor and food for construction projects.

1928 **September 16:** President (Misi Sēmisi) Newell J. Cutler, his wife, Floy B. Cutler, and three children, arrives to succeed President and Sister Cahoon.

Elder DaCosta Clark organizes genealogical work throughout mission.

1930 Branch presidents: Timote Langi, Fāhefa; Lisiate Talanoa Maile, Foʻui; Paula Langi, Nukunuku; Sione Taufa, Haʻateiho; Sili Fehi, Houma; Sālesi Toutai, Haʻakame; Sione Maʻu, Fuaʻamotu; Puli Tau Vehikite, Muʻa; Elder Harold Holdaway, Pangai; Filimone Tupou, ʻUiha; Elder Reed Parkinson, Neiafu; Herman Wolfgramm, Mataika; Sione Filipe, Haʻalaufuli; Tēvita Niko,

Chronology

Koloa; Sione 'Ulufonua, 'Otea. Elder Robert Nelson is principal of Makeke.

1931 Relief Society flourishes in Vava'u under the direction of President Ma'ata Wolfgramm.

October: Influenza closes Makeke School.

1932 **April 12:** Elder Mervin Proctor dies of infection on Tongatapu.

August 2: Elder Victor Lee dies of typhoid fever in Ha'alaufuli.

Elder Verl Stubbs is acting president, while President Cutler takes Sister Cutler, sick with jaundice, to Samoa for treatment.

Ma'ata Wolfgramm called as Mission Relief Society president.

1933 **June 22:** Makeke College Theatrical Society presents popular concert.

December 4: Reuben M. Wiberg arrives to succeed Elder Stubbs.

Saints somewhat demoralized over severe misconduct of four American elders.

1934 President Wiberg restores confidence in Church leadership.

District presidents: Charles A. Wolfgramm, Tongatapu; Misitana Vea, Ha'apai; Elder C. Raymond Childs, Vava'u.

Nakolo Branch organized (first president, Sālesi Vānisi).

1935 Tēvita Maile set apart as president of Vava'u District.

The Mutual Improvement Association introduces debate, dances, storytelling, choral competitions, etc.

Samuela Fakatou called as mission translator and secretary of mission conferences.

Makeke School Board first organized, composed of Samuela V. Fakatou (chair), Siosaia Maile, Pauliasi Pīkula, Misitana Vea, Sione Tuita Vehikite, Sione 'Esau, and Tēvita Pita Pauni.

1936 **March 12:** Emile C. Dunn, accompanied by wife, Evelyn Hyde Dunn, and two children, arrives to replace President Wiberg.

1937 **February 22:** Hurricane destroys Makeke School buildings, rebuilt by local members within a few months.

LDS Boy Scouts and Beehive girls visit Queen Sālote at her invitation.

November: Elder Floyd C. Fletcher directs Tonga-wide jamboree for LDS Scouts.

President Dunn translates and distributes pamphlet, "The Contributions of Joseph Smith."

1938 Severe drought causes food shortage.

April: Faleloa Branch organized in Haʻapai (first president, ʻIsileli Fehoko).

May 10: Apostle George Albert Smith and Seventy Rufus K. Hardy arrive for conferences; dedicate chapel in Neiafu and recreation hall in Haʻalaufuli.

Sioeli Kauvaka and ʻEpalahame Kumā Tuaʻone called as missionaries to Niuatoputapu; they baptize Sēmisi and Kasimia Sika in Vaipoa, December 18, and organize branch in Vaipoa with ʻEpalahame Kumā Tuaʻone as president.

Convert baptisms recorded for the year: 117.

1939 Halaloto Branch organized (first president, Samuela Fakatou).

Elder Ermel J. Morton, assisted by Tēvita Mapa and Tuʻiketei Pule, completes first-draft translation of the Book of Mormon.

1940 Six converts baptized in ʻEua.

October 24: All American missionaries except President Dunn leave because of World War II; local men and women take full leadership.

Tongan district presidents: Vuna Wolfgramm (Vavaʻu), Tēvita Fīnau Tafuna (Haʻapai), Tēvita Mapa (Tongatapu).

Tēvita Pita Pauni and Siaosi Palauni called as teachers at Makeke, with Samuela Fakatou as principal. Sister Dunn teaches older students preparing for government exams.

1941 Church membership exceeds 2,000.

Sister Dunn and children are evacuated to New Zealand.

1942 Thousands of American troops stationed throughout Tonga.

A large traditional-style *fale* Tonga (chapel) at Makeke accommodates 500 Saints for conference.

Relief Society centennial celebrated in each island group.

Sūlia Tuʻiketei Pule serves as Mission Relief Society president.

Twelve Tongan missionaries and families called.

1943 143 students enroll in Makeke, the largest group ever in a Church school. Sione Tuita Vehikite and Sinisā Fakalata assigned as teachers. Paula and Lesieli Malupō appointed as caretakers and dorm parents of the students.

Nukumovahaʻi and Sela Tonga called as missionaries on Niuafoʻou with Samuela and Heleine Fakatou.

November: Penisimani Lātūsela Mapa authorized to visit members and hold Sunday School in Suva, Fiji, while attending medical school. The Suva Branch would not be officially organized until September 5, 1954, under the direction of the Samoan Mission.

1944 Severe famine in Niuafoʻou. Saints receive relief from Church.

American soldiers withdrawn.

1945 January 15: Tēvita Mapa, secretary to the Premier of Tonga and prominent LDS leader, dies.

Church branches organized for the first time at Makeke (first president, Sione Mōleni); at Malapo (first president, Siaosi Loiti Talakai); and at Folaha (first president, ʻAtonio Tuʻiʻāsoa).

1946 June 7: Evon W. Huntsman, accompanied by wife Martha and three children, replaces Emile Dunn.

Tongan translation of the Book of Mormon published; presented to Queen Sālote and several nobles.

Volcanic eruptions destroy many buildings in Niuafoʻou, causing severe drought and food shortages.

September 9: Church parachutes food and supplies.

December: Niuafoʻou population evacuated to Tongatapu and ʻEua.

At year's end, the records show 31 branches and 2,422 members.

1947 **February 4:** Future foreign missionaries limited by government policy to three, plus mission president.

President Huntsman leases property for school in Halaloto.

Apostle Matthew Cowley approves property for the construction of Liahona College (high school).

December: Emile C. Dunn appointed building supervisor and returns with his family to Tonga; Rudi Wolfgramm becomes building committee chairman; Siosaia Hola and Samuela Fakatou caretakers.

Tongatapu divided into East District (president, Misitana Vea) and West District (president, Lisiate Talanoa Maile).

Tuʻanekivale Branch and Ngāʻunoho Branch organized in Vavaʻu (first presidents, ʻInoke Mataele and Tuʻivakanō Fisi).

1948 **February 15:** Makeke College opens at the Liahona site, with seventy-five boys and thirty-four girls. Principal: Elder Bevan Blake. Missionary-teachers: Elder Rudi Wolfgramm, Sione Filipe, Vaea Tangitau, Fauniteni Ikakoula, Siaosi Loiti, Viliami Pasi, and ʻAtonio Tuʼiʻāsoa. Nafetalai ʻAlusa supervises the boys; Sister Faʻalupenga Sanft the girls.

July 14: Emile Dunn replaces President Huntsman, released because of illness.

First building supplies and equipment arrive for Liahona College.

November 5: Church Architect Edward O. Anderson, school designer, presides at groundbreaking. Dozens of local labor missionaries called – beginning of the Building Missionary Program in Tonga.

1949 **May:** Tongamamaʻo Branch organized on ʻEua (first president, Sonatane Vāvasa Fehoko).

August 29: Matthew Cowley, assisted by Elders Mosese Muti and Reuben M. Flynn, lays the cornerstone of Liahona High School.

December: By the end of the year, Church membership reaches 2,820 with 37 missionaries, mostly married Tongans, in the field.

Chronology

1950 **May 17:** Elder Lionel Gowing becomes Liahona building supervisor.

June 12: Evon Huntsman replaces Dunn as mission president, with Alexander Wishart and Samuela Fakatou as counselors.

1951 **February 20:** Ermel J. Morton, new principal of Liahona School, accompanied by wife Lena and family, arrives.

March 19: With most of the first-phase construction completed, Liahona opens with upper forms (grades) 3, 4, 5, and 6.

August 6: Forms 2 and 3 added at Liahona; enrollment 170.

Twenty Tongan men called to serve missions, accompanied by their wives and children.

1952 **February 11:** Liahona opens with complete contingent of classes and staff.

February 20: D'Monte Coombs, accompanied by wife, Joan Winegar Coombs, and family, replaces President Huntsman.

Nukuleka Branch organized in Tongatapu (first president, Sione Pauni).

Translation Committee organized: Elder Thomas Hansen, Samuela Fakatou, Viliami Sovea Kioa, Sēmisi Taumoepeau, and Siosaia Tupou.

August 27: Hihifo Branch organized on Lifuka, Ha'apai (first president, Sione Vea).

1953 Principal Ermel Morton translates twelve tracts, "The Rays of Living Light" by Charles W. Penrose.

September: President Coombs organizes first training school for local missionaries.

Liahona Band performs at palace for Queen Sālote.

December 1: Apostle LeGrand Richards dedicates Liahona, with Queen Sālote in attendance.

December 19: Queen Elizabeth and the Duke of Edinburgh visit Tonga.

1954 **February 7:** Falevai Branch organized in Vava'u (first president, Mafua 'Uluaki'ahoia).

Liahona students' boat shows assist missionary/public relations.

July 15: Niue islands become part of the Tongan Mission.

1955 **January 15:** President David O. McKay visits, says a temple will someday stand in "these islands."

January 28: First Presidency authorizes construction of twenty-one brick chapels.

December 19: President Fred W. Stone, accompanied by wife, Sylvia Stone, and son David, arrives to replace President and Sister Coombs.

1956 **January:** President Fred Stone sets apart fifty Tongan labor missionaries.

Wendell B. Mendenhall, chairman of the Church Building Committee, visits Tonga.

March 1: Extensive building program launched with groundbreaking for Matahau chapel, Tongatapu; includes mission home and office complex in Fasi, Nuku'alofa. General supervision of the building/labor mission program assigned to Elder Franklin R. Knowlton with Joseph Archie Cottle as assistant, Jack W. Dowdle as treasurer, and Fakatou Vaitai as local coordinator.

March 26: Siosifa Tu'iketei Pule and Misitana Vea counselors in mission presidency.

Ermel Morton completes first draft translation of the Doctrine and Covenants and Pearl of Great Price, assisted by Sovea Kioa, 'Atonio Tu'i'āsoa, and Sione Tuita Vehikite.

District presidents: Maile Mataele (East Tongatapu), 'Epalahame Kumā Tua'one (West Tongatapu); Elder Charles Woodworth (Niue); Elder John H. Groberg (Ha'apai); Elder James P. Christensen (Vava'u); 'Aisake Hoatatau (Niuatoputapu).

1957 **January:** Ralph Olson replaces Morton as principal of Liahona.

February: Hurricanes destroy four chapels on Niue island.

Church primary schools open in Pangai, Ha'apai, and Ha'alaufuli, Vava'u.

Eleven foreign builders and supervisors and seventy-five labor missionaries participate in building program.

June 12: Pioneer Siosaia Mataele dies.

October 14: Pacific Board of Education established, Wendell B. Mendenhall as chair. Teachers are salaried employees, not missionaries; schools separated from mission.

1958 Fiji becomes part of the Tongan Mission.

January 15: First conference in Suva.

February: Twenty-six Americans arrive to teach at Liahona.

May 4: President David O. McKay visits Fiji and dedicates Suva chapel.

May 26: Apostle Marion G. Romney dedicates the Nukuʻalofa and Matahau chapels.

July 13: The Eastern District on Tongatapu is divided into the Eastern (Hahake) and the Central (Vahe Loto) districts (district presidents: Elder Duane Hiatt and Maile Mataele respectively).

October 13: Owen Cook, executive secretary of the Pacific Board of Education, arrives in Tonga and closes Church primary schools.

Chapels dedicated in Vainī, Nukunuku, Fuaʻamotu, Pangai, Kolonga, Neiafu, and ʻUiha.

December 15: First Tongan excursion (thirty-five Saints) to New Zealand Temple.

Liahona enrollment: 485.

1959 **January:** Chapels dedicated in Leimātuʻa, ʻOtea, and Tuʻanuku (Vavaʻu).

February 18: Elders Gideon Dolo, Fijian, and Kami Pāsoni, Tongan, open missionary work in the Lau Group, Fiji.

June 7: New mission home dedicated in Fasi, Nukuʻalofa.

June 22: M. Vernon Coombs and LaVera Coombs arrive to replace President and Sister Stone, their third mission to the South Pacific.

May 25: Kenneth Powell Lindsay replaces Ralph Olson as principal of Liahona.

September 8: Liahona Advisory Board organized: Lisiate Talanoa Maile, Hale Vete, Tēvita Kitekei'aho, and Manase Nau.

September 22: Liahona acquires Niumate plantation.

1960 **January 18:** Hurricane devastates Niue; four thousand left homeless; Church sends relief.

March 2: Thirty-one experienced Tongan labor missionaries called to build chapels and Church College in Hawaii.

Copies of the Tongan translation of Doctrine and Covenants and Pearl of Great Price arrive.

June 17: Vaotu'u Branch organized on Tongatapu (first president, Nafetalai 'Alusa).

October 26: First seminary graduation at Liahona.

Elder John Longden, Assistant to the Council of the Twelve, and LaRue C. Longden, first counselor in the YWMIA general presidency, spend ten days in Tonga.

First mission council (analogous to a stake high council) organized: Siosifa Tu'iketei Pule, Misitana Vea, Maile Mataele, and Penisimani Lātūsela Mapa.

1961 **March 16:** Vava'u and Ha'apai suffer from a severe hurricane; many chapels damaged; Church provides welfare supplies. Fakatou Vaitai supervises repairs.

Masilamea Branch organized on Tongatapu, Tui'one Matelau, president.

'Eueiki island branch organized, Kēlepi Tu'avao, president.

September: Vava'u divided into North District (president, Malakai Manu 'Unga) and South District (president, Tonga Pōteki Mālohifo'ou).

October: Hōfoa Branch organized on Tongatapu (first president, 'Asi Lolohea Folau).

November 5: Nuku'alofa Branch divided, presidents Hale Vete and Siaosi Loiti Talakai.

Chronology

Convert baptisms recorded for the year: 519—over three times those of the previous year, and over five times the average annual baptisms in the previous decade.

1962 Apostle Mark E. Petersen visits Tongatapu and Ha'apai. Twenty-two hundred attend conference at Liahona.

1963 **February 7:** Patrick Dalton, accompanied by his wife Lela and two children, arrives to replace President Coombs.

April 28: Mission Home Teaching Committee organized to encourage home teaching among the Saints mission-wide, 'Inoke Kolo secretary.

Student branches organized at Liahona.

November 9: All men graduating from Liahona received a full-time mission call along with their diploma; two-thirds accept.

Convert baptisms recorded for the year: 554.

Rondo Harmon replaces Kenneth Lindsay as principal of Liahona.

1964 **February:** First seminary class organized and taught at the Tongan Government High School (instructor, Elder Emil Wolfgramm, a Tongan raised abroad, son of Charles Wolfgramm).

July 20: Liahona High School District organized with Rondo S. Harmon as president.

October 25: Large numbers of single Tongan women called as missionaries for the first time.

November 23: Apostle Delbert L. Stapley visits.

December 16: Construction begins on three new chapels.

Student enrollment at Liahona stands at 400.

Convert baptisms recorded for the year: 838.

1965 **January:** Elders Rodney S. Fakatou and 'Ofisi Pututau organize Tongan Mission into proselyting zones and districts.

President Dalton emphasizes need to strengthen the national Boy Scout Program, directed by the Honourable Vaea, governor of Ha'apai.

November 2: Apostle Thomas S. Monson challenges Tongan Saints to prepare for stakehood, dedicates the Tokomololo and the Houma chapels, holds special conference with 179 full-time missionaries.

December 15: Queen Sālote Pilolevu Tupou III dies.

December: 217 full-time Tongan missionaries serving.

Convert baptisms recorded for the year: 1,019.

1966 **May 12:** Church boat *Faifekau* constructed under supervision of Fakatou Vaitai.

May: Former building missionary Archie Cottle returns as construction and maintenance supervisor.

July 5: John H. Groberg, accompanied by wife, Jean, and five daughters, arrives to replace President Dalton.

December 31: Mission officers appointed: Sovea Kioa, legal matters; Fakatou Vaitai, building; 'Uliti Uata, business; Peni Mapa, translation; Viliami Pasi, organization; and Mosese Muti, fellowship program.

Convert baptisms recorded for the year: 600.

1967 **March 16:** Seventy S. Dilworth Young and wife, Huldah Parker Young, visit Tongan Mission for conferences.

July 4: Coronation of King Taufaʻafau Tupou IV. Tupou Pulu and Maile Niu appointed to Church translating team.

September 12: Orson Hyde White, accompanied by wife, Barbara, and children, arrives, to be the first superintendent of Church Schools.

December: Ermel Morton returns to Tonga to write missionary discussion plans in the Tongan and the Niuean languages.

Convert baptisms recorded for the year: 833.

1968 **January:** Niue Island District transferred to the Samoan Mission.

February 28: Sunday School and Mutual Improvement Association general board members conduct leadership training sessions.

Chronology

April: Thomas S. Monson visits.

September 5: Nuku'alofa Tonga Stake organized under direction of Apostles Howard W. Hunter and Thomas S. Monson; stake presidency: Orson H. White, Tonga Toutai Pāletu'a, and 'Uliti Uata; stake clerks Mark Cloward and Taniela Pasi. High councilors: Peni Mapa, Sovea Kioa, Albert Pope, Mosese Muti, Tēvita Uatahausi Mapa, Arson Hatch, 'Alikisānita Vimahi, Lynn E. Haskell, Kaulave 'Olive, and Viliami Sika. Bishops: Tēvita Ka'ili, Nuku'alofa Ward; Tēvita 'Asi Lolohea Folau, Nuku'alofa Second Ward; Sione Sika, Haveluloto Ward; Moli Ngatuvai, Tokomololo Ward; Tēvita Folau Mahu'inga, Pea and Ha'ateiho Ward; Mosese Langi, Matangiake Ward; Keith Albrecht, Liahona Ward; 'Atonio Tu'i'āsoa, Ha'akame Ward. Director of translation: Sione Tu'alau Lātū.

December: Jubilee celebration of the Tonga Mission. Mission contains ten districts and fifty independent branches; 700 students registered in Liahona and the middle schools.

Convert baptisms recorded for the year: 1,767.

1969 **July 1:** James P. Christensen, accompanied by his wife, Metta Heder Christensen, and four children, arrives to replace President Groberg.

General Authorities begin visiting the stake quarterly conferences regularly, including Elders Howard W. Hunter, LeGrand Richards, James Cullimore, ElRay L. Christiansen, and Henry D. Taylor in 1969.

Chapels dedicated in Fāhefa, Vaotu'u, Tokomololo, Faleloa, Fotua, and Ta'anea.

1970 **July 26:** Nuku'alofa Tonga West and Nuku'alofa Tonga South stakes created with Orson White and Tēvita Mahu'inga as stake presidents; Tēvita Ka'ili called to preside over the original Nuku'alofa Tonga Stake.

Mission home in Sopu, Tongatapu, dedicated.

Queen Elizabeth II of Britain visits Tonga.

Chapels dedicated in Te'ekiu and Fatai.

1971 Tonga Toutai Pāletu'a becomes president of Nuku'alofa Tonga West Stake, replacing Orson White.

July 21: Nuku'alofa Tonga East Stake is created, Vili Pele Folau, president.

July 23: Fiji Mission separated from Tonga Mission, Sherman Lindholm president.

1972 **July 1:** Charles Woodworth, accompanied by his wife, Marsha, and their children, arrives to replace President Christensen.

July 1: Ebbie L. Davis, a teacher at Liahona High School, called to preside over the Fiji Mission.

Chapels dedicated in Ha'atu'a, Tongamama'o, Kolomotu'a, Havelu, Talafo'ou, and Navutoka.

1974 **July 1:** Tonga Toutai Pāletu'a, the first Tongan mission president, replaces Charles Woodworth as president of the Tonga Nuku'alofa Mission.

September 6: Vaikalafi Lutui sustained as president of Nuku'alofa Tonga West Stake.

1975 James William Harris appointed superintendent of Church Educational System in Tonga, the first Tongan to assume this position.

Sione Tu'alau Lātū replaces Tēvita F. Mahu'inga as president of Nuku'alofa Tonga South Stake.

Pita Hopoate replaces Vili Pele Folau as president of Nuku'alofa Tonga East Stake.

December 4: Neiafu Vava'u Tonga Stake created, Mosese Hetau Langi president.

1976 **February 24–25:** First Area Conference in Tonga; President Spencer W. Kimball present.

Viliami Pasi replaces Tēvita Ka'ili as president of Nuku'alofa Tonga Stake.

1977 Viliami Sika replaces Sione Tu'alau Lātū as president of Nuku'alofa Tonga South Stake.

July 1: Sione Tu'alau Lātū replaces Tonga Toutai Pāletu'a as president of Tonga Nuku'alofa Mission.

Tonga Toutai Pāletu'a called as the first Tongan regional representative of the Twelve.

Chronology

1978 **February:** Early morning seminary introduced throughout Tonga; Penisimani Muti appointed director of Religious Education and called as president of Nukuʻalofa Tonga South Stake (March 24), replacing Viliami Sika.

May: Elder John H. Groberg of the First Quorum of the Seventy dedicates Sainehā High School in Neiafu, Vavaʻu.

Twenty-two Tongan missionaries sent to Bolivia, Philippines, and Fiji. Over the next two decades, hundreds of native Tongans would serve on missions worldwide.

1979 Convert baptisms recorded for the year: over two thousand.

1980 **April:** President Spencer W. Kimball announces that a temple will be built in Tonga.

June: ʻUluʻamu Tuʻifua sustained as president of the Nukuʻalofa Tonga East Stake, replacing Pita F. Hopoate.

July 1: Pita F. Hopoate replaces Sione Tuʻalau Lātū as president of the Tonga Nukuʻalofa Mission; Sione Lātū called as regional representative and is appointed Area Director of Temporal Affairs for the Church.

August 27: Neiafu Vavaʻu Tonga Stake divided, creating Neiafu Vavaʻu Tonga North Stake, presidents Samisioni Uasilaʻā and Mosese Langi respectively.

August 31: ʻIsileli Lolo Tuiaki sustained president of Nukuʻalofa Tonga West Stake. Nukuʻalofa Tonga Liahona Stake also created, Vaikalafi Lutui first president.

September: The *Fetuʻumoana* sinks between Lofanga and Haʻafeva, drowning Elder Hanipale Kinikini, Sister Mele Mafileʻo, and her two children; the baby of another missionary couple, Elder and Sister Seleti Hopoate, also died in the disaster.

Chapels dedicated in Lotofoa, Nomuka, ʻOʻua, ʻUtungake, Tefisi, Hunga, Nuapapu, and Haʻakio.

1981 Vuki Tangitau appointed as superintendent of Church Educational System Tonga, replacing James William Harris.

February 18: President Kimball presides at groundbreaking service for Nuku'alofa Tonga Temple, King Taufa'ahau Tupou IV participating.

April: Tonga Toutai Pāletu'a called as the first Tongan temple president.

December: Tēvita Ka'ili called as regional representative.

1982 **March 3:** Hurricane Isaac hits Tonga. Church supplies extensive relief.

Chapels dedicated in Makeke, Lakepa, Malapo, and Holonga.

1983 **June 14:** Ha'apai Tonga Stake created, Fanongonongo Vaitai, president.

July 15: Nuku'alofa Tonga Vainī Stake created, Samuela 'Iloa, president.

July 19: Melvin Butler, accompanied by wife, Carol, and their six children, arrives to replace President Hopoate.

August 9: Gordon B. Hinckley, first counselor in the First Presidency, dedicates the Nuku'alofa Tonga Temple.

August 13: Mosese Naeata becomes president of Nuku'alofa Tonga Liahona Stake.

October 9: Nuku'alofa Tonga North Stake created, Sione Moala Fineanganofo, president.

Chapels dedicated in Ha'ateiho and Nuku'alofa.

Convert baptisms recorded for the year: 2,261.

1984 Over four hundred Tongan elders and sisters called as full-time missionaries.

June 24: South Pacific Area Presidency created, headquartered in Sidney, Australia, Elder Robert L. Simpson, president, Elders Devere Harris and Philip T. Sonntag, first and second counselors.

1985 **May 19:** Second Area Conference held at Liahona; over 13,000 attend.

Chapels dedicated in Neiafu, Falevai, Pangaimotu, and Longolongo.

September: Hāmani Wolfgramm replaces Mosese Langi as president of the Neiafu Vava'u Tonga North Stake.

1986 **January 17:** Vaikalafi Lutui called as regional representative.

Mōleni Tanginoa Fonua replaces Fanongonongo Vaitai as president of Ha'apai Tonga Stake.

March: 'Uiha Tu'ikolovatu sustained as president of the Nuku'alofa Tonga Stake, replacing Viliami Pasi.

July 1: Eric B. Shumway, accompanied by wife, Carolyn Merrill Shumway, and four children, arrives to replace President Butler.

Chapels dedicated in Talihau, Lavengatonga, Ha'alalo, Tungua, Tofoa, Afā, Nukuleka, and Hoi.

Convert baptisms recorded for the year: 1,024.

1987 Full-time missionaries hold a series of devotionals with King Taufa'ahau Tupou IV.

Church establishes a Missionary Training Center, replacing former center run by the mission; Pita Hopoate, president.

Nukumovaha'i Tonga replaces Tonga Toutai Pāletu'a as president of the Tonga Temple.

Veuki Kaumatule sustained as president of Nuku'alofa Tonga West Stake, replacing 'Isileli Lolo Tuiaki.

Chapels dedicated in 'Ohonua and Nuku'alofa.

1988 **May:** Simeni Tu'ivai sustained president of Nuku'alofa Tonga East Stake, replacing 'Ulu'amū Tu'ifua.

June 16: Sioeli Iketau sustained as president of Nuku'alofa Tonga South Stake replacing Penisimani Muti.

June 28: Six thousand Saints gather at the palace to celebrate King Taufa'ahau Tupou IV's seventieth birthday.

Convert baptisms recorded for the year: fourteen hundred.

1989 **May:** Regional Conference for the seven Tongatapu stakes.

July 1: 'Isileli Kongaika replaces Eric B. Shumway as president of Tonga Nuku'alofa Mission.

Fe'ao Talivakaola sustained as president of the Neiafu Vava'u Tonga Stake, replacing Samisoni Uasila'ā.

Chapels dedicated in Mataika and Feletoa, Vava'u.

Patrick Dalton called as president of the Tonga Temple.

New Missionary Training Center (MTC) dedicated in Liahona.

Convert baptisms recorded for the year: over two thousand.

1990 Tēvita Ka'ili replaces Sione Tu'alau Lātū as regional manager of temporal affairs.

Tonga Toutai Pāletu'a replaces Pita Hopoate as president of the MTC.

Tonga Nuku'alofa Mission launches extensive nation-wide service projects.

Church in Tonga prepares for ten-day centennial celebration, August 16–26, 1991.

Acknowledgements

There is a widely used saying in Tonga, *Ko e koloa 'a Tonga ko e fakamālō* ("The true reward in Tonga is just a simple thank you"). Tongans place a high value on the expression of gratitude, and so do I, especially to all those who have contributed to this labor of love, *Tongan Saints: Legacy of Faith*.

Along with the many thousands of Tongan Saints and leaders in The Church of Jesus Christ of Latter-day Saints, I express gratitude to their Majesties Taufa'ahau Tupou IV and Queen Halaevalu Mata'aho for their friendship to the Church and their intelligent leadership in the Kingdom of Tonga. Also to Princess Sālote-Pilolevu and her husband, Ma'ulupekotofa Tuita, I extend a deep affection and appreciation for their innumerable attentions and kindnesses to Church members.

Appreciation goes to Tēvita Ka'ili and the Church Centennial Committee for their confidence in me and invitation to produce a commemorative publication for the Church's hundredth birthday in Tonga. I thank also the hundreds of Saints who rallied to record and submit their histories for possible inclusion in this centennial volume. For many of them, it was their first experience in recording a written history.

Important assistance was rendered by many people in each phase of the project. Folau Kioa of Ta'anea, Vava'u, conducted oral history interviews and gathered other important data. President 'Isileli Kongaika of the Tonga Nuku'alofa Mission offered much valuable advice and material. Dozens of full-time missionaries transcribed audio tapes and documented vital historical information. V. Lynn Tyler of the David M. Kennedy Center was in charge of gathering photographs appropriate for the book. He also made excellent suggestions regarding the manuscript.

A special thanks goes to Lynn McMurray and Brent Anderson, former missionaries in Tonga, who submitted important primary documents and provided several initial translations of personal histories, and to Riley Moffat for help in preparing the maps of Tonga.

The photographs used in the book have been taken from the collections of Emile C. Dunn, Ermel Morton, Kenneth P. Lindsay, Kākolosi Pulotu, M. Vernon Coombs, Evon Huntsman, D'Monte Coombs, Patrick Dalton, and V. Lynn Tyler. We thank these people and their families for their contributions.

Appreciation is extended to the Charles M. Redd Center, Brigham Young University, Provo, Utah, for copies of the oral histories of Ada Layne Cahoon and Joan Winegar Coombs; and to Verda Nelson Jensen and her daughter, Carol Jensen Lasson, for the life history of John Alexander Nelson, Jr.

Many thanks must also go to Uinise Tua'one Langi for her hours of recording, transcribing, translating, gathering photographs, and proofreading. Her enthusiasm for the project has helped sustain me for the duration.

Drs. R. Lanier Britsch and Lance Chase read much of the manuscript in its early stages, giving encouragement and suggesting many ways to improve it. Nedra Overstreet has done all the word processing, persevering cheerfully after hours and on weekends to meet the publication deadlines. To her I give a special *fakafeta'i*.

I am most grateful to Drs. Jerry Loveland and Dale Robertson of The Institute of Polynesian Studies (IPS) for their interest and for the sponsorship that made this project possible. I am particularly indebted to Sharlene Rohter of the IPS, and to Lavina Fielding Anderson and Signature Books, for their professional competence and editorial diligence in bringing this book to its present form.

To my secretary Sally Hall who went the second mile in her professional responsibilities and to BYU–Hawaii President Alton Wade who looked the other way when writing deadlines occasionally kept me away from my desk, I express my sincere gratitude.

I thank my beloved wife and missionary companion, Carolyn, and our seven supportive children, both for their sustaining love and for their example of faith, which is the legacy of our own family circle.

Finally, and most importantly, I express the *loto hounga'ia* (deep, abiding gratitude) of all the Tongan Saints to the leadership of The Church of Jesus Christ of Latter-day Saints, the prophets, seers, and revelators, and those who have represented them in Tonga, for their immense generosity, care, and loving attention for the members of the Church in Tonga over the past one hundred years.

Preface

This book is dedicated to the thousands of Saints and missionaries whose faith and testimony have nurtured The Church of Jesus Christ of Latter-day Saints in the Kingdom of Tonga for a hundred years (1891–1991). *Tongan Saints: Legacy of Faith* is not a history *per se*. It does not follow a chronology of dates and events. Rather it is a compilation of the personal experiences and testimonies of ordinary men and women who have been a living part of the Church's history in the Friendly Islands. In their own voices, they tell of courage and conversion, endurance, priesthood power, visions, sacrifice, obedience, testimony, revelation, and their love for God and for each other. These are personal statements that give substance and meaning to the dates and events marking the growth of the Church in each generation. Together they capture the essence of faith among some of the Church's most faithful and loving people in the world.

Eighty-five percent of the accounts published here are excerpted from family and personal histories produced in the last two years as part of an oral history project launched in December 1988, while I was still president of the Tonga Nukuʻalofa Mission. Supported by local Church leaders and full-time missionaries, the project generated over three hundred such histories now deposited in the Pacific Collection of the Joseph F. Smith Library, BYU-Hawaii, Laie, Hawaii.

As editor and chief translator for the project, my task has been to review these histories and translate into English those portions which seemed appropriate for the inclusion in this commemorative volume. I have endeavored to be faithful to the original accounts, if not in precise word-for-word renditions, then always in the spirit of the intended meaning. In most cases, I have reviewed each translation with the author for verification of content and meaning. Previously published sources have been edited for consistency in matters of punctuation and capitalization.

Although this book has been a deeply gratifying project, I am aware of its imperfections. For one thing, many prominent Saints and leaders in the Church over the years do not appear in these pages or are mentioned only briefly in the stories of others. Constraints of time, workers, and deadlines made it impossible to secure appropriate information from all these noteworthy persons or their families. Likewise, limited space in this volume prohibited the inclusion of many excellent histories submitted for consideration. I hope that a sequel to this book or other histories of Tonga will make use of these materials. My main regret, of course, is that many faithful Tongan Saints, like their Book of Mormon ancestors (Ether 12:23–25), were mighty in speech but weak (or at least inexperienced) in writing. Their magnificent personal experiences and testimonies rang from the pulpit for generations but did not find their way into accessible personal journals, diaries, or family histories. We hope they are not lost forever.

Yet despite these impediments, that which is most characteristic of the spirit and faith of the Tongan people is communicated clearly, even profoundly by those whose stories lie within this volume. These Saints are revealed as they really were and are, not merely as stereotypical "humble natives" or the "sweet, gentle, simple folk of Polynesia," but as powerful human beings, as intelligent and admirable in their setting as Saints anywhere in Church history. Their collective stories over a hundred years are not unlike those of their ancestors as recorded in the scriptures, or those of the early Mormon pioneers as recorded in LDS Church history.

Although the purpose of this volume is to feature extraordinary spiritual moments in the lives of ordinary Saints, it does not imply that Church history in Tonga is devoid of villains, defections, conflicts, and sin. Far from it. But on balance, the emergence of the Church in the twentieth century and the assimilation of gospel principles among the Tongan Saints generally is a remarkable, even glorious legacy of righteousness and faith within the world Church of Jesus Christ of Latter-day Saints.

Eric B. Shumway
Faivaola

Introduction

The early foundations of The Church of Jesus Christ of Latter-day Saints were laid in the Kingdom of Tonga by devout Christian missionaries who knew little or nothing of the restoration of the fulness of the gospel of Jesus Christ. Yet they were an essential part of the Lord's grand design in preparing the Friendly Islands to receive the fullness of his Church after much tribulation.

Yielding to spiritual guidance, these evangelical men and women courageously put the Lord Jesus Christ into the hearts and onto the lips of a people lacking that knowledge. They pressed the need for Christ and salvation. They taught the fundamentals of prayer and translated the Holy Bible. Organizing schools and congregations, they nourished and enlightened minds. They taught the principles of leadership which would perpetuate faith and instruction over coming generations.

In effect, those missionaries were the *kau fakamelomelo* (those who went before to prepare the way). In the Lord's plan, their role was to *tā e fihi,* cut down the tangled timber of darkness so that the full garden of the Lord might eventually be planted. Thus, any celebration of the growth and stature of The Church of Jesus Christ of Latter-day Saints in Tonga today should include appropriate recognition of those men and women—especially the Wesleyan missionaries—who helped to bring Christianity and Western civilization to the Tongan Islands. A brief overview of some of the key events and people in nineteenth-century Tonga will provide a better understanding of the magnitude of the Lord's work in the Friendly Islands. It will also establish the social, religious, and political context in which the LDS missionaries found themselves when they first landed in Nuku'alofa, July 15, 1891.

I

The story of the introduction and early growth of Christianity in the Tongan Islands is a study in contrast and conflict. On the one hand, it is a tale of civil war, malicious sailors, bloodthirsty chiefs, renegade ministers, threats and murder, sickness and famine, failed missions, political strife, massacres, disasters at sea, arrogance and jealousy, religious intolerance, powermongering, intrigue among the brethren, persecution, betrayal and defection.

On the other hand, it is also a chronicle of courage, relentless evangelical zeal in an immensely hostile environment, indefatigable dedication, patient perseverance in suffering, pentecostal outpourings, the gift of tongues, literacy and education, and finally the complete transformation of a polytheistic "nation of wreckers" to a peaceful Christian country governed by the rule of law and the Holy Bible – the Jewel of the Pacific.[1]

This mighty transformation occurred in the lifetime of one man, the principal player in this nineteenth century saga, Taufaʻahau, who became King George Tupou I.

The swift emergence of this peaceful, modernized nation out of its conflicted past is one of the wonders of the world. The Reverend Thomas West, who served ten years in Tonga as a Wesleyan missionary (1846–56), called this transformation a "change so stupendous, and rapid" that it defies reason and the imagination. He continued:

> The numerous islands, occupied by its people, contain 169 Protestant places of worship. Connected with these there are 24 Resident European and Native Ministers; 13 Catechists; 214 Day-School Teachers; 676 Sabbath-School Teachers; 856 Lay Preachers; 9,822 Church Members; and 248 Day Schools, containing 9,712 Scholars. The number of regular attendants upon public worship is about 30,000, and more than £3,000 per annum are contributed voluntarily by the people for religious purposes.
>
> Forty years ago there was not one Christian throughout the whole of that same region. At that time gross and unbroken darkness prevailed. The people were universally given up to a vile system of

---

[1] The principal information sources are A. Harold Wood, *Overseas Missions of the Australian Methodist Church* (Melbourne: Aldergate Press, 1975), Sione Lātūkefu's *Church and State in Tonga* (Canberra: Australian National University Press, 1974), Ermel Morton, *Brief History of the Tongan Mission of the Church of Jesus Christ of Latter-day Saints*, condensed by Carol P. Fletch for the Golden Jubilee Conference of the Tongan Mission, December 1, 1968, and R. Lanier Britsch, *Unto the Isles of the Sea: A History of the Latter-day Saints in the Pacific* (Salt Lake City: Deseret Book, 1986). The quoted phrase comes from Wood, p. 14.

Introduction

heathenism, and the land was steeped in blood, shed during intestine wars, and by the deeds of a rapacious despotism.[2]

The enormous contributions of the early Wesleyan missionaries in the Friendly Islands are evoked by the names of John Thomas (1826–50, 1855–59), Nathaniel Turner (1827–31), William Cross (1827–35), James Watkin (1831–37), David Cargill (1834–35, 1842–43), Stephen Rabone (1836–50), William Webb (1841–53), Thomas West (1846–55), and Richard Amos (1847–58), not to mention the later genius of Dr. James Egan Moulton (1865–88, 1895–99, 1895–1905) whose intellectual, musical, and linguistic gifts greatly enhanced the quality of Wesleyan worship and schools.

Even more effective than the *pālangi* (white) missionaries in persuasive instruction were such Tongan ministers as Peter Vī, who preached in the first public Christian service held in Vava'u in April 1831 before the chief, Finau 'Ulukālala.

Despite the gallant efforts of the Wesleyan missionaries, it was not only the testimony of Christ but allegiance to their newly converted paramount chiefs that encouraged the Tongan people to venture in large numbers to the white man's *lotu* (religion). The people of Ha'apai and Vava'u submitted completely to Taufa'ahau's vigorous campaign against the old indigenous religion, ridiculing priests and destroying shrines and idols of heathen worship.

Baptized in August 1831, Taufa'ahau took the Christian name of George, became fully literate, and functioned as a regular preacher in the Wesleyan Church. An exceedingly intelligent man with a commanding presence, he was a driving force within the church and the principal protector of the missionaries from outside threats. When he became the *Tu'i Kanokupolu* (King of all Tonga) in 1845, the political and non-Christian alliances against him were severely weakened. By 1852 they ceased to exist as a significant power against him. Thereafter King George Tupou I was the undisputed King of Tonga, and the Wesleyan Church was the accepted national religion. In 1875 with the assistance of the presiding Wesleyan minister, Shirley Baker, King George Tupou I granted his people a constitution which is still the basic governing document of the Kingdom of Tonga.

Ironically, the *lotu* that helped create civil order in the country suffered from its own internal strife, fomented at first by jealousy and overweening ambition among several key *pālangi* missionaries, and later

---

[2] *Ten Years in South Central Polynesia* (London: James Nisbet and Co., 1865), vii.

by their conflicts with the general Wesleyan Conference in Australia. Much of this dissension surrounded Shirley Baker, chairman of the Tongan Wesleyan District (1870–79) and later Premier of Tonga (1880–89). The result was Tonga's eventual secession from the Wesleyan Australian Conference and the establishment of the independent Free Church of Tonga, January 4, 1885. The new Free Church was still Wesleyan in form and doctrine but independent in the management of its own affairs, including its finances. Again it was the dynamism and authority of King George Tupou I that brought the chiefs and almost the entire body of the Wesleyan congregations to the Free Church, for reasons both political and personal with the king. Indeed, the royal command to join the Free Church was tantamount to a test of loyalty to His Majesty and to the fundamental principle on which the Tongan society was based, namely, unwavering allegiance to the *Tu'i Kanokupolu*. This test was carried out with much emotion and a show of force in every village and island throughout the kingdom.

For many Tongans, especially those with long and deep attachments to the mother church and her missionaries, it was a wrenching time. A remnant refused to leave the Wesleyan Church and suffered the hand of persecution for their loyalty. Others found their way into the Catholic faith. However, with feelings of great nationalistic fervor, the vast majority embraced the Free Church of Tonga, the chiefly church, the king's church. Interwoven into the controversies surrounding the secession of the Free Church were fears that Tonga was in danger of annexation by England or Germany. Hence an independent church would help ensure the Tonga-for-Tonga (*Tonga ma'a Tonga*) course the king had long determined to follow. Although it would eventually sign a friendship treaty with Britain and become a protectorate (May 8, 1900), the Kingdom of Tonga would never be a colony. The British High Commission would regulate certain aspects of commerce and government finances, but Tonga would admirably remain the only independent native country in the Pacific.

The social, religious, and political aftershocks from this mighty split, plus increasing dissatisfaction with Premier Baker, created a milieu of confusion, religious intolerance, and ongoing resentments. In fact, much of the turmoil of the period can be attributed both to Baker's controversial public policies and to his own personal animosities against the Wesleyan Church over which he formerly presided in Tonga. An unsuccessful attempt on his life in 1887 by a politically motivated group from Mu'a only exacerbated the country's turmoil.

Introduction

When Baker, a British citizen, was finally removed in 1890 by the British High Commission as a danger to peace and order in this island country, there was a collective sigh of relief, even in high places. The king, then in his ninety-third year, welcomed the respite from Baker's quarrels which had divided the nation but remained adamant in his support of the free and independent status of the Free Church of Tonga.

Despite the enormous respect the entire nation felt for its aged king, the country in the early 1890s was still suffering from the ominous tremors of conflicting loyalties, clan rivalries, and bitter remembrances of persecution. The Wesleyans, though very small in number, were the more united for their trials. The large Free Church was solidly grounded on the Tongan values of loyalty to the king and self-determinism. The Catholics were a well-ordered but unthreatening minority. Indeed, the Tongan longing for *melino mo e fe'ofo'ofani* (peace and harmony) made the prospect of more disruption, change, or new religious causes unappealing.

It was into this setting that the first two elders from The Church of Jesus Christ of Latter-day Saints arrived on board the *S. S. Wainui* on July 15, 1891. Their purpose was to announce a new gospel dispensation, to preach the restored gospel of Jesus Christ, and to testify that God had revealed himself to a living Prophet. They meant to proclaim the restoration of the holy priesthood, enabling men on earth to act for God in teaching and saving humankind. No doubt these men hoped to see branches of the Church established throughout the kingdom.

Not fully aware of all the trauma this island nation had experienced, Elders Brigham Smoot and Alva Butler optimistically called upon King George Tupou I the day after their arrival. The old king received the two Americans with his customary graciousness and listened intently as they read the Mormon Articles of Faith to him. His kind response was the same that he had given many times before to other visitors—that religious freedom was guaranteed by Tongan law and the people could make up their own minds whichever church they wanted to join.

The king was no doubt sincere in stating the legal guarantees for religious freedom, but the LDS missionaries soon discovered a less liberal reality. Although the Tongan people were curious about them, even friendly, they kept their distance from the American missionaries who testified that The Church of Jesus Christ of Latter-day Saints was the "only true and living church upon the face of the whole earth, with which I, the Lord, am well pleased" (D&C 1:30), taught a new mode of baptism, described a new scripture to accompany the Bible (the

Book of Mormon), and announced the presence of a living prophet on the earth in their faraway Zion. Besides the anti-Mormon stories circulated by some Europeans, Tongan ministers were also watchful over their flocks, never hesitating to use the test of loyalty to king and country to keep them safely in the fold.

A case in point was the baptism of Poasi Niu and his wife Mele Sisifā from 'Alaki. They were the second and third Mormon converts in Tonga after nearly two years of effort by the LDS missionaries. The couple were subsequently disciplined by Church officials for "apostasy." Before any formal action was taken against them, Elder Olonzo Merrill asked why they quit attending meetings and returned to the Free Church; they simply said it was no longer possible for them to withstand the outrage of their extended family. "Their friends mocked and scoffed at them so much they could not bear it."[3]

In effect, the dynamics of village life and the ceremonial obligations to family, chief, and king that made the Tongan people such a strong society severely handicapped those interested in a new religion. The couple, like other investigators, were part of a complicated, interdependent, and closed system which resisted disruption and change, especially in view of the recent traumas in both church and state.

Over the years, many have found LDS doctrines appealing yet hesitated to become baptized, not because of theological difficulties or lack of faith but because of *fatongia* (societal obligations) or their extended family relations. *Ko ho'o papi he siasi ko iá, he na'e mate ai ho'o kui?* ("You're getting baptized in that church? Did your grandfather die there?") Only a Tongan knows the sting of that implied accusation. Thus, for many in Tonga, baptism in The Church of Jesus Christ of Latter-day Saints was a supreme act of courage, a rending of the traditional customs and relationships which bound them to family and community, and an acceptance of profound disruption.

In short, in the first half of the 1890s, the Friendly Islands were a less than fertile field for preaching the restored gospel. Approximately twenty missionaries labored there for five years and nine months, baptizing only fifteen persons, ordaining only one to the Aaronic Priesthood and none to the Melchizedek Priesthood. Most of these converts lived in Ha'apai. By 1897, only one member of the Church remained on Tongatapu. The little LDS day school in Mu'a struggled to survive

---

[3] Olonzo Merrill, Daily Record No. 5, 18 July 1894–31 December 1894. Photocopy in possession of Eric B. Shumway.

between its founding in 1892 and 1896, shutting down at different times for lack of students.

With heavy hearts and mixed feelings, the final team of Mormon missionaries sailed back to Samoa in April 1897, closing, at least for the time being, the Tongan Conference of the Samoan mission. Given the limitations of their youth, their inexperience with the Tongan language, and the inhospitable conditions offered by Tongan society at that point in history, these men and women served faithfully and well. Their gospel seeds did not all fall in rocky places. Other missionaries would return periodically to nourish the Saints and even baptize. And in 1907 the presence of the Church would again be established, growing in strength, gradually at first, then mushrooming into the mighty congregation of Saints which is so visible today in Tonga and wherever else in the world there are Tongan members of The Church of Jesus Christ of Latter-day Saints.

With what different feelings would those Mormon missionaries have sailed away from Tonga in 1897 had they been able to envision the Church's future in the Friendly Islands? Many of them had witnessed the power of God manifest in remarkable ways, but it would have overtaxed their imagination to behold the present-day Church of over thirty thousand members, ten stakes, ninety shining chapels, a dozen middle schools, two high schools, and a temple—all before the hundredth anniversary of the first landing of Elders Smoot and Butler in 1891.

II

Why has The Church of Jesus Christ of Latter-day Saints become such a conspicuous presence in Tonga today, not just in congregational numbers, but in the activity and devotion of the members? What is its appeal, the reasons for its growth, the energy behind its staying power? These questions and questions like them occur frequently in the minds of local Tongans and foreign visitors alike.

Some observers have offered quick and not altogether complimentary answers to these questions. For them it is a simple matter of material prosperity. The Mormon Church is rich, the buildings are beautiful and well kept, the Church pays top salaries to local employees, and Mormon students get Church sponsorship to study in the USA, which opens the door to fortune and future security for them. Therefore, these observers conclude, people must join the Church for mercenary reasons. They stay there for physical comfort and for relief from the financial burdens of *fatongia* (duty) in their former churches. Others say it must be the persistent proselytizing of the missionaries, the hard-sell preaching, or the zeal to baptize which overwhelms an emotional and gullible public.

Although it is impossible to scrutinize every new member's heart for ulterior motives, these responses are obviously too simplistic and do not bear up under rational inquiry. Answers much closer to reality are found in the personal histories and the living testimonials of the members themselves over the last century, such as appear in this commemorative volume.

The overriding collective theme of these historical accounts is profound religious faith. It is faith motivated and sustained by an assurance that The Church of Jesus Christ of Latter-day Saints is in very fact the only "true and living church" on the face of the earth. As Patriarch Mosese Muti records: "This knowledge is as much a part of me as my right hand and my left hand, even as my whole body." It is a faith that recognizes the good and the worth of other denominations, as expressed in the histories of Samuela 'Iloa and Tēvita Pōme'e, but declares that the *fulness* of the gospel, with its priesthood authority, ordinances, organization, and keys to full salvation are vested only in one church. It is a faith in the Lord Jesus Christ and in the leaders of his church. It is faith in the spiritual energy of personal prayer and in God's actual participation in the lives of his children on earth. It is faith that God speaks to men and women according to their need and spirituality, and that he honors and protects those he calls to his service. It is faith in the power of the holy priesthood of God to heal and be healed and to control the elements of nature. It is faith in the redemptive power of the temple.

The authors of these vignettes out of history come from a variety of backgrounds and experiences spanning four generations. Bound by a common belief, some are university graduates with degrees in medicine and educational administration, while others are subsistence farmers who never studied beyond primary school. Some joined the Church in their young adulthood, some in their late seventies, while others have been nurtured in the faith from childhood. Several were respected leaders in other churches before they were baptized, well acquainted with the Bible. Others had little formal religious training of any kind. Several persecuted the Church, then, like Paul the Apostle, became eloquent defenders of it. A few are young returned missionaries, others are long deceased, speaking from past generations. They are chiefs, housewives, accountants, teachers, businessmen, fishermen, students, bakers, policemen, carpenters, mechanics, and district officers. All of them speak in the same irresistible spirit of faith and testimony.

Besides religious faith, other important qualities which characterize the Saints of Tonga permeate these historical selections. For example, the immense love of the Saints for the missionaries, both foreign and local, is illustrated throughout. No one who has ever felt the love of the Tongan people will forget it. Pī Feleti Maile confesses that the beginning of testimony for his father, Kitione Maile, was his love for the strapping young *kau pālangi* (white men) who regularly walked by his home in Nukunuku in 1910. These missionaries were *anga faingofua* (easy natured) and fluent in the language. He could not resist inviting them in for refreshment—a green coconut or a baked taro. Inevitably, their conversations led to the restored gospel, and Kitione and his family were baptized.

The contrast between the stiff formality of many older Protestant ministers from British Commonwealth countries and the easy warmth of the Mormon missionaries from America was not lost on the Tongans. It is a subject of conversation even today. These young Latter-day Saint men relished Tongan lifestyle, sat crosslegged on mats, ate with their fingers, slept on the floor, played with Tongan children, and, with gusto, ate everything on their plate from *hihi* (snails) to *kolukalu* (jellyfish) to *siaine kili* (boiled green bananas). Each generation of Tongans have looked upon the missionaries as their own children, as expressed in the histories of Pita Hopoate, Muli Lisala, 'Isileli Kongaika, and Muli Kinikini.[4]

The young Tongans serving missions enjoy the same regard from their fellow Saints. For instance, in June 1989 the Saints of Ta'anea and Ha'alaufuli, Vava'u, entertained Elder Joseph B. Wirthlin of the Council of the Twelve with a massive feast at a stake conference. The tables were laden with literally hundreds of island delicacies, for food in the

---

[4] Single Caucasian women were never called as proselyting missionaries because of the strenuous living situations, the government quotas on Caucasian missionaries, and the feeling in Tongan society that it is not proper for single women to be away from the supervision of their families. When it became possible for pairs of sister missionaries to begin proselyting in the mid-1960s, young Tongan sisters greatly strengthened the missionary effort. A few single Caucasian sisters have served from time to time as teachers in the Church schools; and wives of mission presidents played a key role in fostering the work in general and overseeing the auxiliaries in particular.

Tongan culture is an emblem of love. Volume and quality are equally important in the presentation. The following week, the same Saints prepared a meal for our sixty local missionaries serving in Vava'u after a regular zone meeting. I was amazed to see almost the same food presentations as the week before at the stake conference. When I mentioned this to some of the members, they answered almost amazed, "You know we don't make distinctions between apostles and our own missionaries. We honor them equally."

Some may say this response is typical of Vava'u *laukau* (showing off), but it does actually represent a pervasive Tongan attitude toward all missionaries. Other prime instances of this fact have occurred numerous times in my own missionary work. I remember an invitation to eat supper with the Tēvita Muli Kinikini family back in 1961. A 'Uiha, Ha'apai, family, the Kinikinis were living temporarily in Nuku'alofa close to the Fanga'uta lagoon. Tēvita Muli was a full-time proselyting missionary with me and therefore had no salary. Several of the Kinikini children were still at home at the time. I was thus aware of the family's austere living conditions and tried to refuse a request to join them for supper but Tēvita Muli would not allow me to refuse.

Now the Kinikini family had no plantation and no animals on Tongatapu, except for a small flock of ducks that eventually dwindled to one little duckling. When I sat down on the floor in the family circle that night, four young children watched their mother put pieces of boiled breadfruit before each one of us. Then, before me, she put a freshly boiled duckling. The sight and the aroma of this delicacy made a visible impression on the children who were sitting quietly with their hands clasped in their lap. It was clear that the duckling was for me.

"I'll not eat this by myself," I said to Tēvita Muli. "We will all share."

Before I could start dividing it, Tēvita Muli quickly interrupted, "No, you will eat it by yourself. It is yours!"

"But your children?" I protested.

"They do not want to touch it," he continued. "You honor them by eating it yourself. Some day they will be proud to tell their children they went without *kiki* (meat), so that a servant of the Lord might eat and be filled."

Although times and attitudes are changing in Tonga today, there is still a difference between Tongan and Western attitudes toward poverty and wealth. The typical Westerner measures wealth by the things he or she accumulates and stores for personal use. A Tongan is wealthy in what he or she gives away. Conversely, a Westerner feels the bite of poverty in what he or she lacks personally. A Tongan suffers poverty only when he or she has nothing to give someone he or she loves. Hence the outpouring of gifts, mats, tapa cloth, food, compliments, friendship, and love upon the missionaries.

The loving and honoring of the LDS missionaries has always crossed denominational boundaries. Obviously if it had not been for the generosity of people of other faiths, the Mormon missionaries would have suffered severe privation, especially in villages where no branch of the Church existed. One of the poignant moments in Mosese Naeata's history is a description of the love of an elderly Falevai woman. After the hurricane of 1961, virtually everyone in Vavaʻu was reduced to abject poverty. Still this lady insisted that Mosese and his companion turn aside into her hut to eat a tiny morsel of coconut meat and a *sī* root.

The cheerful ability of the Tongan Saints to sacrifice all they possess for the Church and to endure severe hardship for their faith is evident in many recorded histories. Indeed, some foreign readers may be shocked by their willingness or by the quiet assumption of some presiding foreign leaders that they can count on this willingness no matter what personal circumstances are involved. Extreme examples appear in the stories of how Mosese and Salavia Muti received their mission call to Niue and in Manase Nau's "orders" to transfer to Haʻapai, leaving his wife, Salina, to care for their deathly ill child. The frequency with which the mission presidents called couples with small children on missions to remote and primitive places may seem unfeeling today. But nothing strengthened the Church faster and empowered the Saints more with an abiding testimony of the restored gospel than their collective years of sacrifice in voluntary missionary service. Of those years were great family legacies created, and now children remember the faith of their parents and witness how the Lord guides and cares for his own. And far from being critical of their leaders, local and foreign, the Tongan Saints have always been exceedingly supportive, even reverential towards them, if not adoring.

The willingness to consecrate all things for a great cause was no more evident among the Tongan Saints than in their desire to receive their temple blessings in the New Zealand Temple. Lela Dalton records President David O. McKay telling a congregation in Vavaʻu in 1955 that he envisioned a temple in Tonga someday. Many Saints clung to that prophecy. And when in 1980 the formal announcement of a temple for Tonga was made, there was universal joy among the Saints which can only be described in the language of the poet: *"Ko 'emau haka he langi kuo tau!"* ("We dance in the ultimate perfection of the singing!").

Stories abound in family histories of personal sacrifice and spiritual preparation to enter the house of the Lord. Dr. Sālesi Havili tells of the profound test of his faith in the surgery amphitheater in Vava'u. Lu'isa Kongaika describes how her husband disassembled their house, sold it piecemeal, and added every article they possessed to pay their fare to New Zealand. Leni Tu'ihalangingie records the succession of "heavenly coincidences" that allowed him and his family to travel to the temple in New Zealand. Tēvita Folau Mahu'inga recounts how his father was inspired in 1973 to consecrate his property next to Liahona, the Church school, as the site for the Lord's house.

The curiosity which the Nuku'alofa Tonga Temple inspires among the general Tongan public has occasionally spilled over into unsavory comments or even verbal attacks, accusing the temple ordinances of violating traditional Tongan decorum and modesty. If not, detractors argue, why are temple ceremonies secret? The Saints themselves, without revealing the sacred details of the temple ceremony, simply dismiss what they call *laulaunoa ni* (this nonsense) with a categorical refutation. Indeed, for them nothing emphasizes or validates traditional Tongan family values and ideal human relationships as the presentations within the house of the Lord.

Another vital component within the society of Tongan Saints is the strength of the Church's women as leaders and nurturers of the faith. Tonga Toutai Pāletu'a credits the survival of the Church in Faleloa, Ha'apai, to the "faith and force of four women." Tonga Mālohifo'ou's praise of his wife 'Ana ("I came to consider her as a mother to me, as well as a wife") is a fair assessment of the thousands of LDS women who mothered children, husbands, and fellow Saints in the various branches of the Church.

The Tongan concept of mothering is expressed most poignantly in the proverbial phrase *mohe ofi* (sleeping close). The image is of a child lying close to his or her mother on the bed, head resting on her forearm, listening to her wisdom. A supreme compliment to a child (and the parents) is, *"Fie lau he na'a ke mohe ofi"* ("No wonder you excel. You slept close"). In this sense, the growing Church "slept close" to its mothers. Lu'isa Kongaika's encounter with the Savior and subsequent personality change, Sela Feinga's courage at sea, Ada Layne Cahoon's radiant faith that overcame the terrors of cultural shock, Sela Tāfisi's devotion in the midst of persecution, and Sālome 'Ulu'ave's conversion that opened the gospel doors to an entire island—all are unforgettable portraits of heroic womanhood.

The priesthood's power and its reverent use is another theme that glows throughout the history of the Tongan Saints. A simple explanation of priesthood is that it is the sacred authority of God, given to men to act for him in bringing about the happiness and salvation of his children. Jesus Christ's ancient apostles returned to earth under his direction to bestow this priesthood upon the Prophet Joseph Smith; and through him, it extended widely and freely in the Church. Today all worthy men in the Church may hold the same priesthood regardless of education or social position.

The concept of a lay, non-professional priesthood suggested a kind of equality which was initially foreign to such a rank-conscious society as Tonga. However, in the Church it was an equality before God which allowed an illiterate like Kitione Maile, for example, to preside effectively over congregations and give wise counsel to the educated.[5] More importantly, the gifts of the Spirit were readily apparent in those who righteously used their priesthood authority. Thus the priesthood generated confidence among the members and, through the proper exercise of it, opened their minds and hearts to an understanding of Christlike leadership that they could have never attained through formal study.

Thus the spread of the gospel by the Mormon missionaries was not just in word, but in power. President John A. Nelson, Jr., (1913–16) offers a stirring account of the gift of tongues in his history. Sela Tāfisi, Sālome 'Ulu'ave, Teleita Fakatou, Senivia Tu'ikolovatu, Tohi Fonua, and Havea Māsila are examples of hundreds of converts to the Church who were first miraculously healed from serious physical afflictions by their faith, united with that of the elders, and by the power of the missionaries' priesthood. Their testimonies are recorded as one aspect of the power that moved the work of the Lord to its present status. Perhaps the most awe-inspiring of these stories is that of Tonga Mālohifo'ou during the fury of the 1961 hurricane which devastated Vava'u. Reasoning that he had priesthood power to heal the body, he

---

[5] Ralph Olson, former missionary to Tonga in the late twenties and later principal of Liahona High School, reminiscing with me in August 1990, admiringly remembered, "Kitione Maile *was* the Church in those days. And you know I would rather preach with him than anyone else, because of his power at the pulpit. He couldn't read or write a lick, but he knew the Bible and the gospel. When he spoke he held the congregation with the strength of his words and ideas."

saw no reason why he could not also "heal" the storm. His dramatic blessing at the peak of the hurricane saved his home and the people who took refuge there. Obviously different circumstances require different uses of the spiritual gifts inherent in the priesthood of God. The histories of Muli Lisala, 'Iohani Wolfgramm, Tonu Naeata, Charles Wolfgramm, Leni Tu'ihalangingie, Tēvita Folau Mahu'inga, Muli Kinikini, Tonga Toutai Pāletu'a, Lolo Tuiaki, Joan Winegar Coombs, and others reveal new dimensions to a phenomenon in The Church of Jesus Christ of Latter-day Saints that loses nothing of its sacredness by its frequency.

In addition to the spiritual highlights in the history of the Tongan Saints, there is also much of local color and cultural flavor. Some of this flavor may be subtle, but it increases our delight in the stories and sharpens our vision of what is typically humor (*hua*) or Tongan rivalry (*fakavahavaha'a*) or fear of the supernatural (*ilifia tēvolo*), etc. Who can resist a smile at the antics of Lātū Makaafi swearing publicly he will never join the Mormon Church? It was not enough for him to raise his right arm high (*Ko hoku nimá ē!*) in the traditional gesture of oath-making. He lifted his left arm to underscore his promise, then sat down on the grass and mockingly raised both his feet toward heaven. The irony of this ridiculous oath is that, despite his vows, he accepted the gospel, was baptized, and became a fine member of the Church.

Mosese Muti's touching account of crossing the deadly 'Auhangamea channel at night in a miraculously prepared outrigger canoe is countered by the quip of a practical relative who wasn't impressed by such daring: "Muti," he says, "true religion is not so very stupid as that!"

Mosese Naeata's fear of ghosts and evil spirits strikes a responsive chord in every Tongan raised in the lore of old Tonga. Whole villages can still be worked up over any suspicious sign of a lurking shadow from the underworld. The moment of redemption for Mosese came when he realized he would rather face the spurious ghosts of the Vava'u forests than his very real mother if he failed to return home that night.

Hungry school girls at Makeke barking like dogs in chase of wild pigs; Presidents Mōleni Fonua and Folau Moehau making an elaborate ceremonial food presentation to express "gratitude" to a boat captain for forcing them to jump overboard in deep water; Sela Kioa dragging her husband to see a fortune teller; John Alexander Nelson, Jr., president of the Samoan Mission, brooding over Tongan pride, which smarted

Introduction

at being "governed" by Church leaders from Samoa—are all colored with cultural overtones which make each history more readable, more human, and more Tongan.

III

The spectacular growth of the institutional Church of Jesus Christ of Latter-day Saints with its office buildings, chapels, schools, and temple tends to preoccupy many observers who overlook the spiritual impact of the gospel in the private lives of the members. Even as Saints, we must be careful that *polepole* (boasting) or *loto hikisia* (pride) in our outward blessings never becomes a substitute for true spirituality. President David O. McKay often made the point that our fine buildings and grounds and monuments must be symbols of an inner morality and goodness without which material prosperity become nothing but a husk and a shell.[6]

As we contemplate a hundred years of the Church's existence in Tonga, especially in view of immense changes which have occurred and will yet occur in the Kingdom of Tonga, the Saints must grip all the more tightly the iron rod of the gospel of Jesus Christ. Today's challenge is not the enforced distance of society from religion but the challenge of having the form of religion (*fakangali lotu*) without the substance of faith. It is the turmoil of dishonesty, greed, and immorality. If, as A. Harold Wood says, the pre-Christian Tongans of the early nineteenth century were a "nation of wreckers," then Tonga today, following the heartless example of the world, may be becoming a "nation of family breakers." The answer is to heed the gospel message which can save both family and nation.

Many Tongan customs are eroding under the abrasion of modern technology and modern thought. Many cultural fixtures will inevitably become relics of the past. What must continue—and increase—is the legacy of faith so abundantly preserved in the lives of the Saints in The Church of Jesus Christ of Latter-day Saints. With that faith we must preserve also the classic Tongan virtues which have traditionally characterized the ideal nature every Tongan (indeed every person everywhere) should aspire to: *anga'ofa* (a loving nature), *anga faka'apa'apa* (a respectful, reverent disposition), *mamahi'i me'a* (zealousness in a good cause

---

[6] Reuben D. Law, *The Founding and Development of the Church College of Hawaii* (St. George, Utah: Dixie College Press, 1972), 68.

to the point of pain), *tauhi vahaʻa* (maintaining good relations, being eager to mend fences), and *loto tō* (to be humbly willing, deferential, but keenly committed).

IV

I learned to admire and revere these qualities, to emulate them in a way that always seemed fumbling compared to the sincere graciousness and ease of the Tongans who opened their homes and hearts to me. It is to pay an unfeigned, though halting, tribute to these people that I include this personal history of my experiences in Tonga, not because I have any importance in myself nor any desire to intrude into these narratives. Rather, I see myself as a voice for the hundreds of non-Tongan missionaries and teachers called by the Church to labor in the Friendly Islands over the last hundred years. My experiences, impressions, and rites of passage are widely typical of all the *kau faifekau papālangi* (white missionaries) who struggled in the service of God to assimilate a new culture, language, diet, and climate.

I served my first mission to Tonga between 1959 and 1962, returned to Tonga in 1968 as a language training coordinator and Tongan linguist for the United States Peace Corps, then conducted several research projects in Tongan oral culture throughout the 1970s. In July 1986, I was called as president of the Tonga Nukuʻalofa Mission. Carolyn and I took four of our seven children with us to this beloved second home.

Missionary life is composed of sunshine and shadow. It calls those set apart to that work to mature spiritually in a distant environment which is in many ways alien to their own. I testify of the power of Christ in transforming weak vessels, fractured with limitations, into messengers of light equal to the task of preaching his gospel in a "strange tongue." Finally, I celebrate the profound love and thanksgiving that anyone who has worked among the Tongan people feels for them, for the charm and generosity of their character, and for the strength of their faith.

My arrival in Tonga November 9, 1959 was a painful awakening. I arrived with a romantic vision of Tonga as an exotic paradise inhabited by a sweet and simple people. As the old passenger boat, the *Tōfua*, glided cautiously toward the Nukuʻalofa wharf, I wrote down my first impressions of the Tongan Islands: "I thrill at the beauty of this place. We are passing many small islands close enough to see the beaches and the palm trees silhouetted against the morning sky. Two or three sailboats are scurrying afar to some little island in the chain."

Introduction

What peace, what serenity! And what a jarring change of point of view just a few minutes later as Elder Boyd Helquist, my traveling companion, and I were being jostled down the gangplank onto a dock milling with a dark, foreign-speaking multitude. I was overwhelmed by the humidity, the stench of rancid copra, and the guttural, staccato speech of the dock workers. This first encounter with the incomprehensible, alien language terrified me.

Several minutes later, we noticed a portly, elderly man moving toward us, dressed meticulously in white trousers, a gray coat, and dark glasses, and swinging an umbrella. I would soon learn to love and revere President M. Vernon Coombs, a tough veteran who was serving his third mission in the South Pacific. He had presided over the Tonga Mission from 1920 to 1926 in perhaps its darkest hour. When a 1922 law prohibited Mormon missionaries from entering the country, thus threatening the existence of the Church, he spearheaded a two-year effort by members and Church representatives that resulted in its repeal. But on first impression, I sensed only what seemed to be gruffness and found him more businesslike than warm.

President Coombs informed Elder Helquist that because of a visa problem he would be the mission secretary for his entire mission. It was a terrible disappointment to Elder Helquist. I was somewhat disappointed myself in *not* being given that assignment, for I admitted real fears about proselyting in such a primitive place.

My fears were exacerbated by President Coomb's brusque announcement: "Elder Shumway, you will be going out to the bush early tomorrow. You will be stationed at Muʻa and will be in charge at first of eight married Tongan missionaries. Don't stick your head in Liahona [the Church school], and don't come down here to Nukuʻalofa until you can speak Tongan. We've not got room for you here." Then he added that no Tongan missionary lessons and no language learning materials were available except for the Tongan Bible and the Book of Mormon. I felt the first wave of intense homesickness. I knew exactly how Elder W. O. Facer felt when he wrote, soon after he arrived in Tonga in 1907: "When you get that kind of homesickness you wish your Mother hadn't had you."

My November 9th entry concluded, "Tomorrow I hit the bush with my native companion Vakapuna ʻAlatini. The language seems impossible and never have I felt more need for the Lord." The next four weeks overwhelmed me—cultural shock, identity crisis, unbearable homesickness, and downright despair. My emotional balance was so precarious that I consciously avoided any reminders of home. Even the sight of a Church magazine, a *Be Honest With Yourself* poster, or a *Church News* brought waves of hopelessness.

The Tongans were immensely friendly and hospitable, but I lacked the experience to understand and appreciate it. That first week, a family in Haʻapulou invited us to share their evening meal, which featured the species of large bat known as a flying fox, baked whole in coconut milk, and wrapped in taro leaves. I shall never forget opening the little bundle and staring at the tiny skull grinning back at me.

Endless visitors streamed unannounced to our missionary quarters, ostensibly to practice their English but really responding to my obvious misery. Several months later, I realized that the Tongan cure for homesickness is to be constantly in the presence of friends. For them there is no comfort in privacy. Many of these visitors were returned missionaries themselves, full of stories of the heroic exploits of former missionaries from Zion: "No one will ever match Elder John Groberg!" or "Ah, if only you could speak Tongan like Elder Douglas Banks." I did not, at first, understand these comments as encouragement that I, too, would survive these first awful days to become a successful missonary. I resented this constant praising of former elders and felt my knees buckling under the burden of my own fears. These Tongans had a great deal of love for me from the beginning but no pity. They knew that I must change to succeed, and they checked every effort I made, consciously or unconsciously, to avoid dealing with the reality of Tonga.

I attended my first public meeting with the Saints just days after I arrived. As I sat on the stand looking at the congregation and feeling that everyone was staring back at me, I asked myself: Why do they stare at me so? How will I learn this impossible language and teach these staring people anything? I could not hold back tears of despair. Ironically, the Tongan Saints also wept because, as several commented later, they "saw that I was touched by the spirit of the meeting." When I found *that* out, then I added the guilt of seeming hypocrisy to my burdens.

The first time I tried to wash my own clothes outside our quarters I received a reprimand from ʻAna Mālohifoʻou, the wife of the Tongan missionary who lived in a little Tongan *fale* (hut) behind the missionary apartment. Apparently I had publicly insulted the sisters of the branch. "What will the nonmembers think of us if they see our elder from Zion scrubbing his own clothes?" she demanded. I resisted briefly, trying to explain through my Tongan companion, Vakapuna, about wash-and-wear clothing, drip drying, the need to be careful with delicate fabric. Even to myself, it sounded patronizing.

The physical problems included the humidity, adjustment to strange food, the incessant rain, and—perhaps the most grueling—the constant noise as mulberry bark was pounded into tapa cloth. The whole village seemed to be one huge percussion section that made my ears ring for days. I heard it in my frequently broken sleep.

Thus, just in that first week I felt myself fast becoming a nonperson as my American identity shattered under the repeated assaults of culture shock. I did not realize that the breaking would allow the emergence of the Eric Shumway I wanted to be. I desperately wanted to be loved and accepted by these people but felt so bad about myself that I was sure they were talking about me. The raised eyebrows, the snickers, the frequent use of *pālangi*, the only word I could recognize, the movement of people at will in and out of the missionary headquarters—all became a form of tyranny that increased my loneliness. I was forced to accept that I must become fluent in Tongan.

This awareness was my immediate salvation. I spent many hours memorizing a three-line talk and testimony which I gave the first Sunday I was in Tonga. The positive acclaim I received from the people for that little sermon far exceeded my deserts. And the Tongan people never failed to reward with praise and expressions of appreciation every stumbling effort I made to speak the language. I gave that same talk every Sunday and many times in between, adding a line here and a new expression there. My spirit fed on the compliments, *"'Oiaue, 'oku vave 'ene poto 'i he lea faka-Tonga"* ("My, how fast he is learning to speak Tongan").

What really cured my depression, however, was not my intellectual achievement but the first unmistakable, genuine, spiritual communication I had had in my life. It came as comfort in the fourth week when my feelings of worthlessness and humiliation were so intense I thought I could not continue my mission. There was no visitation, no thunderclap—only a quiet, inexplicably sweet force penetrating my heart and making impressions on my mind in words of promise that I could understand: reassuring me that I was acceptable before the Lord now, that I would love these people as my own flesh, that I would learn to speak their tongue fluently, that my words would be sweet to them. In turn I promised to use the gift in a single-minded effort to testify of the truth of the gospel to as many people as might cross my path.

While this experience did not totally eliminate my homesickness and my occasional fears of failure, I felt a surge of faith and energy I had never known. My desire to learn Tongan was rewarded a hundredfold. Some days I memorized and retained as many as seventy-five new words. In the next few weeks, I experienced a series of euphoric incidents, as the Lord blessed my efforts. Five weeks after my arrival, President Coombs announced at district conference that I had learned the language by the gift of tongues. I wrote in my journal: "I was filled at that time with the most real sense of appreciation to Heavenly Father for the spiritual help and gift I received that day, for I had truly given all I had, in energy, study and practice, which was a small percent, but the Lord made up the rest."

My mastery of the language was, of course, far from complete. I made my share of embarrassing mistakes. One day I proclaimed to a group of well-wishers at a wedding celebration that the custom of kissing the bride after the ceremony was similar in both Tonga and America. Unfortunately, instead of saying *kiss* I said *circumcise*. Another time when I was saying goodbye to a sweet lady we had taught, I thought I was saying, "It is too bad that we have to part." What I actually said was, "It is too bad that I must now be weaned from your breast."

Still, after the first seven or eight weeks of struggle, prayer, fasting, and arduous labor, the spirit of missionary work filled me with a passion that sustained itself throughout my two and a half years in Tonga, especially in those early months when the challenges of the language and newness of the culture kept me humbled constantly before the Lord. Nearly every entry in my journal during this period of time concludes with a prayer of gratitude and a plea for help. These written prayers were sometimes in English, sometimes in Tongan; but I ceased praying verbally in English after the first month.

Early in 1960 at a mission conference in Liahona, I experienced another wonderful moment of discovery and enlightenment which helped dissolve in me any remaining shred of racial prejudice toward the Tongan people. It was a moment in which I was taught feelingly the meaning of the Apostle Peter's vision of the descending net through which he learned that the gospel should be preached to Gentiles as well as to Jews (see Acts 10:9–16), that the human soul is infinitely precious, and that color and custom are simply external trappings.

After a late afternoon meeting, the visiting authority, Elder John Longden, Assistant to the Council of the Twelve, retired to the home of the school principal. Soon a large group of Saints from Vava'u gathered on the front lawn to perform a *lakalaka* dance in honor of this General Authority from Salt Lake City. As with all *lakalaka* performances, this one began in majesty and ended in exaltation, the voices of two hundred singers reverberating through the grounds of the school.

The group dance concluded with a male solo dance, a *tau'olunga* performed by the Vava'u district president, Malakai Manu 'Unga. It was fascinating to me to see a man dance with such graceful movements and warmth. Elder Longden sat forward in his lawn chair, clearly animated by the beauty of the performance. Suddenly he sprang to his feet and commenced his own version of the *tau'olunga,* imitating Brother 'Unga's every movement, including the whirls, the nods, and the bows. I nearly swallowed my tongue with surprise. Whatever grave dignity Elder Longden had conveyed from his chair as a travel-weary but interested spectator was now transformed into overflowing and overwhelming love and appreciation that manifested itself through the movements of his whole body. Here the white man, knowing little of the ways of the brown, and the brown, knowing less of the ways of the white, were caught in a glorious moment of harmonious feeling which transcended color, race, or culture.

Slowly they gravitated together in the movements of the dance, until they embraced – equals, brothers, co-stewards in God's kingdom, communicating a love and wisdom that surpassed words. For me it was as if the barriers of race, ignorance, and prejudice had fallen, and I stood bathed in the insight of Peter's vision: "Of a truth I perceive that God is no respecter of persons" (Acts 10:34).

One of the greatest blessings of my mission was the unqualified loyalty and love of my fellow Tongan missionaries. Most of them were married men with families. In 1946, the Tongan government limited the number of foreign elders to three, according to the number of total Church members. By 1959, only four proselyting Caucasian elders were allowed in Tonga, including the mission president. Non-proselyting teachers were allowed entrance to staff Liahona High School. This government policy turned out to be a blessing in disguise by giving Tongan converts a marvelous missonary challenge to which they rose magnificently. The two other Caucasian elders were stationed on different island groups. The Tongan elders loved me enough to transform me – pushing me, molding me, and keeping me constantly speaking before the public.

At first I felt persecuted by this insistence that I "go public," but it kept me humble and forced me to constantly try to speak my best.

My fourth companion, fifty-seven-year-old Tēvita Muli Kinikini, was both my most pitiless and greatest teacher in the Tongan language and custom. One day we were traveling by tugboat across the channel from Tongatapu to 'Eua. The voyage, though but a few hours, was nauseatingly rough. When I stepped on to the little boat early that morning, the stench of diesel oil and farm animals was so heavy I felt my gorge rising. The deck was full of people, animals, and plantation crops. I resigned myself to the tortures of seasickness.

As we moved out to sea, I gripped the rail tightly and leaned over, braced for the inevitable. Suddenly I could hear Elder Kinikini speaking to the crowded passengers in a voice that rang above the din of the engine and the sounds of animals: "My dear countrymen, we are most fortunate today to have as our fellow traveler a young white man from America, who is here to give you a special message in our own tongue. He is dying to address you. He is learning our language and has asked for this opportunity. I introduce to you Elder Eric Shumway from America."

I felt great irritation at Elder Kinikini's lack of consideration for my illness. He literally pulled me away from the railing and bade me speak. The Spirit came to my rescue. I spoke for the entire length of the crossing. Words came easily and fluently. The nausea receded.

I had heard all my life about the faith of the Polynesians, but I was unprepared for the depth of belief which many of them possess. I had never before seen such faith to heal and to be healed. A missionary is constantly being called upon to fast for, pray with, or administer to someone in distress. One shining experience involved Laukau Toki, the wife of one of our missionaries, Sāmiu Toki. She was eight months pregnant when I visited them in Fatai village to go house preaching with her husband and had not been well since a severe fall in the village copra shed several days earlier.

When we returned from our work that day, she told us she had been to see the doctor because she had not felt the baby move for many days. The doctor who examined her told her the baby was dead and must be removed immediately by surgery or her own life would be in danger. Laukau flatly told the doctor that there would be no operation. She would simply ask her missionary from Zion to give her a blessing.

It was fearsome for me to lay my hands upon a woman of such faith, but I did as she insisted, pleading mightily unto the Lord to spare the child. The next evening Sāmiu came to Nukuʻalofa to tell me that at 4:00 A.M. his wife had been awakened by sharp kicks in her womb. The baby was alive and well. The doctors were amazed that the baby was even alive but then told Laukau she would never deliver it normally—that the baby must be removed by Caesarean section. I wrote in my journal: "I met Laukau the next week. She was overjoyed at seeing me and insisted I allow her to fix me a meal. She cried and fussed over me, mumbling all the time, 'I just haven't got enough to give this servant of the Lord who saved my baby.' "

After I had finished the meal Laukau asked me to administer to her again, blessing her that she could birth the baby normally. She had been already—I gulped—in the early stages of labor for several hours. We blessed her again and rushed her to the hospital. Her healthy daughter was born without pain to the mother and so fast that only the nurse was present. Laukau and Sāmiu named her *Fuahelotu* (Fruit of prayer and worship).

In my two and a half years as a missionary, I had five native Tongan companions with whom I lived in the elders' quarters. For about nine months, I lived in the mission home in Nukuʻalofa without a companion. I tracted each day of the week with one of the married missionaries living in the various villages on Tongatapu. President Coombs, who had seemed gruff in the very beginning, became a close and loving influence in my life, trusting me implicitly to set my own schedule and work priorities as a supervising elder. It was a wonderful time to be a missionary. Convert baptisms in 1960 and 1961 were several times the average annual baptisms of the entire previous decade. During the 1950s, baptisms averaged about a hundred per year; but in 1961, over five hundred people joined the Church.[7] The success was due to one principal cause: we missionaries were concentrating on working with investigators, rather than giving the bulk of our time to administrative responsibilities in the branches with the members.

It was my blessing to work in every major island group and most of the outer islands including Niuatoputapu. I absorbed the Tongan culture and language by the method of careful observation and imitation. My Tongan mannerisms frequently irritated Elder Boyd Helquist, the mission secretary, who needled me for what he called my "oratorical railings" instead of speeches. After one large public meeting held in an entertainment house in downtown Nukuʻalofa in which I was the

---

[7] Britsch, *Unto the Isles of the Sea*, 469.

concluding speaker, he told me that he would never go hear me preach again, then added, "Elder, you'll never convert anybody by yelling and waving your arms at him." I realized then that I had too thoroughly assimilated Tongan pulpit manners. Obviously, I was overdoing it. Thanks to Elder Helquist, I toned down a lot.

My desire to learn and do as Tongans did led me into the ceremonial aspects of the Tongan society. My older Tongan missionaries (*mātuʻa*) introduced me early to many chiefs and nobles. I eventually became friends with such honorables as ʻUlukālala, Fielakepa, Fakafanua, Kalaniuvalu, Tuʻivakanō, Veʻehala, Luani, Vahaʻi, Tuʻiʻāfitu, Malupō, Vaea, Tuita, Nuku, and Tungī who is now King Taufaʻahau Tupou IV. In almost every case, down to the present, these scions of Tonga's nobility and royalty have been hospitable and kind to the Church and its leaders, both foreign and local. They have known the mission presidents by their first names and have facilitated many projects essential to the growth of the Church and its membership.

My access to the higher ceremonial circles of Tongan society was greatly enhanced by a fortuitous first encounter with a high noble, the Honorable Nuku (Feʻao) at a kava ceremony in Kolonga, Tongatapu in May of 1961, just a year and a half after my arrival in Tonga. I had been tutored early in my mission about the importance of these ceremonies in building trust in a village or district. President Coombs encouraged ceremonial participations as settings for preaching the gospel. As I became fluent in the language, I sought opportunities to sit in *haʻofanga* (assembly) with chiefs and village elders to learn the lore and the elevated language of the country.

With my missionary companions, Vehikite, the queen's *matāpule* (chiefly spokesman) from ʻOtea, Vavaʻu, and a fine member of the Church, taught me the inviolable protocol of the kava ceremony and especially how to protect myself against the *tālanga* or verbal attacks of those chiefly attendants who are looking for ways to aggrandize themselves by putting down other chiefs. It is their duty also to protect the dignity of the presiding paramount chief by insisting that no interloper intrude upon the circle and by ensuring that no ceremonial rules are violated.

Thus, when my *kava teletele* (long-stemmed dried kava plant) was presented at the Honorable Nuku's *ʻilo kava* (kava ceremony) and I took a place in the solemn circle, I felt confident I could handle myself and perhaps lead the conversation to my purpose for being in Tonga and to the gospel of Jesus Christ. My Tongan companion for that day was Piliote Toutai, an older fellow missionary who had a legitimate *matāpule* title, Sāpoi. He also sat in the kava circle with me.

The chiefs in the circle seemed pleasantly taken by the novelty of a young white foreigner answering questions and telling stories about his experiences in Tonga. But they were not going to let me sit comfortably too long without a "fight" of some kind. When asked what ceremonial name I would use in the kava circle, I answered with a Tongan name instead of with "Elder Shumway." I had used several different Tongan titles, all unofficial, in less formal circles. But this revelation brought an instant challenge from the chiefs. Why was I using a Tongan ceremonial title instead of my real name as a minister of the gospel? Who gave me that title? Was it legitimate? Had I gone through the appropriate investiture proceedings? Why was I there under false pretenses? Why did I act like a *matāpule* by using the title when I wasn't a chief? Did I know I was belittling the Honorable Nuku by this sham?

I fended them off as best I could, but it was obvious I was struggling in deep water. The chiefs and chiefly spokesmen were not actually angry; rather they were heartily amused by the game of "exposing" me and burying me under their flamboyant debate. The uneven word battle was finally ended by Nuku himself when he declared in a long speech that he would bestow on me the chiefly title of Faivaola (One Whose Talents Produce Success), a title that would be honored even in the highest traditional circles in the Kingdom of Tonga. The debate was over. Nuku explained that a title of *matāpule* (chiefly spokesman) bestowed by him was very significant in traditional Tongan society, since he, along with Queen Sālote herself and the Honorable Niukapu, was one of the *'ulu tolu*—the three ceremonial heads or paramount chiefs in the whole kingdom. That is, a *matāpule* of Nuku was entitled to actually speak for the queen in ceremonial functions. Nuku seemed genuinely touched by the idea of a foreign Mormon missionary, groomed and trained by his Tongan colleagues, participating in the most important traditions of the society. Unlike the modern kava club which focuses on heavy kava drinking, entertainment, and fund-raising activities, the traditional kava circle symbolized unity, brotherhood, and stability in Tongan society. It was a forum of debate, resolution, and reconciliation, as well as a repository of Tongan oral culture, history, and thought. A central feature of any major event—wedding, funeral, birthday party, church conference, village work project, or reception of a distinguished guest—the kava circle ensured that a certain dignity prevailed for the occasion. It also served as a principal means of transmitting Tongan values from generation to generation.

The Saints in Kolonga were delighted at the prospects of my official investiture, or *pongipongi*, and promised to provide the appropriate gifts or *hāʻunga* to Nuku, which included a pig or *puaka hula*, kava plants, sugar cane or *tō*, fine mats, tapa cloth, and baskets of food. In July of 1961 the actual investiture ceremony was conducted at Kolonga with all of Nuku's *kau matāpule* in the circle.

It was a grand and solemn affair. After the gift presentation to Nuku, the conducting *matāpule*, Maumau, ordered the kava mixers to pound the root of the pepper plant and mix the kava in the huge *tānoʻa*, or kava bowl. Several orations were given by other chiefs during the preparation of the kava. Normally, a new *matāpule* does not speak during his own investiture ceremony, but Nuku insisted on an exception. He wanted his people to hear my oration in the chiefly language to show, as he said, that Faivaola was deserving of his new title. Guiding me throughout the preparations and in the ceremony itself was Viliami Sovea Kioa himself, Hihifo District president of the Church, and one of the queen's most respected *matāpule*.

The title Faivaola was instantly useful in opening the doors to missionary work, a kind of passport in circles otherwise closed. The story of my investiture became a leading conversational topic in my first encounters with people. Everyone wanted to hear it, even those who did not initially want to hear about the Church. The Tongans seemed genuinely pleased that a Caucasian would assume an official *matāpule* title and then actually conduct (*fai fatongia*) kava ceremonies, speak in public forums, mingle with the nobility, and challenge other chiefs on matters of custom and protocol. I never introduced myself by my title or used it, except on ceremonial occasions; but I'm sure that it gave me more confidence. The Tongans listened more respectfully to my gospel conversations and open-air sermons. Later the title was immensely valuable to me as a Peace Corps Language Training Coordinator in Tonga, a scholarly researcher in Tongan oral culture, an educator, and finally as mission president.

As valuable as the title Faivaola was in ceremonial settings and important public occasions, the quality that touched the Tongan people the most was a robust, overt friendliness toward them. An amazingly friendly people themselves, they cannot resist an interested, gregarious foreigner who is anxious to greet them in their own language and engage them on their own terms. More than one possible conflict was disarmed by showing an *anga fakakaumeʻa* (a friendly nature). For example, one of our new converts and an elderly missionary were harassed and chased out after a night *malanga* (preaching service) in a little town on Tongatapu. Apparently the missionary had been over-zealous, indeed, combative in his sermons, which fueled village antagonism against the Church. When we later baptized five people in the community, there seemed to be real cause for a town emergency. New and old members alike felt the threat of persecution.

The village was full of young men who were neither employed nor in school. They were subsistence farmers who spent afternoons drinking *kava* and doing mischief. After the Mormon missionaries had been run out of town, this gang of young men told one of our long-standing members of the Church in the community that the next Mormon missionary, white or brown, who set foot in their village would be shot. The following account is taken from my missionary journal:

> One Monday afternoon I and Sione Koka went out to the village to see the Saints and the new converts. As we parked the car in front of the home of Tuʻipulotu, she came running out wringing her hands and crying, "Oh, Elder Shumway, you can't visit here today. You must go. This is a wicked village. These evil men are just waiting for you or any other Mormon. It would be terrible if they did anything to you!" She begged and cried for us to leave.
>
> I assured her that no one was going to be hurt and asked her to show me where this so-called "murderous" clique was. She pointed to a vacant lot about 100 yards away where ten or so large Tongan fellows were sprawled out on the grass, beating the ground with bush knives and whittling sticks. They had seen us drive up in the little car.
>
> I told Tuʻipolotu I wanted to go talk to them. "Oh, no you're not," she said. She made a move to stop me, but I assured her again that no one would dare do anything to me, Faivaola.
>
> The whole situation seemed comical to me, even my own bravado. My Tongan companion, however, was glad to stay at the car. Leaving my basket full of books in the car I walked across the street toward this group of young men. I marched right toward them. My apparent boldness took them by surprise. Giving no one a chance to speak first, I introduced myself, shaking each of their hands, and sat down on the ground in their midst. We were friends in an instant. They were very willing to laugh at my stories and asked questions about America, Arizona, and Indians.
>
> For one hour we laughed and joked and they seemed to forget their hatred and their threat to shoot the Mormons. When I got up

to leave I extended them an invitation to attend our *malanga* that night. "There's nothing wrong with just coming to listen," I said.

"You bet!" they chorused together.

"And you men can help us keep the peace," I invited.

"You can count on us, *Samuei!*" they said.

A few weeks later a branch of the Church was established formally in this village. Counting the children, over 20 members of the Church were present.

This kind of linguistic and social success was a heady combination for a young man. I admit that it was fun to be the only white person in many of the islands where I lived and visited. I enjoyed the celebrity, especially after having received my title. It was flattering to be welcome everywhere I went. I was not immune to vanity and pride. Frankly, I must have been pretty insufferable at times. I'm glad I kept an honest and uncensored journal, even though I still occasionally flinch at reading it, for it recounts numerous cycles of humility, success, pride, failure, despair, and then humility again.

My vanity was especially deadly to missionary work. I was brought to my knees many times and reminded of the real source of my ability. Many of my journal entries are prayers for forgiveness and pleas for help in overcoming special problems. One of these problems was a near crisis of faith about the death of Hola Mataele Motuʻapuaka, granddaughter of Church pioneer Siosaia Mataele who first invited Mormon missionaries to Tongatapu in 1910.

Hola was the wife of Motuʻapuaka, the highest-ranking *matāpule* in all of Queen Sālote's retinue of chiefly spokesmen. Since her consort had died suddenly on July 21, 1942, she had relied heavily on Motuʻapuaka in all traditional ceremonial events. After marrying Motuʻapuaka, Hola had attended the Wesleyan Church for years, and had just returned to activity in The Church of Jesus Christ of Latter-day Saints when I became acquainted with them. During a very difficult pregnancy, Hola had become so ill that she was repeatedly hospitalized and was actually in danger of death. I never fully understood the cause of her illness and intense pain, but the excessive nausea caused dehydration, in itself potentially fatal. My companion and I had visited her many times in her home and in the hospital. We fasted for her several times and administered to her. Each time she was anointed, she would rally but then become ill again. With each anointing, we promised life to her and the baby.

My young heart was wrenched by pity for the intensity of Hola's suffering and the helplessness of her husband and the doctors. I deeply desired to help them in any way I could. But at the same time, I saw the situation as something of a morality play. A miraculous recovery by this influential woman would inspire the nobility with respect for the Church and lead to important baptisms. Surely, Motuʻapuaka would join the Church if Hola recovered. As I recall, I made this point several times in my prayers. I felt no joy in my work as long as Hola was ill. I was sure the Lord would not let us down. Everything was at stake.

Then a message came that Hola was in distress. Would I please come and give her a blessing? I realized that the request had come from Motuʻapuaka himself. We arrived at the hospital to find Hola in a deep coma. Her husband stood at her bedside, as dignified and grave as always. Only his eyes showed his grief and fear. We blessed Hola again, then went aside to offer what comfort we could to Motuʻapuaka. The nurses hovered around Hola, very alarmed. Three of the best physicians in the kingdom entered as we spoke. As they checked Hola, they became visibly perturbed. I heard one of them say she must be brought out of her coma. He seized her by the shoulders, called her name, slapped her face, called her name again, and shook her. There was no response. A few hours later, I learned that Hola had died. I was devastated. I went to bed and wept for hours. I felt completely alone, betrayed, and unworthy, as depressed as I had ever felt during my first week in Tonga. It was my darkest hour as a missionary. Thanks to a very wise and tender mission president, I was saved from complete despair. President Coombs opened my door, walked in, and sat on the bed. I remember nothing that he said specifically, but his words spoke peace to my heart.

Graveside funerals are the custom in Tonga. When Motuʻapuaka announced that his wife was having a Mormon funeral at the graveside and requested that President Coombs and I be the speakers, I was able to respond, gratefully and humbly. We spoke at the funeral to over five thousand Tongans, most of whom were not members of the Church. Motuʻapuaka never remarried and was baptized a member of the Church in 1979. To his dying day we remained fast friends.

My experience with Hola and Motuʻapuaka taught me again that God's ways are, in some ways, opaque to our human eyes. I had thought it was my faith that shattered under the blow of Hola's death, but it was my human pride and my desire to, of myself, busily arrange matters as I thought best. I learned from that experience to accept Heav-

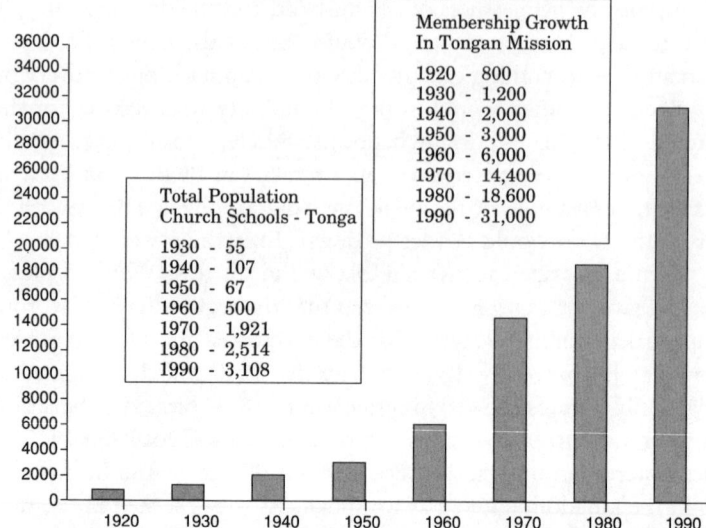

Sources: Britsch, *Unto the Isles of the Sea*, 450, 469; *Deseret News Church Almanac*, entries under Tongan Mission in 1975, 1981, 1991–92; plus additional information confirmed by telephone from Church Education System office, Church Office Building, Salt Lake City, Utah.

enly Father's will with trust and patience, sensing underneath the apparent reverses and denials his divine, sustaining power that has become as real to me as breath itself.

Twenty-four years after my release as a missionary, I was called to preside over the Tonga Nuku'alofa Mission. Arriving with Carolyn and our children on Tongatapu June 30, 1986, I saw instantly the obvious changes in the Church. The physical presence of chapels, schools, and the temple spoke of the Church's strength. The ten stakes were staffed completely with competent local leadership, and the missionary force consisted of 350 single Tongan men and women between eighteen and twenty-one, three Caucasian elders, two Caucasian couples, and five Tongan missionary couples and their families. Three of the four mission presidents preceding me were local Tongan brethren. The Saints as a whole were better educated, but also much more preoccupied than before with the economic necessities of making a living.

In 1959 one main problem for the Church in Tonga had been finding enough local priesthood brethren to meet the demands of struggling branches. Today the problem is finding enough places to locate the many full-time local missionaries. Despite the large numbers of local Tongans being called abroad to serve missions in foreign countries, including the United States, the real but wonderful problem of being saturated with local missionaries will be with the Tonga Mission for some time to come. Other challenges are the ongoing training and motivation of a missionary force twice the normal size, organizing for community service, financial and other material support, travel by sea, and communication with the remote islands.

Whatever the problems or joys during my tenure as mission president, I often found myself looking admiringly up on my office walls at the pictures of past mission presidents and their wives. As I contemplated them and the other men and women who served faithfully over the years in Tonga, I felt a kind of awe and reverence, not just because of who they were but because of what God made of them once they accepted his call. Who can measure the vast goodness of an Emile C. Dunn, an Ermel Morton, a D'Monte Coombs, a James P. Christensen, a W. O. Facer, a Frank Winn, an Evon Huntsman, a Patrick Dalton, or a Vernon and a LaVera Coombs? Who can assess the mighty and ongoing spiritual influence of a John H. Groberg?

And what about the everlasting contributions of their fellow servants and equals among the Tongans whose names also stir feelings of gratitude in the collective memory of the Saints of God: Siosifa Naeata, Kitione Maile, Tēvita Pita Pauni, Samuela Fakatou, Paula Malupō, Misitana Vea, Siosifa Tuʻiketei Pule, Maile Mataele, Lisiate Talanoa Maile, Mosese Muti, Viliami Sovea Kioa, Tonga Toutai Pāletuʻa, Nukumovahaʻi Tonga, Sione Tuʻalau Lātū, Tēvita Kaʻili, and Pita Hopoate? As one observer described the faithful Tongan leaders, "Their hearts were mountains of love and oceans of faith."

A more compelling thought for me in contemplating these giants and many more like them in the Church is that they were all tutored and supported by the same Spirit of Christ which sustains the Saints and the leaders today, including our youthful missionaries who still baptize over a thousand converts a year. Heavenly Father still works his miracles among them and still honors them as he did the prophet Jeremiah in the Old Testament. When Jeremiah protested, "Ah, Lord God! behold, I cannot speak: for I am a child," God rebuked him:

> Say not, I am a child: for thou shalt go to all that I shall send thee, and whatsoever I shall command thee thou shalt speak.
> Be not afraid of their faces: for I am with thee to deliver thee, saith the Lord. (Jeremiah 1:6–8)

These words have a tender application to our missionaries who sometimes struggle under a societal attitude that youth and wisdom are contradictions in terms, expressed in the proverb, *potopoto 'a niu mui* (wisdom of the immature coconut). Yet I witnessed among my own missionaries from my experiences as a young elder that God speaks and works through his appointed servants, despite their youth and weaknesses. Timid, frustrated, and immature in the beginning, these young people in a matter of months develop into dynamic, articulate teachers of the gospel. Giggly eighteen-year-old girls become models of modesty and dignity almost overnight.[8] Missionaries lacking functional reading and writing skills acquire them. Many who never progressed beyond middle school perform as effectively as those who attended university abroad. They heal the sick, control the elements, and bring the light of truth into the lives of thousands at home and abroad. The hand of the Lord rests conspicuously upon them. Wearing the traditional dress of the kingdom, they inspire admiration even among those who may have lingering animosities toward the Church. In the words of parliamentarian Viliami (Bill) Afeaki, my second counselor in the mission presidency, addressing a stake conference, "Whether they are singing anthems before their king, or cleaning up a village after a whirlwind, or bearing gifts in a funeral procession to present to a grieving family, or teaching a gospel discussion, our young missionaries are irresistibly the hope and the future of Tonga."

---

[8] The age requirement for Tongan sisters serving missions in their homelands was changed, after 1989, to nineteen.

PART I

BEGINNINGS

1891–1926

The Seeds of Faith

Olonzo Merrill, missionary in Tonga, 1892–96, appointed presiding elder in 1892. (Courtesy Elaine Spendlove)

Family traveling in a Tongan pōpao *(outrigger canoe). Despite the skill of the paddler, this early mode of transportation was frequently dangerous. (Courtesy V. Lynn Tyler)*

The James E. Giles family in front of their home at Pangai, Lifuka, Haʻapai, 6 February 1895. Standing left: Ellen Giles, Elders Thomas Adams, William P. Hunter, and Albert S. Jones, and George Giles. Seated left: Emma Giles, Rachel Giles, James E. Giles, and Louisa Giles. Elders Hunter and Adams baptized Giles, an Englishman, 14 October 1894 in Tongatapu. Sister Fatamafi Giles, James's wife, is not shown. Three of the children, Rachel, Louisa, and George, were educated in the United States; a large branch of the family still flourishes in Samoa. (Photograph by M. Walter Batty, original in possession of Murry L. Bohn, Louisa's son, used courtesy of Charlotte M. Bohn)

Son of pioneer Siosaia Mataele, Maile Mataele has been a monument of faithfulness and friendliness in the Church for many decades. Baptized 9 August 1911, only four years after the return of the Church to Tonga, he was sent to school at Sauniatu in Samoa where he became fluent in English. Returning to Tonga in the mid-1920s, he became a prominent businessman, Church leader, and translator. His friendly, outgoing nature became well-known to thousands of foreign visitors to Tonga over the years. He was Nuku'alofa Branch president (1931-44) and Tongatapu District president (1955-58). (Courtesy Maile Mataele)

Missionaries in 1894. Individuals not identified. (Courtesy Bea Johnson)

Apostle David O. McKay greets Pauliasi Fua Matua, June 1921. Elder McKay was the first General Authority to visit Tonga. (Courtesy Emile C. Dunn family)

A ceremonial kava circle honoring American missionaries, 1921. Left: C. A. Oborn, Stirling May, Reuben M. Wiberg, three Tongan kava mixers who have not been identified, Rueben L. Hansen, LaVerra W. Coombs, mission president M. Vernon Coombs, and J. K. Rallison. (Courtesy M. Vernon Coombs family)

Relief Society leaders in Vava'u, 1921. Back left: Fine [surname not known], Levaitai Fulivai, Seini Tōnē, and Lesieli Ahivao. Front left: Mā'ele Wolfgramm, Ma'ata Wolfgramm, LaVera Coombs, and Sālome Wolfgramm. (Courtesy Emile C. Dunn family)

American elders and sister missionaries, 1926. Front left: Walter J. Phillips, L. Leavitt, Mary Leavitt holding her child, President M. Vernon Coombs and LaVera Coombs with their three children, Rueben Clark, and Harvey G. Sorenson. Back left: Althen Rasmussen, Clarence Henderson, L. Parkin, O. Wilford Olsen, Rueben M. Wiberg, Rueben L. Hansen, and Emile C. Dunn. (Courtesy M. Vernon Coombs family)

1

John Alexander Nelson, Jr.

THE GIFTS OF THE HOLY SPIRIT[1]

One of the persistent themes in the fascinating story of The Church of Jesus Christ of Latter-day Saints in Tonga is the remarkable Tongan language skills acquired by the foreign missionaries. Taken from the history of John Alexander Nelson, Jr., the following story represents the collective experiences of hundreds of foreign missionaries to Tonga over the last century, who have become poto vave 'i he lea faka-Tonga *("fluent very quickly in the Tongan language"). The gifts of language and healing among both the foreign and local missionaries have profoundly influenced the quality of missionary service in each generation.*

On March 12, 1910, twenty-one-year-old John Alexander Nelson, Jr., arrived in Pago Pago to begin his service as a missionary in the Samoan Islands. In 1913, just a few days before he was to return to his home in Canada, he received another mission call, this time to be the president of the Samoan Mission which still had jurisdiction over the Church in the Tongan Islands.

Young, nervous, and unable to speak Tongan, President Nelson made his first six-hundred-mile voyage to Tonga three months after his formal appointment as president of the mission. This visit among the Tongan Saints was less than satisfying. "There seemed to be some discontentment about my being chosen as Mission President," he later

---

[1] From *Heritage and Histories of John Alexander Nelson, Jr., and Vera Wilcox Nelson*, researched and compiled by Verda Nelson Jensen and Carol Jensen Lasson (privately published 1989), 84–91, 111–12. Photocopy in my possession.

wrote in his personal history. "I did not have the understanding of the Tongan language. They felt they were being discriminated against by not having their own president."

President Nelson felt so keenly their disapproval of the "man from Samoa" who could not speak Tongan that, when he returned to 'Apia, he wrote directly to the First Presidency, then Joseph F. Smith, Anthon H. Lund, and Charles W. Penrose:

Dear President Smith and Counselors,

> I have just returned from a tour of the Friendly Islands, or the old Tongan Mission and everywhere I went, this question was put to me: "Why can't we Saints in Tonga have a mission of our own and a president who can speak our language?"
> Sincerely your Brother,
> John A. Nelson

The First Presidency responded by saying that the time was not right to divide the mission and instructing him to continue handling the affairs of the Church in Tonga from the Samoan Mission headquarters: "We want you to go back to Tonga, in the course of your travels, and the Lord will bless you."

President Nelson's next visit to Tonga occurred in the latter part of 1913. Upon his arrival he was invited to speak that very evening to a large congregation of Wesleyans on one of the outer islands, possibly 'Otea. Feeling deeply his inadequacy in the language, President Nelson initially turned the invitation down. "I do not know enough language to do you any good," he said to Elder Jaynes who was pressing him to make an appearance at the meeting. Elder Jaynes persisted, however, and he reluctantly yielded. In his heart, he pondered the promise of the First Presidency of the Church: "The Lord will bless you."

When they arrived at the little island, the villagers with their minister were already filling the large thatched Wesleyan chapel. President Nelson describes the event:

> Elder Jaynes took a seat with me at one end of the large hall, near the only door where a person could enter standing up. The little bench, on which we sat, was the only seat in the Church. . . . After a second song was sung Elder Jaynes gave a discourse on the first principles of the Gospel. When he had finished his sermon, he told the people that President John A. Nelson was going to speak to them in the Samoan language, since he did not understand or speak Tongan. These people did not understand Samoan any more than I understood Tongan.

As I arose to speak, a woman appeared in the doorway to my right. I motioned for her to come inside. Since she was a Tongan woman, I assumed she had come to attend the meeting. She shook her head, indicating that she did not wish to sit down. Consequently, I left her standing near me in the doorway. Elder Jaynes later said that he did not see her.

I had thought I would give a few sentences of greeting in the Tongan language and then switch to Samoan. Just as I had ended the few sentences I knew in Tongan, intending to switch to Samoan, the woman in the doorway seemed to give me the words of the Tongan language. I did not hesitate for a single word. I continued speaking in the Tongan language. It was as though I could see the words as they came from her mouth, from her lips, to me and I grasped them and went right on speaking in Tongan.

It was a revelation to these 300 or more people who were sitting on the grass and in the chapel. Those who were sitting on the outside began to come in. They realized that I had not known the Tongan language, as Elder Jaynes had announced this fact as he introduced me.

When the Lord gives a gift, he doesn't do it haphazardly. It is given in its complete form. I was speaking the Tongan language as fluently as any native. There was no hesitancy in my speech. The natives were astonished. Elder Jaynes looked at me in great wonderment to realize that I was speaking in Tongan.

I bear my testimony to you, that I spoke to that group of people for nearly an hour, in their own language. I told them of the restored gospel. I told them of the Prophet Joseph Smith. I told them of their lineage; that they were Israelites and the Lord loves them. Because of this love, he had called missionaries to come 7,000 miles from America to teach them the great plan of salvation. This plan had been restored to the earth in these latter days, through the instrumentality of the Prophet Joseph Smith.

After the people sang one more beautiful song, Elder Jaynes closed the meeting with prayer. He thanked the Lord for our being there and for the experience we had just witnessed: the gift of tongues to a humble servant of the Lord. It is one of the greatest testimonies of my life.

After the meeting, the minister came up and congratulated me. I told him that the Church of Jesus Christ of Latter-day Saints has all of the gifts and powers that were in the Church when Christ was upon the earth. I told him that the gift of healing and all of the other blessings enjoyed by the prophets of old, had been re-established and sent to the earth again for the benefit and blessings of mankind. He seemed to enjoy our discussion. However, I realize that people do not join the Church just because of a miracle. I never saw the woman in the doorway again. Elder Jaynes repeated that he had never seen her at all. There was a beautiful spirit and wonderful feeling of friendship and love felt and expressed by many.

The next day at our conference, I spoke fluently in the Tongan language, not lacking for a word. I did not need an interpreter. The letter that I had received from the First Presidency of the Church, which said, "Return to Tonga, and the Lord will bless you" was certainly true. He did bless me.

As we traveled from island to island and from branch to branch, many of the people followed us. They were so eager to hear the words of their Mission President, who had been given the gift of tongues, the gift of the Tongan language. This was not only a blessing to me, but also to the Tongan people. I learned to read the Bible translated into the Tongan language and I studied so that my pronunciation would be perfected.

From that time on, I never needed an interpreter to deliver my messages to the Tongan saints. I never heard again the request, "Why can't we have a mission president who can speak our language?" As true as I live today, I bear testimony that the gospel of Jesus Christ, as revealed to us in this day and time, through the instrumentality of Joseph Smith, is true. It is the one and only true plan of salvation that God has revealed to the people on earth today.

When I returned again to Samoa, I wrote the First Presidency of the Church of my gift of the Tongan language, for it was indeed, a gift. I have always recognized this experience as the most precious testimony and gift that the Lord has ever given me.

President Nelson recorded an additional testimony in a letter to his daughters June 15, 1959:

My Dear Daughters:

I have been thinking about a testimony that I desire to write to you about. I have thought of it a hundred times, but have never told it in public. It is very sacred to me and I have always given the Lord the credit for the accomplishment of a very wonderful blessing bestowed upon a very faithful Samoan sister.

In the month of June, 1914, while I was presiding over the Samoan and Tongan Missions, I called a Samoan man and his wife, Afatasi and Losa, to go on a mission to the Tongan Islands, six hundred miles from the Samoan group, where they had to learn a new language.

Afatasi was an elder and a very powerful speaker in his own tongue. Losa was a wonderful mother of several children and a good Latter-day Saint. However, she was blind. We had just finished a missionary meeting in the chapel, where these lovely people were both set apart for their missions to Tonga.

I had gone upstairs to the office. The mission office and several apartments for the missionaries were on the second floor. For some reason, I arose very suddenly from my chair in the office and walked to the head of the stairs, just as Losa was coming up, feeling her way along the side of the wall. Just as she was about to take the last step up, I reached down and put the fingers of my right hand on her eyes and in the name of Jesus Christ, I commanded her to receive her sight.

The outcome of this was she went on her mission with the full vision of her eyes. She could read and write as well as any school girl. She performed a wonderful work among the Tongan women and the Lord gave her another special blessing, the gift of the Tongan language, as well as the gift of her eyesight. Her dear husband was also a wonderful missionary and did a great work among the Tongan people.

I testify that I was but an agent for the Lord. It was not my power that bestowed her eyesight, but the power of Jesus Christ. I heeded the Spirit's direction and I was the instrument in the Lord's hands to perform this sacred miracle.

I know that the gospel of Jesus Christ is true. I bear this testimony to you, my dear daughters, in the name of Jesus Christ, our Savior, Amen.

2

Frank Winn

"LAYING THE FOUNDATION OF A GREAT WORK"
Doctrine and Covenants 64:33

"Elder Winn was a lion!" So remembers Maile Mataele who was baptized a member of the Church in 1911. "He could outdistance a horse when he set out walking—from Ma'ufanga to Fo'ui and back!" Like many of the early missionaries from America, Elder Winn won the trust and affection of the Tongan people because of his easy, friendly manner and his fluency in Tongan. The four entries here from his daily journal, kept during his mission from 1910 to 1913, reveal much of his enthusiasm for the Lord's work just three years after Mormon missionaries came back to Tonga after a ten-year absence. Of particular interest is his record of the dedication of the frame chapel in Nukunuku, which also served as a schoolhouse.

July 22, 1910
After a short stay we returned to Tu'anuku and visited a number of families, but as neither of the town officers were there or any of the big chiefs, we could not make any arrangements for a meeting, and the people were so afraid of us, because of their ministers, that they dare not keep us overnight. So we had to wend our way back toward Neiafu, with no expectations of a stopping place until we got there. This distance was about ten miles over muddy roads from the rain that day, and with nothing to eat since morning. We felt rather tired. We plodded on and after two hours of hard walking we arrived in Tefisi.

We were just about to leave the town when we heard a man running toward us from behind and calling. He said he wished us to come and stay with him overnight. We were only too glad to receive the invitation. When we entered the house, to our surprise, supper was ready. After supper the man brought out a little game that is much played by our American children. We taught him the game and he seemed quite delighted. After spending an enjoyable evening we were put to bed in a regular American iron bedstead with springs and white sheets.

July 15, 1911
We held baptismal services at ten o'clock on the seashore, near to the hospital, where I baptized three, namely Tēvita Fatogia Tau, Mele and Mele Tupou. The latter belongs to the family of the king. The king was also present and witnessed for the first time a baptism by immersion. We indeed felt the honor of His Majesty's presence at our first baptism of this island. In the afternoon the ordinance of the laying on of hands was attended to. President [Don C.] McBride and I also did some visiting.

July 18, 1911
President McBride and I visited the king at ten o'clock and had a short conversation with him. We presented him with a book which he gladly accepted. We also explained to him our work and he sanctioned the same and was glad to know that we had come to enlighten and educate his people without charge. When we left he gave us an invitation to come and visit him at any time. We went visiting in the afternoon.

December 28, 1912
At nine o'clock a meeting was held with all the elders in attendance. Tuʻivakanō, the Premier of Tonga, was present as was Henelē Toliai, the Wesleyan minister. Also in attendance were about 128 saints and friends. The singing was done by the Foʻui and the Nukunuku schools. I spoke on the work we had performed and the possibilities of the future. President [Christian] Jensen followed with a few remarks in Samoan, after which he offered the prayer of dedication of the new school house at Nukunuku. After the dedicatory prayer Brother [C. C.] Wiser spoke for a short while.

Then Tuʻivakanō gave a nice talk, thanking the elders and people for their effort in building the new house, and promising to do all he could to help us. Toliai was then asked to speak and responded with a nice speech. After this meeting a feast was prepared which consisted of sixteen pigs, thirty baskets of food and other edibles. This was divided out among the people and elders.

At four o'clock, school examination was held, and Tu'ivakanō was again in attendance as was Toliai, and also the Free Church minister. In the evening a school concert was held and the house was filled. Many were standing on the outside. One of our number from Mu'a came to me and said that in all his life he had never known such a day of rejoicing. Although he had never met many of the people, yet they were as brothers and sisters to him. We were indeed happy.

3

Tēvita Pita Pauni

"THE PESTILENCE THAT WALKETH IN DARKNESS"
Psalms 91:6

Baptized in July of 1913, Tēvita Pita Pauni was one of the early converts to the Church in Vava'u serving faithfully as branch president and district president for many years. He fulfilled a mission to Tongatapu, laboring in Fua'amotu, Makeke, and Kolonga. His leadership contributed much to the growth of the Church in Vava'u and the building of chapels and Sainehā High School. Brother Pauni was also the Ha'alaufuli town officer for years. As President Tonu Naeata of the Vava'u North Stake Presidency puts it: "When I was growing up in Ha'alaufuli, Pita Pauni, with his kindly handsome features and white hair, always seemed like a living prophet to me. He acted like one, too." The first portion of this excerpt from Brother Pauni's oral history includes an eyewitness account of the flu epidemic of 1918. The second section illustrates Brother Pauni's faith many years later as a seasoned Church leader.

I was born in Hihifo, Niuatoputapu, in 1903 to Tēvita Pauni, a Samoan, and Sangata Pipiena whose mother came from 'Uvea. They were strong Catholics. When I was very small, we came down to Vava'u intending to catch the steamer to Samoa. Unfortunately, my poor parents had a serious quarrel and separated for good, my father running off to Tongatapu, and my mother making her way to Ha'alaufuli.

Before my father left for Tongatapu, he made arrangements with the Catholic priest, Father Sevelio, to take me with him to France when he returned to his homeland. I was at that time boarding at the Catholic primary school in Neiafu. Hearing of my father's plan, Mother went to Father Sevelio and asked if I could spend one Sunday with her in Ha'alaufuli. The Reverend Father agreed but insisted I be back in school Monday morning.

Well, I never went back, even when Father Sevelio came to get me. I insisted on staying with my mother. At that time the little Mormon primary school was in session at Niumui, a place owned by Talikavili in the village of Ha'alaufuli. I well remember the elders who served as teachers in those early years, Elders W. O. Facer, Mark Woolley, Heber J. McKay, an Elder Platt, and a Samoan missionary named Siosefa. I remember the move of our little school from Niumui to another lot called Tapuhia. We disassembled the little building and put it up again at Tapuhia. The missionary house in Neiafu was also removed by boat, piece by piece, to Ha'alaufuli. This was in 1911, as I remember; and in 1912, we started building the chapel in Ha'alaufuli.

On July 13, 1913, at a conference held in Koloa, I was baptized into the Church along with my mother. Elders Westoway and West performed the ordinances of baptism and confirmation. I had by then been active in the Primary and Sunday School for a long time. Although only ten years old, I had developed a strong testimony of the truthfulness of the Church. This testimony has grown continuously to the present day. When the elders established a school (called *Maamafo'ou* or New Light) in Neiafu, with the more advanced grades, I continued my education there.

At fifteen I was still in school, playing baritone horn in the school band. Elder Stirling May was the principal. What excitement when we learned our band had been invited to perform at the mission conference in Tongatapu. Despite the difficulty of securing any vessel fit for transporting the Saints from Vava'u to Nuku'alofa, the Church was finally able to rent the *Fetu'u'aho* and a locally built boat from 'Utungake called the *Hikutamole*. On the Saturday afternoon of our departure, I boarded the *Hikutamole* with part of our group and set sail for 'Otea island. There we gathered green coconuts for our water and food supply.

The plan was that we would secure the coconuts and wait for the *Fetu'u'aho*. However, a boat carrying the harbor master appeared in the channel signaling to us to return to Neiafu. There would be no voyage. The government would not give us permission to sail, claiming we were dangerously overloaded. Elder May ordered us all to disembark with our goods and wait for a large steamer that was arriving soon from abroad. It would take us all to the conference.

This was the infamous vessel that would bring the influenza to Tonga and kill thousands. It landed in Neiafu the next day and we all boarded her and took our voyage to Tonga. Landing in Nukuʻalofa, we were met by the Tongatapu Saints and others in their horse-drawn carts. They took us and our goods first to the mission home where our band played several numbers for the Saints gathered there. After this impromptu concert, we made our way to our previously assigned homes. The band members stayed in homes in Kolomotuʻa.

That very night the death knell sounded across Kolomotuʻa, announcing the passing of a man named Matoka, the first victim of this devastating disease. The next night our tuba player died, then our snare drummer, and then Lupe, wife of Talikavili, who had allowed the Church to start a little primary school in his home. Every day from then on bells would ring announcing more deaths. The government finally put a stop to the bell ringing altogether for fear the whole population would succumb from terror at its sound.

Everyone was ill. I remember a huge caldron being set up at the police station. In it they made a powerful soup to distribute to the homes of the sick. This was to help cure us of the flu. My father, who had not gone to Samoa but had stayed in Tongatapu and married another woman, came and took me to his home in Fasi. His poor wife was deathly ill with the flu, also. She lay in the main room and I in the bedroom. Her suffering was intense. I'll not forget when she died. Some men pulled up to the house in a large open cart and just carried her out, put her on the cart, took her off, and buried her.

The widespread sickness and death throughout Tonga left very few people to bury the dead. Burials were often quick and sloppy with the graves too shallow and many people in one grave. Dogs mangled the poorly interred corpses and a ghastly smell permeated the villages. I begged Father to take me back to Vavaʻu.

I was reunited with my mother shortly thereafter and continued to grow in faith and testimony.

Years later, on July 7, 1962, in Feletoa, Vavaʻu, Viliami and ʻAna Uasilaʻā and their daughter Pelepetua died suddenly from eating the toxic flesh of a very poisonous fish called in Tongan *peʻe moana*. Viliami and ʻAna were members of the Tonga Free Church, but their oldest son, Samisoni, was a Latter-day Saint student at Liahona High School.

On the day of the funeral, I happened to be visiting the LDS branch in Feletoa in my capacity as district Sunday School president. As the meeting was about to begin, the branch president received word that Kalatiola Lātū, another member of the Uasilaʻā household, was still deathly ill from the poisoning and wanted Mormon elders to come and give her a blessing. I suggested to the branch president that we postpone Sunday School and respond to the plea from this non-member family.

The village of Feletoa was nearly overrun with people from everywhere in Vavaʻu who had come to the funeral. Many of these people had their own home cures for fish poisoning and were anxious to give them to Kalatiola. Her condition was desperate, and it appeared she would be the fourth in the family to die. A man from Leimātuʻa stood at the doorway shouting, "A medicine is wanted. Bring medicine!"

When we reached the house, many people, knowing we were Mormons, exclaimed: "And what can you possibly do for the little girl? We've tried everything!" We answered nothing but pressed our way into the already crowded living room. The little girl lay at the far end, surrounded by curious visitors.

Suddenly I felt a profound feeling that the girl would completely recover through a priesthood blessing. This quickening of my own faith gave me courage to speak to the people and say: "Honored chiefs and citizens, you are all here no doubt because you want to help. I speak frankly to you all. We are going to bestow a blessing upon this girl. If there is anyone here who does not believe in this sacred ordinance, please leave the room. If you think you can sustain with your faith this blessing of the sick, you may remain." They were all quiet and still.

As the sacred anointing took place, I felt a sensation of warmth in my heart I had never felt before. And when we put our hands upon her head, I uttered the words of blessing that came by inspiration to my mind. In less than five minutes after this blessing, Kalatiola asked for water and drank nearly a pitcherful. She said she felt better. Later after the funeral, we discovered that she was sleeping peacefully, completely well from the affliction which nearly took her life.

4

Talitaufa Vaha Uasilaʻā

"DEATH, WHERE IS THY STING?"
1 Corinthians 15:55

Talitaufa Vaha Uasilaʻā offers a special insight regarding the death of his parents and the healing of his auntie Kalatiola Lātū, as recorded in the preceding account by Tēvita Pita Pauni. Talitaufa witnessed this event as a child and comments on its significance to their family.

The death of my parents and sister from toxic fish poisoning caused a great sensation in Vavaʻu. They passed away Saturday night, July 7, 1962, and thousands attended the funeral the next day in Feletoa. It was a new thing for the people, I suppose, and very pitiful. My own most vivid memory of the event, however, was the miraculous recovery of Kalatiola Lātū, my mother's sister, who was anointed and blessed by the Mormon elders. She too had ingested a large amount of the lethal fish and was on the verge of death for many hours. Her wonderful healing confirmed my faith in The Church of Jesus Christ of Latter-day Saints. I was baptized in August of the same year.

Mother and Father were strong members of the Tonga Free Church in Feletoa at the time, and Kalatiola had come to live with us as one of the children in the family.

Dad purchased a large fish called *peʻe moana* from fishermen in Leimātuʻa on Saturday afternoon and had distributed substantial pieces of it to several households of his extended family for their Sabbath meal. We cooked our portion, however, for the Saturday evening meal.

We all ate the fish and became acutely ill. The smaller children were able to vomit it up; but poor Dad, Mom, and Peleputua passed away within a few hours. The other families who had expected to prepare the fish for Sunday were spared perhaps a similar fate.

After the funeral, conducted by ministers in the Tonga Free Church, there was much talk of tragedy, heartache, and eight orphaned children. But Heavenly Father took care of us in ways that will bless our family throughout eternity. Every one of the eight children, including Kalatiola, joined the Church, went on missions, and married in the temple. I was ordained a high priest at the age of twenty-one; and Samisoni, the oldest, was president of the Vava'u Neiafu Stake for many years. We were all sealed to our parents in the temple in 1984.

5

Pī Feleti Maile

THE FAITH OF MY FATHER

Pī Feleti Maile has been a faithful member of the Church since his baptism in 1911, serving as a proselyting missionary, branch president, district president, and labor missionary. Pī still lives with a large posterity in Veitongo, Tongatapu. The following excerpt from his personal history provides insights into the lives and faith of a first-generation Latter-day Saint family on Tongatapu. He is the son of pioneer Kitione Maile, also baptized in 1911, who became a profound source of strength in the Church between 1911 and 1940.

My father was Kitione Maile and my mother Lose Feleti. I was the fifth child in a family of twelve children. Kitione was a man of faith and great strength, supporting his large family from his own industry, even though he could not read a word or write his own name. The fruits of his labors showed in his extensive plantation and the number of his animals, pigs, goats, ducks, chickens. Honored by the whole community of Nukunuku before he became a Mormon, he was fiercely disliked by many after he was baptized and brought the Church to our village in 1911. However, the high chief Tuʻivakanō honored him still because of father's willingness and ability to fulfill his ceremonial obligations to his chief and to the village.

"Don't bother Maile in matters of religion," Tuʻivakanō would say to the villagers who complained about him and the new church he had brought to Nukunuku. "Let him do as he pleases. He carries his weight in our community and more."

Father's conversion to the Church was prompted at first by the pleasure of his acquaintance with the Mormon elders from America who passed through Nukunuku, walking from Ma'ufanga to Fo'ui. Father would invite them to stop and refresh themselves with ripe bananas and a fresh coconut. Soon our home became a permanent refreshment stop for the Mormon missionaries, Elders Frank Winn, C. C. Wiser, an "Elder Charles," and others. Father liked their easy-going nature and their language fluency. What amazed him about these white men was their humility and their willingness to mingle with the Tongans. They taught him the gospel of faith and repentance, and he soon longed for a Church school in Nukunuku, just as there were Mormon schools in Ma'ufanga and Fo'ui.

I was baptized in 1911, at age eight. A branch of the Church had already been established in our home at Nukunuku. I remember the service held in our single frame twenty-four-foot-long house.

Father's illiteracy was compensated for by a brilliance of speech, a powerful mind, and an extensive memorized knowledge of the Bible. He spoke with eloquence and power, using the old style of sermonizing, calling out biblical references to be read out loud on the spot by members of the congregation. He knew the Bible from Genesis to Revelation. If someone misread a scripture, he would correct the reader. His faith in the power of the priesthood and of prayer matched his knowledge of scripture. He seldom took us to a doctor of any kind. Even when my brother Vaisa became deathly ill with a bloated stomach, Kitione would not accept the doctor's prognosis of certain death. He simply declared to the doctor, "Fine, I'll take this boy back home with me, and three months hence I will bring him back to you healed."

After three months, Kitione took Vaisa back to the doctor. In amazement the doctor asked, "What did you do for him?"

"It was nothing I did," my father replied, "I just asked God to heal him and he did."

Kitione was one of the first Tongan brethren who went on preaching tours around the island. His early companion was Paula (Tongan for Paul) Langi from 'Uiha, a caretaker at the prison on Tongatapu. Years later in 1937, he was called to serve a formal mission in Vava'u. In fact, he replaced me and my family. We had been called there to replace my older brother, Lisiate Talanoa Maile, who later became a counselor in the mission presidency.

On that same mission, Kitione was transferred to Ha'apai, where he was instrumental in bringing one of the great and courageous future missionaries of the Church into the waters of baptism, Viliami Fakataha. Viliami was a minister at the time in the Church of Tonga, in Tongaleleka, Ha'apai. A man with a clever, stubborn mind and great strength of body, Viliami had been very ill for some time. Kitione went to visit him and learned that the minister had over a hundred coconut trees on his plantation which had been neglected a long time because of his illness. The ripe nuts were dropping, but there was no one to split them and cut out the meat to dry into copra, the only source of income for the family.

Without saying a word, Kitione borrowed a copra knife from the family in Pangai he was living with, went to the minister's bush plantation, and attacked the huge pile of coconuts. For two solid days and nights, he stuck to the task of digging out the coconut meat to dry. After two days, family members of the minister came to the plantation site to harvest some crops and found Kitione in the middle of this labor of love.

The minister was so touched by this act of charity that his heart was softened to the gospel message, and he finally said simply to Kitione: "Maile, baptize me." Later Viliami (Vili) Fakataha was called to serve several proselyting missions in Tongatapu and brought scores of people into the Church. . . .

On June 6, 1934, about a year before we were called on our first mission, I went to the doctor with a chronic lung problem. The problem was diagnosed as tuberculosis, and the doctor gave me the sad news that my lungs were ruined by the disease. I left the doctor and went straight to the mission president's office to convey the news to President James Cutler.

"President Cutler (Misi Sēmisi)," I said, "I am here to tell you the doctor says my lungs are useless from T.B. Could you please give me new lungs by the power of your priesthood?"

I looked steadfastly at the president and saw tears begin to roll down his cheeks. He laid his hands on my head and blessed me and I have been healthy ever since. I am eighty-seven years old this year (1990).

Our greatest joy as a family was to accept the mission call in 1935 to serve in Vava'u. My wife and I and six children embarked with six shillings in our pocket. This system of calling poor families on missions to labor for two and a half years without pay was happily embraced by the faithful members. During our years of service my wife and I lacked in nothing, feeling neither poor nor neglected.

6

'Elenoa Mē Mataele

"THE LORD GAVE AND THE LORD HATH TAKEN AWAY"
Job 1:21

Sione Lolo Manaʻia and ʻElenoa Mē Palauni Mataele are parents of fifteen children. It was Lolo's father, Siosaia Mataele, who in 1910 brought the Mormon missionaries to Foʻui, Tongatapu, to provide a school for his children. He and his wife Lolohea were soon baptized, and both a school and a branch of the Church were established in Foʻui in 1911. The Church owes much to these pioneers.

Siosaia Mataele was a man of influence on Tongatapu because of his nima mālohi, *his industry, his good business sense, and his driving personality. As Elder Frank Winn (1910–13) put it, "Without Siosaia and Lolohea Mataele, the Church would have never made it on Tongatapu in those early days."*

Not only was Mataele a compelling preacher himself, he constantly opened doors for the missionaries to preach. As just one example, when farmers of his area came to weigh their copra for sale, he often prepared food for the occasion. Then during the meal, he would invite the missionaries to speak to his guests. Mataele was also helpful in the Church's successful effort to repeal the 1922 law banning Mormon missionaries from entering Tonga.

Lolo Mataele, Siosaia's second son, and his wife, ʻElenoa Mē Mataele, served in the Church in many capacities. They labored as missionaries in Niuatoputapu in their later years. Mē describes some of the harsh realities of missionary life just after the hurricane of 1961. This excerpt from her history reflects the total consecration of the missionaries to the Lord's work.

After we returned from the temple in New Zealand in 1960, we were called on a mission and assigned to Niuatoputapu in 1961. There we experienced the love of God through many hardships. Lolo was sickly much of the time, but he worked hard so we could survive.

Several things combined to keep us guessing about just how effective we were. For one thing, the strong Catholic influence made it difficult to do any actual preaching. The people were very kind to us but absolutely refused to listen to a Mormon sermon. The fishermen of the village shared their marvelous catches with us but turned a deaf ear to our message.

Therefore, our missionaries performed a lot of community service. Lolo and the other missionaries planted huge amounts of *manioke* (cassava or tapioca root) on a large acreage of land. At harvest time he distributed it to the people. This made us part of village life and curbed the prospects of famine. One missionary by the name of Tītali Tavake performed the much-needed but lowly task of improving the outhouses in the village. Tītali was the hardest worker one could ever meet and was not afraid or too proud to tackle any task. Many outhouse pits were full and overflowing. Tītali dug new holes in new locations, moved the houses, and covered over the old pits with mounds of dirt. It was a tremendous blessing to the community. This kind of service gradually overcame the prejudice of many people against us. Soon the homes of Niuatoputapu were opened to us.

I'll never forget a man named Sione Vuki who let us take whatever we wanted from his store. At the end of the month when Lolo went to pay our bill for the month, Sione Vuki would not take the money. It was his gift of friendship. The people regarded us highly.

But there was also much sadness for us during our mission in Niuatoputapu. One day we received a letter from my sister that our oldest daughter Hola, married to the high chief Motuʻapuaka, was very ill, and might not live. She was suffering from complications of a dangerous pregnancy. I was instantly fearful for my beloved daughter's life and made plans to go to her. Of course, communication with Niuatoputapu in those days was limited to telegraph and an occasional boat.

On the next boat, however, we met Dr. Sione Tapa from Tonga who told us Hola was in her fourth month of pregnancy. Though her condition was still precarious, she seemed to be doing a little better. We felt encouraged and decided I should stay in Niuatoputapu on the mission. You can imagine the unspeakable shock of sorrow when we received the news that Hola and the baby had both died. It was the saddest thing that ever happened to me.

The extended family in Tongatapu wanted me to come to Tonga on the next boat. Even though the funeral had to be the day after Hola's death, the mourning, and the family responsibilities according to Tongan custom, would extend many weeks. Besides, it would be a comfort and solace to me to be with my kin and my other children. Perhaps only Tongans can understand the pain of such deep grieving in isolation from family.

But my dear husband spoke these words to me: "Mē, everything is in the Lord's hands. The Lord has taken our Hola. Let our family in Tongatapu take care of all the ceremonies and obligations to the dead and to the community. The Lord's work here is more important now. It was our blessing to receive this call in our old age. Let us return to Tonga only when our work is accomplished."

This counsel was coming from a person who himself had experienced much sickness. I sought comfort in the Lord and continued our service in Niuatoputapu.

We were released from our mission and returned to Fo'ui in June 1962. In October of the following year, Lolo passed away leaving me a widow.

Despite the problems and sorrows, my life has been sweet in the gospel. I know it is the only true way to happiness. The Church has been generous with the Tongans. I'm thinking of our daughter Kalo who left Tonga to attend the Church College of Hawaii. Many people tried to discourage us, but Lolo said he trusted the Church and knew she would be taken well care of in Hawaii. Well, Kalo has since become an enormous blessing to our family and to Tongans everywhere.

PART II

MAKEKE

1926-47

The Growing Tree

School girls at Makeke dine on meager fare, 1938. (Courtesy Ermel Morton)

Samuela and Heleine Fakatou. Samuela was a preeminent teacher, missionary, translator, branch president, and counselor in the mission presidency. A graduate of the Church's Maori Agricultural College in New Zealand, he was the first Tongan teacher at Makeke School in 1926 and had great influence in preparing local Church members to bear leadership responsibilities in the growing Church. Heleine served in every Church auxiliary. (Courtesy Mele Fakatou Brown)

Sālote and 'Iohani Wolfgramm, devout and effective missionaries. 'Iohani is a renowned genealogist. The Wolfgramms are the grandparents of the Jets, a current popular singing group. (Courtesy Tisinā Wolfgramm Gerber)

Sālome and Solomone 'Uluʻave. Baptized in Niuafoʻou they nurtured the Church there and in 'Eua. (Courtesy Sālome 'Uluʻave)

Le'o Kinikini and Tēvita Muli Kinikini. Tēvita Muli was a perennial missionary, a branch president, and a poet of renown. His grand composition, a lakalaka *(large group performance combining poetry, melody, and dance)* depicting the history of Joseph Smith, premiered in Tonga in the early 1950s and became a feature at the Polynesian Cultural Center in the 1960s. *(Courtesy Kime Kinikini)*

'Inoke Mataele, son of pioneer Siosaia Mataele, was an eloquent speaker and perennial missionary; he taught and baptized in every island group in Tonga during three decades, 1930-60. *(Courtesy Lilevai Tua'one)*

Ermel Morton, missionary, teacher, translator of the Book of Mormon, Doctrine and Covenants, and Pearl of Great Price, and the first full-time principal of Liahona High School. (Courtesy Ermel Morton)

Large Tongan fale *built in Ha'apai for the Church's centennial celebration, 6 April 1930. (Courtesy Ralph Olson)*

Ha'apai Relief Society, 1935. Front row left: 'Alisi Fasi, Finau Malakai Lavulo, Melesisi Kapetaua, Selu Vili Feru'u, unidentified, and Vaikato Tavutu. Second row left: Palu Talai, Sulieti Ula Fo'aoso, Meleseini 'Ilo'ilo Vea, Mele Lavaka, Fifita Kavafau, Mele'ana Tō'anguvu, Le'o Langi Kinikini, and Silika Fasi. Third row left: 'Amelia Tapu, Tema Tu'ile'ila, Sulieti Laa'afi Talakai, Mele Feru'u'aho, Simaima 'Asilasi, 'Ala Satuala, Ane Lupe Pulotu holding her daughter Sela, unidentified. Back row left: Soko Siaosi Pulauni, Lesieli Tuita Vehikite, unidentified, Lu'isa Pulauni, Seini Mafi, 'Ofa Simote, and two unidentified sisters.

Siosifa Tuʻiketei Pule and wife Sūlia Foliaki Pule. Tuʻiketei was a branch president and counselor in several mission presidencies. A superior teacher, Sūlia presided in Relief Society and Primary organizations. Tuʻiketei held a respected post in the government and worked closely with Ermel Morton in translating the LDS scriptures. (Courtesy Tēvita Kaʻili)

Chapel in Neiafu, Vavaʻu, dedicated in 1938. (Courtesy Ermel Morton)

Tēvita Mapa, who died in 1945, was president of Tongatapu District, and secretary to the Premier of Tonga. He refused a noble's title to serve in the Church. (Courtesy Taupeavai Mapa Hemaloto)

Saints at mission conference in Matavaimoʻui, Nukuʻalofa, with Apostle George Albert Smith, in May of 1938. (Courtesy Ermel Morton)

Saints in Muʻa, Tongatapu, in front of chapel, 1939. The Church's headquarters and first day school were established in Muʻa (1891), the ancient capital of Tonga. (Courtesy Ermel Morton)

7

Ada Layne Cahoon

"WITH GOD NOTHING SHALL BE IMPOSSIBLE"[1]
Luke 1:37

Jay and Ada Cahoon were nineteen-year-old newlyweds when they arrived in Tonga on a Church mission in February 1925. Eighteen months later, they received a letter from President Heber J. Grant, appointing Elder Cahoon president of the Tongan Mission to replace M. Vernon Coombs. The following experiences from Sister Cahoon's personal history typify the intelligence, courage, and strength of the women who presided with their husbands over the Tongan Mission. Because of their wide influence for good among the Tongan women, the extent of their impact on the growth and spirituality of the Church in each generation can hardly be measured.

I was born in Cardston, Alberta, Canada, in 1905. I grew up there in a very large family. Before I was born, my parents had three boys and two girls, and they lost all five of them at once with diphtheria in their throats. The oldest was six and the baby was six months, and they all died. My mother died in childbirth with the thirteenth baby. So I guess life was pretty hard for parents in those days. . . .

When I went into high school, I met Jay Cahoon. It was about the ninth grade, I guess. He came in from out of town to school. He was so shy and so quiet, we teased him unmercifully. The girls would

---

[1] Ada Layne Cahoon, Oral History, interviewed by Vai Lātū, July 1980, Oral History Project, Charles Redd Center of Western Studies, Harold B. Lee Library, Brigham Young University, Provo, Utah.

just say, "Jay, what are you blushing for?" [and] his face would just go red. After he had been in school maybe a year and a half or maybe two years, we started going out to school things together.

One day when we were both out of the twelfth grade his father, who was the bishop of the ward he lived in, sent in [Jay's] papers for a mission. Bishop Cahoon didn't want his son getting serious about me so he was going to send him away. When Jay found out he was going on this mission, he said, "Then I'm taking Ada with me." That wasn't the idea at all. Neither his father nor my father thought too much of that idea, but they finally gave their consent, and I was called to serve a mission with Jay. We were married on January 2, 1925.

On January 14 we left for the Tongan Mission, which was the end of the world at that time as far as we were concerned. We only knew one person who had ever been there and he was our stake president. He loved it!

We left Cardston on January 14, 1925, and it was forty degrees below zero, dressed in heavy winter clothes and coats. We came to Salt Lake and stayed in the first mission home before they ever held a missionary class in it. Then we went by train to San Francisco where we took a steamer to Tonga. We got there on February 14, exactly one month after we left our home. That was the fastest trip that had ever been made at that time.

When we got to Samoa, there were some who tried to talk us out of going on to Tonga because the government in Tonga had passed a law banning any future Mormon missionaries.[2] There was a lot of trouble stirred up by the churches in Tonga. Well, the day we got into Nuku'alofa we discovered that the law was rescinded and we were able to land. We were the first missionaries in three years who had been able to come in.

The people in the Church were so wonderful to us. When I think of bananas, I can't help thinking of that time. They came with bunches of bananas, food, oranges, and everything. It was just so beautiful. I couldn't believe it.

We were only nineteen at this time and here we [were] in the other end of the world. I was twenty on March 8, and Jay was twenty May 18.

---

[2] The law, passed in 1922, had been repealed on 3 July 1924 after a two-year battle. But many Tongans still had negative feelings against the Church, and concern among Latter-day Saints remained high.

The mission president at that time was Vernon Coombs. We stayed at the mission home for about three weeks waiting for a boat, the *Tofua*, to come and take us to Vava'u to teach school. But when the *Tofua* came in, she was quarantined.

Now you don't sail on a quarantined boat, so President Coombs arranged for us to go on a sailboat, the *Makamaile*. Ninety Tongans crowded onto this little boat, plus Brother Coombs, Brother Cahoon, and myself. That is ninety-three people besides the crew. There wasn't even standing-up room, let alone sitting-down room, it was so crowded. We had our lunch with us and thought we would get along nicely for two days until we arrived in Ha'apai. They were expecting us.

We landed in Ha'apai just fine, and the Saints made a great big feast for us. But that evening a strong breeze came up. The captain seemed quite anxious to get on our way and use that wind. It was March and the weather was tricky. So we got on the boat and took off. The sailing was just fine until about sunset when the wind died and we just sat becalmed in nearly ninety-degree weather. It was hot! Oh, it was hot!

Then suddenly a breeze came up from the other direction and the waves started coming in. By morning we were in a full-fledged hurricane. For eight days we rolled in that hurricane in the Pacific with no food, no water, nothing. The water was washing over the boat. The captain put us all down in the bottom where there were two little rooms and two bunks. One room was a mail room. I don't know what the other was for. An old toilet had stood in the corner at one time, but it was no longer in use. Once during this eight days I was finally able to get on one of those bunks and lie down. An old water tank with big rivets sticking out about a half inch stood along one wall. Jay lay on that thing for two or three days.

Everybody was seasick, deathly sick. The stench down there in that hold was so terrible I can't tell you how bad it was. If I could have got out and walked all the way back to Canada I would have gladly done it.

Finally after about eight days, I think on March 16, we were becalmed again. The sea died down, the wind disappeared, and there we sat in that awful heat again. But by this time we were close enough that people in Neiafu knew that we were coming. They sent a motor launch out to pull us into shore.

The two missionaries who were in Vava'u at that time were Lawrence Leavitt and his wife, Mary Ann. They came down to meet us at the wharf. We were so weak we couldn't even walk to the waiting truck. People had to help us all the way.

Many people were deathly seasick. They had needed fresh air but couldn't get up on to the top deck. Anyway, it was nasty. The Leavitts took us to their place, and we had the best meal that I have ever eaten in my life. That was fried potatoes and "bully beef," a can of corned beef. I don't think I'll ever find food so good again, after more than eight days of starving at sea.

That afternoon after things had cleared up, Brother Leavitt said, "Now tomorrow you'll go out to Ha'alaufuli and teach school. You'll take over the school."

I had the chapel to teach school in, and my husband had the schoolhouse. He had grades six, seven, and eight. Those kids all spoke a little English. It was not much but a little, which helped him a great deal. As for me, I was in a room of thirty-two children under twelve years old. They were sitting on the floor waiting for me to say something intelligent. I didn't know anything to say. They looked at me, and I looked at them. I thought, "Well, I guess it is my move. If I don't do something, nobody will. I'll find out their names; I can do that." I had learned to say one or two other little things. I could say, "What is your name? How old are you?" and so on.

So here was this first row of six-year-old children. I thought, "Well, start at the first." I couldn't read the writing in the roll book. So I started with the little girl on the end. I asked her what her name was, and she ducked her head and giggled. So I said, "Come on. Tell me what is your name!" She wouldn't say a word. One of the older girls finally said, "Her name is Vaipapālangi."

I put in my days trying to teach those kids, but it was pretty hard. Because I associated with these young children, I learned Tongan very fast. I wasn't very old myself, so it was really no great problem for me to learn that language. I could speak it when I was down there. Before I left, you wouldn't have known whether I was Tongan or somebody else. At least they all told me that.

I didn't like coconut milk in my food at first. I just didn't like it. I'm not really fond of it yet. But I couldn't eat it then. To make matters worse I was pregnant at the time. However, after the first two or three months, I got so I could eat anything. I just ate and ate. Our oldest daughter was born on December 31, 1925. We had been there almost a year. I had a very hard time with her. Because it was New

Year's Eve, the doctor had been drinking at a big party. The labor was long and painful, but everything came out all right.

Our daughter was five months old when word came from Salt Lake that my husband was to take over the mission. He was not sent there in the first place as the mission president, but he got a letter from President Grant who told him that when Brother Coombs left for home he would be in charge of that mission. He was to take over and he would do what they wanted done.

When we got down to Tongatapu from Vava'u, President Coombs was about ready to leave. So it was all just dumped right on to us and here we were, barely twenty-one.

That was quite an experience. They made me at this time president of the mission Relief Society. I had never been to Relief Society in my life. I had all these women who thought I knew something, and I didn't. I'm not the first one who has been in that position, I know. But then there was Mutual. I had the Beehive girls out at Makeke. That meant a weekly trip up there to teach Beehive girls. Then we had Relief Society besides that. To help things out, there were no lessons in the Tongan language. Every lesson had to be translated from English into Tongan. That is how I spent the next three years, translating lessons and getting them out to organizations.

We had wonderful Tongan girls in the mission home who took care of our children. I had given birth to another baby daughter in 1927. But I didn't ever have to do anything with them. I couldn't. I didn't have time. I was busy, busy, busy all the time. These Tongan nannies were so wonderful you would have thought they belonged to our children. They were so sweet with them. They did all the cooking and the cleaning and they did it almost for nothing. It was just really pitiful. They should have been paid something more because they were certainly worth a lot to us.

The Tongan people were absolutely wonderful. They would come in to pay their tithing. I remember a man from Ha'alaufuli who used to come in with a watermelon under each arm. "One for my tithing, and one for the missionaries," he would say. He paid his tithing that way. It was all English money then. Many, many Tongan people did things like that. We were as poor as they were and they couldn't afford to give to us, but they did. The sisters in our Relief Society used to come and bring me lovely pieces of silk material. It was just beautiful the way people were. Everybody seemed to love everybody at that time.

When I see the elders and the sisters today being trained and taught down at the Missionary Training Center, I think it is marvelous. I wouldn't necessarily wish the same experiences I had onto anyone. That hurricane was traumatic. So was going into that room full of small Tongan children and wondering, "What will I do?" I tell you, you go home and you pray a lot and you cry a lot and you wish you were out of there. But you're there. You cannot give up. You've got to do something. It is up to you. Nobody else is going to do it for you. That is just about the best way I can tell you. That is about the way we've always built our lives. Where we can help, we help. If we think we can't help, we just get busy and do it. We feel it is the way you should do. You shouldn't be dependent on somebody else for everything all the time. It is just a little bit like having your charge card and never paying for anything.

8

Sālesi Vānisi

A LEGACY OF PRAYER

Similati Vānisi, bishop of Kahuku Second Ward in the Laie North Stake, reminisces about several of the spiritual qualities of his pioneer grandfather Sālesi Vānisi (born in 1888), whose conversion was the beginning of the Church in Nakolo, Tongatapu.

Despite the warnings and threats from his friends and extended family, on February 20, 1921, Sālesi and his wife, Meleane Siu, became the first members of the Church in the village. They were very faithful, sending their eleven children to the Church schools in Matavaimoʻui and Makeke and bearing the burdens of the tiny Nakolo branch.

My grandfather, Sālesi Vānisi, was one of the early converts to The Church of Jesus Christ of Latter-day Saints on the eastern side of Tongatapu. As a young boy he loved to read the Bible, so when the missionaries taught him the gospel from the Bible, he knew that this was the Church he had been waiting for. As with many early pioneers of the Church, opposition and persecution from enemies of the Church were a daily trial for him.

When I was six years old, my mother passed away, leaving me and my sister Vavalo for my grandparents, Sālesi and Meleane Siu, to raise. It was during this period of my early life that the seeds of the gospel were planted deep in my heart. Grandpa Vānisi's spirituality inspired an awe in me as a child. I remember following him daily to his plantation. He would always point out to me the very best of his taro, bananas, or yams and say: "These will be for our tithing." His greatest care was given to these "chosen" ones. During the harvest, I was often the one assigned to take our load of tithing to the branch president. I remember sitting on the family horse. Grandfather would lift onto its back a sack of fine taro which I balanced in front of me. Then with a very serious look in his eyes, he said to me, "Simi, be very careful because this is our tithing." From my grandfather I learned early in life that you give only your best to the Lord.

Perhaps the most powerful memory I have of my grandfather was his private and public prayers. One day walking back with Grandmother to Nakolo from our bush plantation, I saw two ripe mangoes hanging by a bird's nest in a mango tree. Grandpa was still working at the plantation. I told Grandmother to go on home, and I would get us some mangoes. Climbing high into the tree, I discovered the nest to be empty, so I picked the mangoes and began my descent. I got halfway down the tree when I noticed Grandpa Vānisi walking toward the mango tree. Fearing he might discover I had not gone on home with Grandmother, I stayed very quiet in the leafy branches. Grandpa came right up to the tree, looked around in every direction, and then knelt down directly below me to pray.

I could hear every word of his prayer and felt the love he had for Heavenly Father. Grandpa expressed that love and vowed he would sacrifice everything he had, even his life, to build the Church on earth. Getting up from his knees, Grandpa went back to his work, leaving me on my branch to ponder what I had seen and heard.

This was my first experience with such personal devotion. Grandpa never found out he had instructed his grandson so profoundly in the value of frequent secret prayer. The result was that I too began to pray secretly, saying the same things my grandfather had said as I remembered them. I experienced, even at this early age, the calmness, the joy, the humility and the assurance that my prayers were received and appreciated by a Father who loves me unconditionally.

Grandpa Sālesi Vānisi was as dedicated to his callings as anybody I have ever known. When he was a branch president, part of his responsibility was to attend leadership meetings and conferences. These meetings were usually held in Foʻui or Nukuʻalofa or other places far from Nakolo. Grandpa would walk the entire distance, usually starting out on his journey the day before the meeting. His provisions were usually a large baked taro and two or three drinking coconuts wrapped in a cloth and tied to a stick, which he carried over his shoulder.

Grandpa rested during his journey under certain trees along the way. Sometimes he would sleep all night under their branches. But always before resuming his walk, he would kneel and thank Heavenly Father for the tree and for strength to travel to the Church meetings.

Years later he said to me: "You know those trees I took refuge under on all my journeys to my Church meetings? They are still standing. Their fellows have been cut down all around them for farming purposes, but not the trees that gave me shade and protection. They are sacred trees because they served as a chapel for all my prayers and pleading."

When it finally came time for me to attend Liahona High School, Grandfather had long passed away, but I recognized some of the sacred trees he had told me about. As I passed them going to school or returning home, I could see in my mind's eye my dear grandfather kneeling underneath them in prayer or lying down for a rest. Sometimes when I walked home from school I would kneel under one of those sacred trees and thank the Lord for a grandfather who set the greatest example of my life.

My grandparents gave their heart and soul and substance for the Church, but they themselves never mentioned the word *sacrifice* or complained about their hardship. They believed that as long as you do what Heavenly Father wants, nothing is a sacrifice. When the Church was looking for a property to build a chapel in Nakolo, they insisted on giving their property, the place with the best view. The beautiful Nakolo chapel stands today on that property, a tribute to Grandpa Vānisi's memory.

9

'Iohani and Sālote Wolfgramm

"AND I WILL GIVE YOU
POWER TO HEAL
ALL MANNER OF SICKNESS"
Matthew 10:1

'Iohani and Sālote Wolfgramm have lived and served faithfully in the Church in Tonga and in America. They filled several proselyting missions for the Church and two labor missions at Liahona. Despite the hardships of missionary service in the forties and fifties, they distinguished themselves as an eminent missionary family in the Church. 'Iohani and Sālote are the grandparents of the current singing stars known as the Jets. Besides testifying to the power of the priesthood, the following accounts capture much of the flavor and local color of Tonga.

Sālote

I was born on June 27, 1915, and was still a tiny baby when my mother, Seluvaia Mafi Fakatou, passed away. On her deathbed she asked my father's sister 'Amelia 'Ofa to care for me as her own child. As did many Tongan mothers in those days who were unable to nurse their children, 'Amelia chewed my food thoroughly, mixing it with her own saliva, and let me suckle from her mouth. That is what kept me alive until I was old enough to eat on my own. When 'Amelia 'Ofa and her husband Kaliopasi Vaitai moved to Pukotala to care for Vaitai's mother, I was given to my grandparents, Teleita and Fakatou, in Felemea. I never longed for my poor dead mother because of so many living parents in our society.

An active member of the Tonga Free Church, Teleita was a very strong woman. One of the powerful images indelibly etched in my memory is of her kneeling by her bed in her private prayers. Sometimes she would disappear during the day; and, in a child's panic, I would search all over for her and finally find her in her room praying aloud. I was the subject of many of her prayers. As I knelt by her, she would ask God to make me a fine and virtuous woman one day. From Teleita I learned the value of offering many private prayers to Heavenly Father, day and night. . . .

My uncle, Samuela Fakatou, was a member of The Church of Jesus Christ of Latter-day Saints and was among the few selected to study in New Zealand at the Mormon Maori Agricultural College. When Samuela returned from New Zealand in 1926, he was called to teach school at the newly established LDS school in Makeke, Tongatapu. I had already become enchanted with the Mormon primary in 'Uiha and would frequently steal away on Sundays and attend the Mormon Sunday School. Threats and spankings from my grandmother could not quell my desire to be a Mormon. Nor could she resist Samuela's insistence that I go to school in Makeke.

I was baptized in Makeke on March 18, 1928. Grandmother Teleita took it hard, but my real father wrote me and said, "I have authority over your physical body, not over your spiritual self. If you feel this Church will bring salvation to your soul, then so be it." I was overjoyed.

Life was both difficult and joyful as a boarding student in Makeke. Our diet was boiled *manioke* (cassava or tapioca root), day in and day out. Occasionally there would be boiled plantains. Actually, we made this fare quite exciting by persuading someone to run down to the ocean and bring back sea water in a bottle. This became our dipping sauce. The salt water gave the *manioke* a taste we all thought heavenly. One day our boys spotted a small herd of wild pigs while we were digging up clumps of grass in the bush to plant in the barren yards of Makeke. We all gave chase, the boys running ahead and the girls following behind, baying like hounds. The shotgun blast made us squeal with delight, knowing we would actually have real meat on our table for once. In fact, the students' portion was ever so small, but still we thought we were in heaven, savoring every piece of skin, every bone, indeed, every morsel.

Toward the end of the 1928 school year, Grandmother Teleita missed me too much to stay any longer in Ha'apai. So she came to Makeke to be close to me. Not long after her arrival, she became deathly ill with pneumonia. She struggled desperately to breathe. At the moment of greatest alarm to her, she cried out to 'Ofa Vaitai: "Go tell Samuela to come and do as he thinks best. As for me I'm going to die."

Soon Samuela arrived with some elders from America who anointed and blessed her to be well. During the blessing, Teleita fell asleep and slept deeply the entire night. All signs of her sickness had disappeared when she awoke the next morning.

"You know what's going to happen today?" she cried. "I'm going to be baptized. I'll not wait any longer. I know the Church is true. I was sure to die last night except for the blessing of the elders."

Well, she was actually baptized the following Sunday at the beach down from Makeke. It was a baptismal service I'll never forget because of the miraculous way the surf was calmed by the presiding elder, Elder Austin Carter. Walking down the steep path to the beach, we could see that the ocean was at full tide and the heavy waves came crashing in at regular intervals. The services began with no sign of the ocean letting up. Our singing was drowned out by the pounding waves. At the very moment the baptisms were to be performed, Elder Carter stepped out and blessed the ocean, commanding it to be still so these sacred ordinances could be accomplished. We were all amazed to see the ocean calm down almost instantly. There were absolutely no more waves. Five people were led into the water and were baptized, including Teleita and Mele Nau, mother of Manase Nau, who became a very prominent leader in the Church.

The services concluded, we started up the path to return to the school. As we departed, the waves came crashing in again over the very spot the sacred ordinances were held.

Teleita's miraculous conversion and baptism had a profound effect on my life. To her dying day, she gave her whole heart and soul to the Lord and his Church. . . .

My marriage with 'Iohani Wolfgramm is what you would call a whirlwind romance and wedding, but it had the approval of both of our families. I first laid eyes on him on a Friday and we were married the following Wednesday. I had gone to Vava'u with a student performing group from Makeke, as part of the mission conference of 1933. I performed several numbers and directed a choir piece composed by Siale Sanft, a tribute to Joseph Smith. I knew 'Iohani's sister, Ella, slightly but had never seen him until Heleine Fakatou, Samuela's wife, told me 'Iohani wanted to speak with me.

"Why have I not seen him with the other youth of Vava'u?" I inquired.

"Well," she said, " 'Iohani is a serious chap and has spent most of his time with the older men who are preparing the food or organizing the conference programs."

I agreed to talk to him and found out very quickly for myself just how serious a young man he was. We had not talked long before he said, "Sālote, I really want you to marry me!"

"What?" I cried, "We have barely met and you want to marry me? Please give me time to think."

It was more than just thinking. I fasted and prayed, sought counsel from my uncle Samuela Fakatou. I was touched by 'Iohani's sincerity and so were Samuela and Heleine. Sunday I fasted again while 'Iohani pressed his case more fervently. I told him I needed more time. On Monday our group which was staying in Neiafu went to Ha'alaufuli to perform. By now I had done much praying and decided that I would devise a way (*talotalo*) the Lord could answer me. I decided that, when our group arrived at Ha'alaufuli, if the first person I saw was a young unmarried person, then I should marry 'Iohani. If that person were an older married person, then that would be a sign I should not marry him. Well, the first person I saw when we arrived was 'Iohani himself, carrying a load of firewood.

The marriage arrangements were formalized the next day when 'Iohani's mother, Sālome, and stepfather, Siosifa Naeata, met with Samuela and Heleine Fakatou, my guardians; and on Wednesday, July 13, 1933, we were married.

This kind of marriage arrangement was not uncommon in the Church at that time since it was vital that Church marriages occur as much as possible. For a girl to marry outside of the Church meant her almost certain loss to Church activity. . . .

We lived happily in Vava'u and were soon blessed with two lovely children, Malina and 'Ana. I knew my new husband was a serious person, but I learned quickly that he was also a man of great faith. He suffered tremendously from boils. One monstrous boil on his thigh had made it nearly impossible for him to stand up for three months. Nothing seemed to help it. The thing had grown nearly to the size of a football and was immensely painful. One afternoon, he called for Tēvita Pita Pauni to come to him.

"Pauni," he said, "come here and read this scripture I have marked. I would like to hear you read it."

The scripture was Matthew 10:1 which recounts Jesus' bestowal of the sacred priesthood power to his disciples. "And he . . . gave them power . . . to heal all manner of sickness and all manner of disease."

"Read it again!" cried 'Iohani, which Pauni did, a second, even a third time, at my husband's request.

"Why do you keep asking me to read this scripture?" asked Pauni.

"Do you believe the scriptures?" replied 'Iohani.

"Of course," said Pauni.

"Well, what do they say?" persisted 'Iohani.

"They say Jesus gave his servants power to heal all manner of sicknesses."

"Do you believe you have that power, Pauni?" continued 'Iohani.

"Yes!"

"Then come administer to me and command me to stand up and be rid of this affliction."

Tēvita Pita Pauni did exactly as 'Iohani told him. Anointing him with the sacred oil, he blessed him and said, " 'Iohani, in the name of Jesus Christ and by the power of the holy Melchizedek Priesthood, I command you to stand up from your bed and walk."

Instantly 'Iohani stood up and walked around. The pain had disappeared. He went to MIA meeting that very night and was off to our family plantation the next day. I begged him not to be so careless, for he was still sick. The next day even the branch president told him to rest. The symptoms of his illness were still obvious.

"I am well," he said, "because of the power of the priesthood. I know for a surety the Church is true, that priesthood power is real, just as the scriptures testify."

'Iohani was right. He felt no more pain and the lump on his leg just quietly disappeared. . . .

'Iohani

We were called on our first mission for the Church during World War II. Thousands of American soldiers were stationed in Tonga in those days, and President Emile C. Dunn stayed in Tonga throughout the war and presided over the Church. Times were hard for the local missionaries who carried the burden of Church work in the various villages. Our little family was growing all the time, and we were absolutely without money.

Our first assignment was to labor in Houma. Thanks to a very fruitful breadfruit tree, we were well supplied at least with this delicious food. There was no money for laundry soap so Sālote would scrape and squeeze the *fihoʻa* plant, the juices of which made fairly decent soap.

I went to work immediately to plant our own extensive garden to sustain ourselves so we would not have to rely on the Saints for food. In six months' time, my garden was truly prosperous with crops of every kind—bananas, yam, sweet potato, taro, tapioca root, and pineapple. Exactly one week before I was to begin harvesting food from my own garden, President Dunn came to Houma with the news that we were being transferred immediately to Foʻui where I would proselyte and preside over the Foʻui Branch.

"Here are the couple [Samu and ʻIlisa Vehikite] who will be replacing you and Sālote. Have you planted your own garden here?"

"Why, yes!" I said.

"Are your plants producing?" he continued.

"Yes, indeed!" I replied.

"Good, but you understand now that you are being transferred elsewhere. You are not to harvest anything out of your garden here in Houma. It's all for this new couple and their children."

So we went happily to Foʻui with nothing. The Lord didn't forsake us, though. We went to work and planted another extensive garden in Foʻui just like the one in Houma. In the meantime, the Saints in Foʻui were very kind to us, donating food to our family needs. I remember Sione Kaifoto driving up to our little home there and unloading a whole cart full of long white yams—each piece over four feet long. Even army surplus food came our way.

The Sēkona family (Makeleta and Fine) and many others saw to it we did not go hungry. Sālote often despaired in trying to patch our children's unpatchable clothing. Without thread, she often used the coarse fibers of the *fau* tree to stitch and patch our clothes.

But poverty meant nothing to us. I loved the preaching opportunities and visiting non-members home-to-home. My visiting companions were Samu Vehikite and Motulalo Tonga.

Perhaps the most profound experience of our mission during this depressed time was the accident that befell our little three-year-old daughter, Tisinā (Disna), who was run over by a taxi full of American soldiers. She and the other children were following behind Sālote on her visit to the sick of our village. It was on Sunday afternoon, and I had remained at home to complete some branch business. The children walked along holding hands for safety when suddenly Tisinā slipped away from them at the roadside and was hit without the driver or the passengers even knowing that they had struck her. The villagers yelled at them that a little girl had been hurt.

Four soldiers carried Tisinā's lifeless body to our home with Sālote and the other children running behind them. I opened the door and saw four foreigners holding my little girl. Her head was crushed and her face was terribly disfigured. It was a traumatic moment for all of us. Sālote explained what had happened. It was clearly an accident. The men in the car were not at fault. They were very moved by what had happened and expressed their sympathy, even offering to take the little girl to the hospital to repair her severely damaged face.

"Will the repair bring her back to life?" I asked.

"No," they replied, "there is probably no hope for her life, but the doctors can fix up her head and face for the funeral."

I told them I did not want them to take her but that I would ask God what I should do and, if it was possible, to give her life back.

The soldiers graciously carried Tisinā's body into the chapel. I asked them to hold her while I gave her a priesthood blessing. By then the curious people of the village were flocking in to see our stricken little daughter. As I was about to proceed with the administration, I felt tongue-tied. Struggling to speak, I got the distinct impression that I should not continue with the ordinance. It was as if a voice were speaking to me saying: "This is not the right time, for the place is full of mockers and unbelievers. Wait for a more private moment."

My speech returned at that moment and I addressed the group: "The Lord has restrained me from blessing this little girl, because there are unbelievers among you who doubt this sacred ordinance. Please help me by leaving so I can bless my child."

The people present left without taking offense at my words. We put Tisinā in her bed by the table, covering her with a sheet. From 5:00 P.M. to 8:00 P.M., there was no movement in our little girl's body. Sālote, of course, was greatly agitated and kept saying: "Why are you waiting to do something? When are you going to bless her? Her body is beginning to harden. Isn't it better to prepare her for burial while her body is still soft and warm?"

I told Sālote I had done nothing because the Lord had restrained me. He would let us know what to do at the appropriate moment.

One curious villager after another had been coming to inquire after our little girl.

Soon the impression came strongly that I should now proceed with the administration. All present in the home at that moment were people with faith in priesthood blessings. The feeling of what I should do and say was so strong within me that I knew Tisinā would recover completely after the blessing. Thus, I anointed her head and blessed her in the name of Jesus Christ to be well and normal. I blessed her head and all her wounds to heal perfectly, thanking God for his goodness to me in allowing me to hold his priesthood and bring life back to my daughter. I asked him to open the doors of Paradise, so I could tell her to come back and receive her body again and live. The Lord then spoke to my heart and said, "She will return to you tomorrow. You will be reunited then."

This last impression filled me with deep emotion and anxiety. I felt the difficulty of the situation as I lay down by my lifeless daughter. But I had blessed her that the Lord's will be accomplished, that her flesh, bones, and blood be restored to normal health.

At ten o'clock, Sālote was still asking me why we let Tisinā just lie there without preparing her for what seemed to her like the inevitable funeral. I said to her, "Go to sleep. She will come back to us tomorrow. The Lord has told me."

Sālote slept by Tisinā and I lay down with our baby. At 3:00 A.M. the following morning, I was awakened by a tiny hand pulling my hair. It was Tisinā alive and well. I grabbed her and examined her, her head and face. They were perfectly normal. All her wounds were healed; and from that day to this, she has experienced no complications from the accident. Her life was the miraculous gift from Heavenly Father during our missionary labors in Fo'ui. Tisinā has been an immense blessing to the family all her life. . . .

10

Filipe Kioa

ONE HEART AND ONE FAITH

Filipe Kioa attended the Mormon primary school in 1918 as a ten-year-old scholar. He attended the first Tongan Mission conference in the same year, presided over by President Willard Smith. Brother Kioa participated in the fasting and prayers of the Saints for the repeal of the law prohibiting Mormon missionaries from entering the kingdom. Finally in 1925 he was baptized a member and has remained faithful to the present day. The following story captures the interesting mix of local culture and spiritual conversion.

It was a strange set of circumstances which finally brought my wife into the Church.

Sela Kava and I were married in 1930. She was a member of another faith and resisted every invitation on my part to hear the gospel or to worship with me in the Church. After sixteen years and eight children, we still went our separate ways on Sunday. By nature I was not aggressive or forceful. My wife did as she pleased.

One day I felt impressed to say to her, "Sela, hear my words for they will be words of prophecy for you. If you don't repent and join with me in the true Church, someday soon you will weep pitifully and there will be nothing like your sorrow in this land, you mark my words!" But Sela continued going to her church, not heeding my words.

Shortly thereafter our little daughter died of a severe infection from a boil on her face. She died at 2:00 A.M.; and at 11:00 A.M., my wife's mother, who lived next door to us, passed away. Sela went back and forth between the two houses wailing uncontrollably, first over the body of our little girl, then over the remains of her mother. It was most pitiful to see. Her sorrow reminded me of my words to her. But she was still determined to have nothing to do with my religion.

The following year (1948) our fourth child, a boy, was stricken with a severe infection which responded to neither a doctor's prescription nor a Tongan home remedy. When the situation became desperate, Sela pleaded with me: "What is to be done?"

Feeling impressed to repeat the previous warning, I said: "Sela, you do whatever you choose; but mark my words, your sorrows are just beginning if you do not repent and come to the Lord's true Church with me."

These words had an effect on my wife, but she could not cast off her resentments and doubts. She finally proposed another idea–to take our son to a well-known psychic or fortune teller on the island of Foa and ask her why these hardships were upon us and what remedy would heal our son. Sela insisted we go.

So we went to the little village of Fangaleʻounga and approached this famous young woman whose name was Vāhoi. "Let us first go," Vāhoi said, "to the house of the Methodist steward and ask him to pray for us."

The prayer accomplished, we sat down in a circle with Vāhoi who stared at Sela for a long time. She then shifted her gaze toward me. Her first words were: "You both attend different churches, do you not?"

"Yes," replied my wife.

"Your family is in turmoil," said Vāhoi, "because you are not of one heart and mind. Sela pulls the children away to her church, and you pull them away to yours. It's this tug of war which is tearing your family apart. The problem is spiritual, not physical."

The young woman then turned to my wife and said, "Sela, you and your husband unite in one church, and speak to God with one voice and your little boy will live."

"And which church is that?" queried Sela.

"Why, the church of your husband. That is the true church. You follow your husband. The Bible teaches that the head of the woman is her husband, just as the head of the church is Christ. And Christ and his church are one. Now go and join his church."

Well, we returned to ʻUiha and Sela was baptized immediately. However, the sickness of our little son continued. This was in 1948 just before the visit of the apostle Matthew Cowley. I said to Sela one day, "You take our son to Tongatapu to the mission conference. When the apostle comes, you ask him to bless our Sēmisi to be healed."

It was just as I had said. The apostle laid his hands on Sēmisi and the boy was made well. When Sela came back from the conference she was truly converted and admitted the error of her ways in the past. Her stalwart service in the Church included a tenure as president of the Relief Society in the 'Uiha branch.

Being together as one in the Church has brought us great sweetness and peace of mind. Service in the Lord's kingdom is our greatest joy.

11

Albin ('Alipini) Johannson

"THE LORD IS GOOD TO ALL"
Psalms 145:9

Albin Johannson is a lay preacher in the Methodist Church, an accountant, the Swedish Consul, and former manager of the Dateline Hotel. The following account illustrates the gratitude many leaders of other faiths have for the Church.

In 1939 when I was ten years old, I became deathly ill with typhoid fever and pneumonia. After weeks of suffering, I was in a condition so severe that both Doctor Pōsesi Fonua and my parents had given up hope for my life. My hair had fallen out, and my body was reduced to skin and bones. It looked as if I would slip away at any time.

During that bleak moment in time, my older brother Feleti, a student at the Mormon school in Makeke, asked my parents if he could bring two Mormon missionary teachers to give me a blessing. My mother, although a strong Wesleyan, said they could come. After all, everything else had failed.

The day the Mormon elders came had been particularly rough for me. I had fallen into a deep coma and it looked as if I was gone, but I revived a little as I became aware of two white men kneeling at the side of my bed. Anointing my head with oil, they placed their hands on my head and prayed for a long time. Afterward we talked briefly, and they left. From that moment on, according to my mother, strength began to return to my body. I took no more medicine and was able to return to school the following year.

Feleti remembers the missionaries, Elder Franklin Spencer and Elder Earl Tew, to whose faith and love I owe my life. I will always be grateful to them and especially to the Lord Jesus Christ.

12

Charles (Siale) 'Ataongo Wolfgramm

THE WORK OF THE CARPENTER

Charles Wolfgramm had the distinction of being the first Tongan bishop in the Church, ordained in May 1958 in Auckland, New Zealand. A master carpenter, he served many labor missions, helping to build chapels in four countries—New Zealand, Tonga, Samoa, and the United States. He also assisted in building the New Zealand Temple and the Polynesian Cultural Center in Laie, Hawaii. His construction and Church leadership skills were greatly appreciated everywhere he lived, Tonga, New Zealand, Samoa, Hawaii, California, Arizona, and Utah. The following account is excerpted from his personal history.

My father, Emil Otto Fredrick Wolfgramm, came to Tonga from Germany at eighteen years of age in 1874. He was one of five Wolfgramm brothers who settled in Vava'u and made Tonga their home. My Tongan mother, Lataheanga, delivered me on August 5, 1905, at our home in the little island of 'Otea where I grew up as a native Tongan boy, riding horses, fishing, and working on our plantation.

Dad was a strong, energetic man. In Germany he had learned the trade of a blacksmith and developed powerful arms. He could climb attic stairs with a 280-pound sack of flour on his shoulders. His industry in Tonga generated prosperity for the family; but with the outbreak of World War I, he lost his store and his fortune. The family moved then to the island of Koloa where he helped his children establish another store. Life was hard. There were few comforts. Survival itself was an achievement.

In 1917 a major hurricane struck Vava'u, causing havoc and destroying much of the island's food supply. People lived on fish and coconut meat until new crops could be planted and harvested. The following year in 1918, the influenza killed thousands of people throughout Tonga. Everyone in our family was ill but me and Dad. I became the caretaker of the family, feeding them exactly what Dad told me, namely, the boiled juice and pulp of mangoes, oranges, bananas, pawpaw, and pineapple. In ten days, everyone began to recover. All survived. . . .

At the age of fifteen, I was baptized by Elder Emile C. Dunn on December 12, 1920 at 'Otualea beach. In 1923 I was invited to attend the Church-sponsored Maori Agriculture College at Korongata, Hawke Bay, in New Zealand. I was one of several Polynesian boys from other South Pacific islands brought to this college. Here my eagerness for the gospel and activity in the Church flourished.

My father had taught me to bake bread in Tonga so I earned my tuition money as a baker. I was lonely at the Maori Agriculture College though, being so far away from home, especially being separated from my mother. One night I dreamed of my mother. She was lying on her bed in her *fale* (hut) and kept calling my name "Siale, Siale." The dream disturbed me so much that I woke up and wrote a letter to my family. At the next mail call there was a letter from Tonga with news of my mother's death. She had died the very night I dreamed of her.

I wanted to quit school but knew I couldn't give up. Knowing that Mother would want me to finish school, I had to keep on. Besides I loved school. Our headmaster was Ariel S. Ballif. I took a speech and drama class from his wife, Sister Arta Ballif. She fed my deep, long-time yearning to learn English, a desire which was born back home in Tonga as I tried to read the English Bible in my father's home. Sister Ballif made us memorize poems and stories and then present them to our class. I spent hours out by a wooded area on the school grounds speaking to the trees, trying to memorize my assignments perfectly. . . .

In 1928 I graduated with honors. The Lord blessed me in my school work, quickening my understanding so I could comprehend and remember things I read. I can never adequately express my gratitude for the education which opened doors for me when I returned home to Tonga and wherever I went throughout my life.

Back in Tonga I married Meletoto Mu'a and started working for Lever Brothers in Nuku'alofa. Later, on January 21, 1934 we were called on a mission, and I was set apart as president of the Tongatapu

District, presiding over the twelve branches on the island. I also taught at Makeke College and proselyted at night. . . .

In 1935 I became the missionary companion of Floyd Fletcher from Boise, Idaho. One day a request came from Nakolo branch for us to come and administer to a woman who had leprosy. She was told she would have to go to the island of Makogai, Fiji, the leper colony in the South Pacific. On a Sunday afternoon we arrived at her home in Nakolo. I anointed her and Elder Fletcher sealed the anointing. In this priesthood blessing, we promised her she would be healed of this terrible disease through the united faith of her and her family. On the following day, the Tongan medical officer ordered her to board the *Tōfua* that would take her to Fiji. When she arrived in Fiji and was examined by two different doctors there, she was declared free of the disease and was released to return immediately to Tonga. This woman was Mele Lea-'a e-Maka Tukikava-'i-Falelahi, a great-grandmother of Sione Vānisi. Sione told me years later in Hawthorne, California, that his great-grandmother had been completely healed and never suffered from the disease again.

We were released from our mission in February 1937 but continued to live in Nuku'alofa for a while before moving to Leimātu'a, Vava'u. Meletoto, who had been such a faithful companion, died eighteen months after the birth of Otto, our last child together. The children were placed temporarily in homes of helpful members of my extended family. At the counsel and encouragement of President Emile C. Dunn I married Hena Langi, September 23, 1940.

In 1946 I wanted to better my life and to have my children acquire an education. Accordingly, I moved my family to New Zealand where I worked on a hydropower project and did some private contracting in building homes. Our own home on Buette Street became a "home away from home" to all Tongans venturing to New Zealand, extended family members and strangers alike.

I was successful as a private contractor in New Zealand, and my work soon attracted the attention of the Church building supervisor who asked me to join with him in building chapels in New Zealand. I have never turned down an opportunity to work in the Church and I accepted this offer with willingness and humility. I felt this was the way I could help build the kingdom. I was put in charge of building many chapels—at Scotia Place, Auckland; Hastings, Gisborne, Tamaki, Mt. Roskill, and many other places throughout New Zealand. Perhaps my greatest joy was helping to build the New Zealand Temple. I was awed by the innumerable hours donated by crews made up of Church members, coming from far and near to build this edifice. . . .

When the first stake in Auckland was organized in May of 1958, Brother George Beisinger was called as president. I was called to be bishop of Auckland Second Ward, the first Tongan bishop in the Church. Despite my feelings of unworthiness, even guilt, I was told the Lord had chosen me and that I was the man he wanted to serve in that holy calling. From this time on, my own knowledge of the power of faith and the priesthood was added upon by a special quality of discernment and the manifestation of the Holy Ghost in my life. Mine was the great blessing of serving families from many lands including the Solomon Islands.

The following is just one of many spiritual experiences. Brother Mitchell, a Rarotongan member, came to me early one morning and asked me to bless his daughter who was in the tuberculosis sanitorium. I asked several ward members to join me in a fast for this young girl, whose condition was very serious. As we entered the sanitorium, the nurse gave us cloaks and masks to wear; and we went into the hospital room where our patient was isolated. A feeding tube was in her throat so she could not talk. We were told she would be returning home as there was nothing more that could be done for her. My counselor anointed this good sister, and I bestowed the blessing. My eyes told me she was truly in a terminal condition; and yet when I laid my hands on her, I heard the Holy Spirit say to me, "Bless her to be well." I obeyed the prompting and blessed her to health. The next day she was taken home and from that time on she proceeded to recover. In fact, she later bore a child and continued to be in good health.

When we decided to migrate to America, Hena worked in a clothing factory to provide money for our son, Emil, to go to school at Church College of New Zealand and to help with our fares to Zion. Our children worked to earn money for their fares. Unfortunately, Hena passed away before her dream was fulfilled. She died the day Otto got married in June 1960.

Our family decided to continue our plans to go to Zion, so in January of 1961 we departed for America. We settled in Mesa, Arizona. I worked for Buehner Block Company in Mesa and did private contracting on the side. Otto and I built cabins in the mountains of Arizona. . . .

While on a short visit to Salt Lake City, I renewed acquaintance with Verna Davis who had served a mission in New Zealand a few years before. We were married in the Manti Temple July 1, 1961. Shortly after our marriage we left to serve yet another building mission, this time in Hawaii. I assisted in building the Polynesian Cultural Center. Among other things I served as the personnel director for the unmarried labor missionaries who were building both at the college and the center. I also supervised the building of the Tongan and Fijian villages.

The gospel is my life's blood. I want to share the gospel with everyone—anywhere, anytime. . . . I can never deny that the Lord blesses us when we exercise our faith in him. Indeed, the priesthood has been restored. From my little island in 'Otea, Vava'u, in Tonga I have traveled and served in other parts of the world. While living among the Caucasian people, I came to love them for their goodness as a people. It was not difficult for me, a Polynesian, to be accepted by them and be treated as one of them. I was accepted in every circle of friendship and was looked upon as a leader among them. There were cultural differences, but I was never intimidated because of my Polynesian culture. What did make the difference, though, was that I was an active Latter-day Saint Polynesian. I gave up parts of my culture not in harmony with the teachings of the gospel of Jesus Christ. . . .

In 1973 Verna was stricken with cancer. We fasted and prayed and asked Heavenly Father to preserve her life. Her recovery was remarkable. To think of this as a trial is absurd. The Lord gives to his children these wonderful challenges because he knows exactly what each must endure and overcome to make his or her faith stronger.

In my seventy-seventh year (1982), I noticed a decline in my health. My strength was leaving me and my body ached. After a doctor's examination, X-rays and many tests, it was determined that I had bone cancer. I wasn't given long to live, according to medical prognosis; but I knew that my time to go was not yet. I still needed to be with my family. I continued to travel, even worked for about six to eight months at the Polynesian Cultural Center in Hawaii, always returning home to my wife who kept the "home fires burning" for me. Priesthood blessings were given by family members and extended family members at different times during this sickness. My cancer went into remission *many* times, and I improved in health with each blessing and each remission. These were challenging days for me. Even in the darkest hour of my sickness, I offered thanks to Heavenly Father for my blessings throughout my life.

Note by Verna Davis Wolfgramm: Charles 'Ataongo Wolfgramm passed away May 16, 1988. He was eighty-three years old. He died five months after he returned from a trip to Israel. He was able to accomplish a number of things he desired to do while in the Holy Land. He wanted to walk where Jesus walked. He wanted to fast so the Holy Ghost would direct his thoughts and actions so he would be worthy to walk on this sacred ground. He wanted to bear his testimony. These three privileges were granted to him. He walked in Nazareth, Capernaum, and to the Mount of Beatitudes. He fasted. He was called to bear his testimony at the Jerusalem Center and the Garden Tomb.

13

Ermel J. Morton

THE GIFT AND POWER OF TRANSLATION

Of all the foreign LDS missionaries sent to Tonga, Ermel J. Morton had one of the keenest minds for language. His gift of speech and translation were a marvel to everyone. On his first mission (1936–39), Brother Morton served for a time as principal of the Makeke primary and secondary schools. Under the direction of President Emile C. Dunn he began the Tongan translation of the Book of Mormon which turned into an eight-year project.

In 1950 Brother Morton was appointed principal of Liahona High School where he continued his translation of the Doctrine and Covenants and the Pearl of Great Price. His able Tongan assistants were Sovea Kioa, ʻAtonio Tuʻiʻāsoa, Sēmisi Nukumovahaʻi Tonga, Siosifa Tuʻiketei Pule, and Sēmisi Taumoepeau. The enduring quality of his translations is much appreciated by the Tongans themselves.

The following excerpts from Ermel Morton's unpublished personal history[1] provide insights into how the Lord prepares his servants for a mighty task.

As soon as I landed in Tonga on October 25, 1936, I began an intensive study of the Tongan language. I received an immediate outpouring of the Holy Spirit, giving my first Tongan speech one week after my arrival. At first I spent hours memorizing and preparing; but in less than two months, I was speaking freely without the crutch of memorization. On December 13, 1936, I gave a fifteen-minute speech

---

[1] Copy of typescript in possession of author, Laie, Hawaii.

I hadn't memorized. On December 18, I spoke for thirty-five minutes in a district conference.

I had heard that President Joseph F. Smith, president of the Church, learned Hawaiian in three months when he was a missionary in the Sandwich Islands. My hope was to be fluent in Tongan within three months as well. I knew it was a gift of the Holy Ghost to me, the gift of tongues, the gift of the Tongan language, and that gift depended on my continued humility, prayer, and diligence.

On January 15, 1937, after a cottage meeting of unusual spiritual power in Vainī, the Holy Spirit whispered to me that my increasing knowledge of the Tongan language would lead me into the work of translating the Book of Mormon. The possibility of this blessing began to occupy my mind, and I dreamed one night that President Dunn told me he would release all the missionaries at their regular time but would keep me longer to translate this sacred book.

Actually President Dunn was hoping to work on the translation himself, but he was so busy with building a new recreation hall in Haʻalaufuli and a new chapel in Neiafu, he never got the opportunity he desired. On November 18, 1938, he instructed me to commence a translation of the Book of Mormon. Half of my time was to be given to translation and half to proselyting. Five months later I had finished the first draft translation of the Book of Mormon. As I had been forewarned, President Dunn asked me to stay in Tonga beyond my time to finish the project.

The completion of the draft translation was a profoundly emotional moment for President Dunn and the Tongan Saints at the April 28, 1939, district conference. The two major projects he had set his heart on as mission president were to complete the Neiafu chapel and to translate the Book of Mormon. He announced the completion of both. He thought revisions and corrections to the translation would be minimal. No one realized at the time that it would take seven more years to get the Book of Mormon published in Tongan.

On May 9, 1939, I left Vavaʻu for Nukuʻalofa for the purpose of revising and correcting the manuscript with the aid of Tēvita Mapa and Siosifa Tuʼiketei Pule. They read the manuscript carefully and suggested corrections. President Dunn and I took turns reading each Tongan and English sentence to make sure the translations were correct. The typing of the final revision was completed August 5, 1939.

In the process of translation, as we read again Moroni 10:3–7, the Holy Spirit bore witness to me that the Book of Mormon is true and is the word of God. The Holy Spirit also bore witness in an overpowering way that Joseph Smith was a true prophet of God and that the Church is true.

I sailed for America with the revised Tongan manuscript on September 22, 1939. Arriving in Salt Lake City October 5, I delivered it to the Office of the First Presidency where it was placed in the vaults of the Church. I met President Grant who had been told of my work. He congratulated me and said, "Keep the harness on, my boy. Keep the harness on." I also had an interview with President David O. McKay, at that time a counselor to President Grant.

Shortly after this time, Elder Floyd C. Fletcher and Elder W. Brent Wright were called to check over the manuscript and to make revisions they thought necessary. A few others who knew Tongan also assisted briefly. Brother Wright and Brother Fletcher went through the Book of Mormon manuscript and suggested changes, but President Dunn did not accept the changes.

After some time, Elder George Albert Smith of the Council of the Twelve and President Rufus [K.] Hardy called me to Salt Lake in January 1942, and turned over to me the entire responsibility of revising the manuscript and preparing the Book for publication. I was given the authority to make final decisions on all matters. Elder Smith and President Hardy were my advisors.

I began to work on the manuscript again, but soon realized I didn't have enough knowledge to do a really good job. So I began to study Tongan again. I had some Tongan books such as *Ko e Ta'u e Teau (One Hundred Years)* and others which had good, idiomatic Tongan in them. I began to prepare a Tongan-English and English-Tongan dictionary of usage from the words and sentences I found in these Tongan books. I made cards for each word and filed them under their Tongan and English meanings. This work on the dictionary went on for a year until I felt that I could resume the revision of the manuscript. The making of the dictionary greatly increased my knowledge of idiomatic Tongan and helped me make many corrections and improvements in the Book of Mormon manuscript.

In addition to the Tongan dictionary I made, I had a copy of the 1884 edition of the Tongan Bible and also a copy of Dr. James Moulton's Tongan translation of the Bible. These materials provided excellent language resources for the translation of the Book of Mormon into Tongan.

They also gave me access to more of the language of the scriptures in Tongan and prepared me for my later task of translating the other LDS scriptures into Tongan.

I retyped the entire Tongan manuscript of the Book of Mormon so as to have a working copy that could be marked up and changes be inserted. The original manuscript I brought from Tonga was kept in the Church vaults for safekeeping.

On September 4, 1944, I received word that the Tongan Cabinet and Privy Council had adopted certain changes in the spelling of Tongan words. Thus I had to begin another retyping of the entire Tongan manuscript to agree with the changes decreed by the Tongan government.

Finally on March 15, 1945, I wrote in my diary: "I finished the Book of Mormon tonight and expect to take the manuscript to Salt Lake City on Saturday to deliver it to the First Presidency for printing." During the time we were revising the manuscript, I sent copies of our revisions to President Dunn in Tonga for his approval.

After delivering the manuscript to the First Presidency, I received word that the Tongan government had again decreed further changes in the spelling of Tongan words. Accordingly I went to Salt Lake City to get the manuscript so that I could copyread it and make the necessary changes in the spelling of the words. I completed these spelling changes during the summer and returned the manuscript to the Church Offices in Salt Lake ready for printing.

The work of typesetting began during the fall. By November 5, 1945, I had begun reading and correcting the proof sheets. Elder Wright assisted in the proof reading. The work of typesetting and correcting the proof sheets continued; and on February 25, 1946, I went to Salt Lake City to work full time on the proofreading, the page makeup, and the final preparations for printing the book.

We finally finished all the preparatory work on March 8, 1946, and the Tongan Book of Mormon was ready to go to press. On April 29, the books were off the press, and President Evon W. Huntsman took the first consignment to Tonga. A few books were bound in black leather for presentation to the Queen of Tonga and other high government officials.

It was evident throughout the translation of the Book of Mormon into the Tongan language that the hand and power of the Lord was manifest in all that happened and all that was done. The spirit of revelation was manifest abundantly to guide the translation. Whatever few mistakes there may be are the mistakes of men. I know that the Lord helped me abundantly and guided my thinking and efforts to translate the book. It contains the word of God.

14

Tēvita Muli Kinikini

"WHATSOEVER
I SHALL COMMAND THEE
THOU SHALT SPEAK"
Jeremiah 1:7

Tēvita Muli Kinikini (1903–84) was an exceptionally fine proselyting missionary and priesthood leader, baptizing hundreds of new converts into the Church. A man of unusual spiritual gifts, including the gifts of healing and preaching, he was also a renowned poet and musician. His famous "History of Joseph Smith" lakalaka *(group dance) was premiered in Tonga in the early fifties and later became a feature performance at the Polynesian Cultural Center in Laie, Hawaii, in the 1960s. Most of the large Kinikini family have migrated to America where they continue to contribute to the Church as leaders, missionaries, and musicians.*

I was born in the island of 'Uiha in 1903 to Taniela Kinikini and Sēlita Valu Malupō. Father and Mother belonged to the Tonga Free Church. Dad was a sort of psychic who amazed everyone with his ability to mentally see lost articles and tell others where to find them. Mom was the sister to the paramount chief, Malupō. Several of her brothers eventually held the title. Our family was well known and well respected. We were expert farmers and fishermen.

In January of 1930 I married Le'o Langi. One day in 1932, Le'o's father Paula Langi, a missionary in the Mormon Church, approached and asked us for lodging for him and his companion during their stay in our island of 'Uiha. I agreed to treat them as guests but insisted that there be no preaching. "I'll feed you, but don't bother me with that doctrine," I said.

Although I declared my wishes to my father-in-law, I really could not resist his request to use our little house for a public meeting. An elder from America, an Elder Scott Miller, would be speaking.

When the meeting was held, the hut, yard, and road were overflowing with people. I stood in the road, angry at my father-in-law and embarrassed that LDS doctrine was being preached from my house.

But a strange sensation occurred within me when Elder Miller stood up and spoke of his mission, bearing testimony that he got no salary or commission from his work. It was a labor of love for him as for all those who ministered in the Church.

I was fascinated and moved closer to hear better. By the time the meeting was over, I was sitting among the few people in the house itself. I felt genuine excitement and asked for the biblical references used by the elders, which Le'o read to me later, after the people had left the premises. I simply said to my wife. "I'll not wait any longer, I am going to be baptized immediately."

Unfortunately, word spread quickly throughout the village that I was being baptized into the Mormon Church. My extended family began to mourn. Mom and Dad went into shock and the paramount chief, Malupō, became so furious he threatened to take away my plantation which was on his estate.

I held to my convictions, but cancelled the baptism when my parents threatened a double suicide if I went through with it. They said, "The day of your baptism we will go to Tatafa island and watch the beach Fale-'a-liku. The moment people begin to show up to your baptism, we will both plunge into the ocean and drown ourselves."

The temporary cancellation of the baptism calmed the troubled waters, so that when I was baptized the next week most of the family had gotten used to the idea. Dad gave me his blessing, charging me to never violate the principles of the gospel I had embraced.

Only Malupō remained angry and inconsolable, worried what the queen and the rest of the nobility would say. When he threatened again to take away both my plantation land and my village residence, I simply said, "Malupō, do as you please. Take the property. I can get earthly property anywhere, Tongatapu, 'Eua, Fiji, Samoa. But a celestial mansion in heaven can be obtained only in the Church of Jesus Christ in which I was baptized today." Actually the whole affair quieted down almost immediately. There were no serious repercussions to the baptism.

In 1933 I became a deacon, a teacher in 1934, and priest in 1936. In those days the leaders were very slow to advance even an active person to the Melchizedek Priesthood. Notwithstanding, my experiences in things spiritual increased wonderfully.

It was in 1938 that my father, the village psychic, dreamed a dream and saw that I would be the father of only boys. When he announced that Le'o would have no female children, we were disappointed because we wanted a girl very badly. Dad's reputation for "seeing" the future and knowing the secrets of existence seemed irrefutable. He had not joined the Church.

This was the year that Apostle George Albert Smith visited Tonga and came to Ha'apai. I was in charge of preparing our island for the arts festival to be held in conjunction with the conference in Pangai. Many people from the Wesleyan and the Tonga Free Churches made up our dance troupe and the choir from 'Uiha.

The festival, consisting of *lakalaka* and *ma'ulu'ulu* dances, the *kailao*, and choir competitions, was absolutely spectacular. Apostle Smith seemed delighted and amazed at the beauty and color of the occasion. Early Sunday morning our choir was scheduled for a final practice before the main session of conference. When they had gathered, I announced: "You go ahead and practice. I'm taking Le'o to the apostle to ask him to bless us to have a baby girl. My father has dreamed that we can produce only males."

My announcement was met with laughter and ridicule from some of our fellow villagers: "So these two presume to ask Jehovah for a little girl? Who do they think they are?"

Elder Smith blessed Le'o that morning and promised us our next baby would be a girl and that we would have other female children as well.

Thus the conflict between the apostle's blessing and my father's prophecy captured the imagination of the citizens of 'Uiha. When Le'o became big with our next child there was much speculation among them. They saw it as a contest of truth. And when she went into labor just after our next district conference, certain people crowded around our residence waiting and listening. They heard the baby cry and the midwife say to Le'o: "You are blessed with a little girl." Silently the people disappeared in an instant. The apostle's promise came true and we named the child Susana 'Auhangamea.

We wept bitterly when President Dunn sent word that all of the American elders were being sent back home because of World War II. This was in 1940. We loved these elders as our own children. But it was a blessing in disguise. After their departure, we had to rely on ourselves in spiritual matters. I tried hard to be worthy of my callings and the Melchizedek Priesthood which I now held.

In 1941 we received our first mission call to preach the gospel and also to serve as branch president in Vava'u. The call came when we were struggling the hardest just to survive. There were ten of us in the family. Money was scarce since there was no market at the time for our copra. Of course we had to pay our own boat passage and sustain ourselves throughout the mission.

But our spirits were high as was our faith. We sold our pigs for eight shillings apiece. The children hired out to large plantations. Le'o made soap, and I processed some coconut oil to be used in an ancient-style lamp so we would have light. Landing in Vava'u, we had eight shillings to our name and began serving in the island village of Koloa.

At that time in Vava'u, the only other missionary was Tēvita Mahu'inga, branch president in Tu'anuku, who often accompanied me on proselyting tours. During the week we visited from village to village, coming home late on Friday night. Saturday was always the day to prepare for Sunday.

One such Saturday I arrived back at Koloa at break of day, just in time to take our four little boys and go fishing for our Sunday meal. The five of us crowded onto one large outrigger and paddled to Faiola island where we caught much fish. When we landed back at Koloa around 7:00 P.M. with our load of fish, Le'o said to me, "We have a funeral on our hands. Three times the family of Vika Fatafehi sent word for you to come quickly and administer to her. I told them you weren't back yet. They just sent word to never mind because poor Vika has passed away."

Now Vika was already over a hundred years old and ready for death, but I felt great anxiety and guilt to have been away at her time of need. As I was cleaning up, suddenly it seemed a small voice whispered to me and said "Go and restore Vika to life." I put on my best clothes. The voice came again: "Go." Picking up my consecrated oil from my clothes box, I left the hut.

"Where are you going?" asked my wife.

"I'm going to bless Vika to live."

"Oh, Muli," she cried. "Come back, you'll be the laughing stock of all Tonga. We'll all be ridiculed if Vika doesn't revive."

I reassured Le'o about what had been revealed for me to do. I walked straight to Vika's house which was full of women sitting in a large circle around Vika's bed. When they saw me the women whispered among themselves, "Here's her minister." Vika's younger sister, who was blind, heard the women and cried out: "Reverend sir, three times we asked for you to no avail and now poor Vika is dead."

I said nothing. I simply knelt by Vika, removed her shroud, and began to anoint her head with consecrated oil. I sensed immediately the reaction of the women, their giggles and their mockery. But I felt calm, because I was only following what had been a clear message to me, to reveal the power of the Almighty among these people. Nevertheless, after the administration I pleaded with the Lord to honor this ordinance.

I returned home and waited, praying. Shortly, a woman arrived with the message that Vika had miraculously revived, telling the people present of her journey into the spirit world. She was met by a man who had come to guide her. Suddenly the man said: "Vika, you are being called back. There is still work in the world you must perform."

I told the messenger that Vika's recovery was through the power of Christ and His holy priesthood vested in the Elders of His Church.

The following morning I put on my waist mat and went to the home of Vika's son, Taufa, where a large number of chiefs and guests were assembled in a kava circle. Word had already spread about Vika's impending death. They had come to the funeral from all over Vava'u. I was presented formally with a cup of kava after which Taufa spoke: "Friends and citizens from mainland Vava'u and those from the outer islands, please stay here in Koloa. Vika will no doubt pass away in a little while, perhaps tonight or tomorrow. We'll hold her funeral and then you will be free to go."

At that moment I heard the same small voice inside me say: "Speak to this people and say Vika will not die."

Guided by this voice I said: "Please pardon me, noble chiefs, but I will speak. Vika will not die. What's more, as long as I serve in this village as branch president, there will not be one LDS member pass away, not even Vika."

The following year, in 1942, the Relief Society celebrated its 100th anniversary with a festival and a conference. Vika Fatafehi was called upon to open conference with prayer. She was indeed alive. We were transferred to 'Otea in October 1942. . . .

In 1946 I had a terrible quarrel with one of my sister's sons who, while I was away in Vava'u had confiscated a large portion of my plantation in the little island of Tatafa. His plantation had been next to mine for many years. The boundaries of the two plots had been clear. I was baffled to find a line of newly planted coconut trees down my property by which he claimed more ground for himself.

I complained to the police inspector, 'Ahome'e, in Pangai, who promised to come and restore the original boundaries. My nephew was furious and vowed he would shoot me and my wife, Le'o, if we ever approached that property.

On Monday the following week, Le'o and I put out for the little island. As we walked along the beach, we saw a huge sea bird harassing a school of mullet. The bird seemed to chase one big mullet right at us. I killed the fish with a blow and put it in our basket. Arriving at our plantation, Le'o began to spread the mature coconuts out for splitting and drying.

Suddenly a shot rang out and the heavy branch behind me virtually exploded. Le'o cried out in fright, "Jesus, save us."

My angry nephew emerged from the bush yelling that he was going to shoot us. I yelled back at him to come to his senses and not to do anything stupid.

He advanced toward us, shoving another shell into the gun, cocking it, and saying again emphatically he was going to kill us.

As he came toward us, I called him by name and said, "Come ahead, but the gun will not fire again. In the name of Jesus Christ and by the power of the priesthood in me, the gun will not fire."

The man kept coming, threatening all the way. He aimed and pulled the trigger. The gun did not fire. He cocked it and pulled the trigger two more times without consequence, after which he put the gun down and began to weep: "Oh Muli, please forgive me my insanity."

I said to him, "You may have my entire plantation. It is no longer important to me. Keep it! I'll find a plot of ground elsewhere. My own life is more important than this soil."

When we got back to 'Uiha, Le'o told the town officer, who was her uncle, of the attempt on our lives. Despite my protests, the man was arrested and charged with assault with a deadly weapon with the intent to kill. Nothing came of it because I refused to prosecute or testify. I insisted on their dropping the charges.

I thank Heavenly Father for his honoring of my priesthood and for bringing to pass the words of my command. The gun did not fire. I knew at the time the Lord had clothed me with the holy priesthood even in my weakness and that it was in his name this miracle occurred. Indeed, it is through his holy name that we are all saved.

15

'Epalahame and Lilevai Tua'one

NO GREATER CAUSE

'Epalahame and Lilevai Tua'one were stalwarts of the Church in the village of Fāhefa on Tongatapu. Son of pioneer Metuisela Tua'one, who established the Church and a school in Fāhefa in 1917, 'Epalahame served two proselyting missions for the Church (one with his wife and family) and several labor missions, for twelve years as branch president, and for six years as district president. 'Epalahame had a reputation for hard work and integrity. The following tribute by his wife Lilevai captures the essence of a great leader.

I was born on the 17th of January 1915 on the island of Felemea in Ha'apai. My parents, Samuela Lelei and Mele Laukau Fifita, were devout members of the Tonga Free Church. In 1932 when I was seventeen, two Mormon missionaries, Paula Langi and Kitione Maile, came to preach in our island. When I heard their sermons, I was amazed at the doctrine they taught. The truth of their words entered my heart with such force that I determined to be baptized by immersion into The Church of Jesus Christ of Latter-day Saints. Jesus himself was baptized by immersion in the River Jordan and the Bible made plain that we should follow his example.

Unfortunately, my father became upset when I told him I knew what the Mormon missionaries were teaching was true. "Look, you have already been baptized as a baby," he chided. "And if you notice, only the most stupid and ignorant of the people are Mormons."

Father's angry response to my testimony of the Mormon Church kept me from being baptized at that time; but from that moment on, I had no peace of mind. I wanted to join the Church more than anything. Sadly, my whole family behaved in an ugly fashion, threatening and ridiculing me. A maternal uncle even came with a gun, swearing he would kill me if I was baptized in the Mormon Church. I knew it was only his effort to frighten me, but the language my family used against me sounded equally violent in my ears. They claimed they would rather see me dead than a Mormon.

I pondered over several possibilities how I might free myself to join the Church. In my youthful mind, I devised schemes for my escape. I even went to Saia Langi and asked him to arrange a marriage with an elderly Mormon bachelor I knew of in 'Uiha. Moved by my desire to join the Church, Saia offered very excellent but different counsel to me. "The man you will marry must be a worthy Latter-day Saint. I promise you, if you keep the faith, the Lord will bless you someday with a strong priesthood holder, for he knows that the desire of your heart is to belong to his Church."

Brother Langi's promise finally came to pass six years later, but not until I had experienced much pain over the Church. I lived under the strict authority of my family, even after my father died in 1934. In 1936 I married a young man from Tongatapu with the understanding that I could have the freedom to become a member of the Mormon Church. That was a foolish hope, for my new husband was even more adamant in his hatred of the Church than my family. It was the cause of contention in our marriage.

One day 'Inoke Mataele, a stalwart Latter-day Saint and missionary, told my husband that because of my strong testimony of the Church, he should allow me to be baptized and, if not, the Lord would provide a way for me to join. Those words did not soften my poor husband's heart at all. Rather, he became even more demanding that I have nothing to do with the Mormons. By then we had a seven-month-old son.

Shortly after this encounter with Brother Mataele and just fifteen months after our wedding day, my husband became ill with typhoid fever. In three days he was dead. I was suddenly free to be baptized but was sadly without a husband.

My eventual baptism into The Church of Jesus Christ of Latter-day Saints was a source of great joy to me. As a young widow with a small child, I experienced hard times; but thanks to my cousin Samuela Fakatou and his wife Heleine, I was introduced to 'Epalahame Kumā

Tua'one, a very honorable man and promising Church leader. There was not a worthier young man in all of Tonga. My problem was that I didn't like his looks. He was not handsome and seemed much older than his twenty-five years. I resisted Heleine's efforts to introduce us but finally gave in to what became a whirlwind arrangement for marriage.

It was through this noble priesthood bearer, 'Epalahame Tua'one, that I learned what it meant to be a member of Christ's true Church, to be a true disciple of Christ. There is much more to being a Mormon than just getting baptized. Unfortunately, at that time in my life I was not prepared for this man's total commitment to the Church and his generous ways with others. A life of such consecration was foreign to me. His time, goods, and talents were all for the Lord's work and for the comfort and prosperity of others. He looked upon everything he had, not as ours to keep, but ours to give and share. His horse, his rusty bicycle, and his cart were readily made available to others. As for me, I just hated to be inconvenienced, and I resented that my comfort was not first with him.

Well, we were married for twenty-three years, and he has been dead now for twenty-seven years. I fear I was a hindrance and a great source of affliction to him. It wasn't until he died that I realized his God-like character and his selfless love.

I will share two remembrances of 'Epalahame Kumā Tua'one which illustrate his character.

I remember with regret the time when I sent my husband to buy some laundry soap with the little money we had from the sale of our copra. Due to a late arriving freighter from abroad, only Panisi's store in Nuku'alofa had any soap, and we were desperate. When 'Epalahame arrived, the place was packed with people. After waiting in a long line, he was just about to buy his soap when a commotion erupted in the crowd. A young woman had collapsed from the heat. 'Epalahame made his way over to her and, with the help of another man, carried her outside for fresh air. They couldn't revive her, so 'Epalahame ran and paid for a taxi to rush her to the hospital. After the examination, the doctor told 'Epalahame the woman was pregnant and was apparently overcome by hunger, heat, and fatigue.

Discovering that she lived in Ha'ateiho, 'Epalahame took her in the taxi to her home. On the way, they stopped at a little shop and bought her a loaf of bread, a can of corned beef, and a bottle of orange soda. She felt better instantly.

The woman's husband was so grateful for the kindness of this stranger that he wanted to kill and roast a pig for 'Epalahame as a gesture of his appreciation. 'Epalahame wouldn't hear of it, but needless to say he came home with no soap and no money. Imagine how I railed against him!

The other remembrance is from our missionary service. We were called on the mission by President Emile Dunn in 1945 and served until 1948. We had five young children at the time. The oldest was eight, the youngest six months. 'Otea, Vava'u, was our first assignment. This beautiful island had been suffering a long time from a severe drought, and food was not plentiful. In the beginning of our service, before we could put a garden in, our daily fare was *'otai*, a local drink made from grated green mangoes and coconut milk.

The baby, Sūnia, was ill most of the time and seemed on the verge of death. In fact we expected him to die. His body was lethargic; his eyes would not dilate. I attribute Sūnia's return to health to 'Epalahame's priesthood blessing and also to his amazing "luck" as a fisherman. He was never a fisherman in Fāhefa, yet here in 'Otea he miraculously was able to bring home the most excellent fish, including marlin. Sūnia would suck on this fresh fish and finally became a healthy child. On the other hand, I became pregnant with my sixth child about this time. Malnutrition took its toll on me. Even when the baby was born, I kept going downhill, collapsing often from sheer weakness. 'Epalahame revived me with his priesthood blessings and tender care. In fact, in a vivid dream one night, two men dressed in white appeared to him and said, "Your wife should have died; but because you called her back in your blessing, we let her return to you."

Nevertheless, I lived in fear that I was going to die. I was short of breath and suffered from insomnia. The doctor insisted I wean the baby, but we had no money for baby milk or for any other kind of food for me. 'Epalahame forced me to eat whatever we had, green mangoes still dripping sap and coconut meat, to produce milk for the baby. I remember walking with 'Epalahame around the village late one night because I couldn't sleep. Coming back to the hut, I beheld Viliami, our nine-year-old, holding the newborn Kalisi. Both were asleep. I cried out, thinking what would happen to my poor children if I died.

The next night, 'Epalahame heard that old man Tausinga had a can of hard biscuits (*mā pakupaku*). He went to Tausinga's home and asked for some biscuits for me. Tausinga gave us seven. I ate five on the spot and had my first good night's sleep in many weeks. When

'Epalahame began to have severe abdominal pains from stomach ulcers, I could not hold back my complaints. I spoke the unspeakable: " 'Epalahame, we should go home!"

His response was simply: "If we should die while serving the Lord, what greater cause could we give our lives for?" These words rang in my soul. My husband made me realize that problems and suffering in the mission field were blessings. We stayed on and endured. Finally, 'Epalahame's garden began to produce and our sufferings were relieved.

In conclusion, I will share a tribute to 'Epalahame Kumā Tua'one given by a Seventh-day Adventist friend named Fīnau Suluka. I met Fīnau in Nukuʻalofa not long after my husband's death. After offering his condolences to me he said: "If there were two Mormons like 'Epalahame Kumā, they would convert this entire land to the Church."

16

Solomone and Sālome 'Ulu'ave

SEEDS OF FAITH AND FRUITS OF COURAGE

Solomone and Sālome 'Ulu'ave were among the first converts to the Church in Niuafo'ou or Tin Can Island. Parents of twelve children, they felt the force of their island's animosity about their joining The Church of Jesus Christ of Latter-day Saints. Solomone and Sālome lived to see many of their children and grandchildren receive university degrees and serve in responsible positions, both in the Church and in universities and departments of education. They themselves served on several proselyting and temple missions. The conversion of this good family had a profound impact on the growth of the Church in Niuafo'ou and later in the island of 'Eua.

Sālome

Solomone (Solo) and I were married June 9, 1935, in our home island of Niuafo'ou. Each of us grew up the oldest child in large families, very active in the Wesleyan Church. True, we were relatively young when we married, but Solo was mature and very responsible for his age. We had ample plantation lands; and because of Solo's industry, we soon became quite prosperous from a Tongan point of view.

Besides our material prosperity, Solo was fast becoming a leader in the Wesleyan Church. He preached regularly and, in 1942, passed the ministerial examination. He served as secretary to our local parish in Mu'a while waiting for his formal assignment in the church. By that time we also had five beautiful children, three boys and two girls. Our lives could not have been happier, we thought.

But then our trials began, along with a profound shift in our lives to the gospel of Christ and The Church of Jesus Christ of Latter-day Saints.

On the 4th of March, 1944, when our youngest son, Pita Seti, was eight months old, I became extremely ill, so ill that everyone thought I was going to die. The medical officer in the island said my blood level was critically low and that all that could be done was for me to eat good food. In providing the best we had, we gradually killed off all of our animals. My condition continued to deteriorate rapidly, and my death seemed inevitable. Solo moved me into a little hut on his parents' lot, and there they cared for me, waiting for my approaching death.

As I lay there, drifting in and out of a coma, I was aware of things around me, including the family discussions of my funeral arrangements. I could see the rock slabs my husband Solo had painstakingly chipped out of the lava cliffs by the ocean to wall the sides of my grave. On the beams right above my bed were rolls of Tongan *koloa*, fine mats and tapa cloths which would decorate my funeral bier.

It was precisely then that a Mormon missionary, Sēmisi Nukumovahaʻi Tonga, known as Vahaʻi, visited us. He told us he possessed special authority from the Lord to heal the sick. He said I would get well through a priesthood blessing which he would bestow. He talked of a great work remaining for me to accomplish. Solo agreed to the blessing only as he might agree to a doctor's last-resort offer to help me. I knew too well his negative feelings about the Mormons.

On Tuesday, March 13, 1944, Vahaʻi, the Mormon missionary, and his wife, Sela, came to give me the blessing, saying that they were fasting for me as well. Vahaʻi anointed me and pronounced the blessing in the name of Jesus Christ and by the authority of the holy priesthood of God.

The next day, Wednesday, March 14th, word was sent out to all of my extended family to assemble, because it was not likely I would survive the day. My family arrived all dressed for the funeral, wearing traditional black mourning clothes and heavy waist mats. The little house I lay in was packed with people. Some wailed loudly, others moaned soft and low.

The Wesleyan minister and the congregation from our parish were also there. After singing and saying last rites over me, the minister turned to my husband and said, "Solo, be strong! Let Sālome go! The winds seem to be blowing right, so let her go!" (*"Ngali matangi lelei ke 'alu ai leva ho mali"*).

Solo hated to hear those words and kept quiet, for he did not want to accept the inevitable.

At that very moment, Vaha'i Tonga came in. He had heard what the Wesleyan minister had said. Making his way over to my bed he said, "Solo, be comforted! Sālome will not die. There is still so much left for her to do."

The presence of the Mormon missionary in this setting caused a stir in the congregation. For him to say I was going to live provoked an angry outcry from the people. Vaha'i spoke as one having authority, and the people considered it an affront to their minister, whose word they revered. In their anger and frustration, they all departed from the house, some kicking and hitting the walls as they left. They seemed to say with one voice, "If your Jesus is true and ours false, let your Jesus heal her. We're rid of her." Even my own mother packed her things and left. The only persons who stayed behind were my maternal grandmother, Solo, and the Mormon missionary.

When everyone had left, Vaha'i again said, "Solo, Sālome will not die. She has been blessed and been given a promise through the holy priesthood that she will live. There is still much she has to do in this world."

He came over to my bed and whispered to me, "Sālome, do not fear for your life! We are still fasting for you."

This was the second day of their fasting. I was deeply moved by this show of compassion from a man who hardly knew me. The fact that he wouldn't let me die, even when my own mother and everyone else had left me, filled my heart with a wonderful warmth and love. This warmth started spreading throughout my lifeless body, driving out the coldness of death.

The next day, Friday, March 16th, I felt strong enough to get out of bed and crawl around in the house. I had such an overwhelming love for the Mormon missionaries that more than anything else, I wanted to see them, to be one with them. I knew absolutely that I had been miraculously healed through the power of God and was determined to become a member of his Church.

One week later I asked Solo to take me back to our home. I told him of my faith in the Mormon Church and asked for permission to be baptized.

Solomone

Miraculously my wife recovered after the blessing. She declared her faith in the LDS Church and asked me if she could be baptized. My reaction was to curse the Church and chase the missionaries from our home. I ordered them never to set foot upon our property or visit my wife again.

My wife's desire to join the Mormon Church upset me terribly. After all I was still the secretary in the Wesleyan parish. I took it upon myself to go from east to west preaching against Joseph Smith and ridiculing him as a false prophet, a thief, a liar, and a polygamist. I said many unworthy things about him.

While I was engaged in defaming the Prophet Joseph, the Mormon missionaries were fasting and praying with my wife for Heavenly Father to soften my heart so she could be baptized.

After the fasting, Vaha'i Tonga came to me and said, "Solo, please forgive me, but I have come because your wife has asked to be baptized a member of The Church of Jesus Christ of Latter-day Saints. We will not baptize her without your consent, for you preside over your family. You are the husband and if you are willing for her to be baptized, then we will baptize her; but if you are not willing, then we will not do it."

"Let her do as she pleases," I said, "for if God has decreed that I am the head of our family, my wife may be baptized now, but she will come back to me and my church. If the church my wife is joining is true, then I too must join with all our children."

On June 25, 1944, Sālome was baptized by immersion at a lake known as Vaivela in Mu'a, Niuafo'ou, Tonga. Vaha'i Tonga roasted a pig to celebrate the occasion and, as a sign of respect for me, sent the choicest portion of the pig to me at my home.

Even though I had given my consent, now that the baptism was accomplished my heart began to fill with humiliation and rage against my wife. It seemed like sheer disobedience to me. For while I was trying to become a Wesleyan minister, she was off getting baptized into the Mormon Church. At one point I led her to the ocean threatening to drown her. I desisted only because of the cries of our little daughter 'Emeline who had followed us. I stole away Sālome's nice clothes and hid them so she would have nothing to wear to church. I threatened divorce.

Divorce seemed to be the only recourse in my state of mind. Friends and family encouraged it. My father offered to pay my fare so that I could escape to Tongatapu. In fact, I was about to board the ship with all my goods to make my departure. No doubt I would have accomplished my designs had it not been for another Mormon, Sovea Kioa, who appealed to the district officer to stop me. As I began to board the boat, Peauafi Pālelei, the district officer, called to me: "Solo, come back and take care of your wife and children. Don't leave, for whom will they cry to for support?"

Frankly, I was relieved to join my family again. Also I began to wonder about the intensity of hateful feelings against my wife among the people she had never spoken ill of or harmed in any way.

One night my wife invited me to a Mormon open-air public meeting. I agreed to attend but purposely stayed as far away as I could from the speaker, not wanting to hear the sermons. However, the missionary who spoke that night, Samuela Fakatou, preached at the top of his lungs in a passionate style, and I could hear every word distinctly. That sermon was the beginning of my intellectual assent to the Church.

As one who had studied the scriptures all his life, I learned in the days that followed what the Mormon missionaries taught was true. The light of that truth slowly drove out the darkness of hatred from my heart. I started enjoying the presence of missionaries in our home and listened to their lessons intently. Further, I began to feel remorse for all the things I had said to defame the Church and the Prophet Joseph. Finally there was my witness to the miraculous healing of my wife through the power of the priesthood.

Sālome had mixed feelings about my wanting to be baptized. "The people will think you are just meekly following me," she cried. But by then my heart was burning with testimony and I said "Let them think what they will. I will not wait."

So on September 12, 1944, I was baptized along with our daughter 'Emeline, my younger brother Sailosi, and Sālome's brother, Penisimani Ika.

Joining the Church brought immense joy to my little family, although our faith was tested severely. Three of our children died in less than two years after my baptism. Many people saw these deaths as evidence of God's wrath against my little family for leaving our traditional faith and embracing The Church of Jesus Christ of Latter-day Saints. My extended family swore that all of our children would be taken away because of our disobedience. For them it was a simple matter of cause and effect. There was considerable mockery throughout Niuafo'ou, suggesting that it was a principle of the Mormon Church for children to die of the common cold.

Yet all of these hardships we were able to shake off. In fact, they gave us courage and strengthened our faith in the Church. We were determined to die in the Church our children had died in. True, we may have lost some of our children in death, but what joy to be members of the only true and living Church on the face of the earth! Besides the Lord blessed us with seven more children.

17

Sēmisi Nukumovahaʻi Tonga

"A REFINER'S FIRE"
Malachi 3:2

Sēmisi Nukumovahaʻi (Vahaʻi) Tonga was the beloved friend of thousands of LDS school children at Liahona. Teacher, musician, missionary, branch leader, and temple president, Brother Tonga has had wide influence among the members of the Church for over forty years. The following excerpt from his oral history stands as a permanent witness to the very real courage of Tonga's early Saints.

My mother's family was prosperous and well established socially in Pangai, Haʻapai. She was intelligent, pretty, and highly cultured according to Tongan standards. She could even converse in English. Thus, when she fell in love with and married Tēvita Tonga from the tiny and distant island of Haʻafeva, it was a bitter pill for her family to swallow.

My mother, Luʻisa Haʻakeli ʻOkusi, first saw Dad at their own Free Church of Tonga conference held in Pangai. Dad conducted the church choir from Haʻafeva and led a church band. He cut a fine figure. More importantly he was sweet dispositioned and humble. When they married he took her to live with his family in Haʻafeva.

The second of seven sons, I was born in 1918, the year Sālote Pilolevu was crowned Queen of Tonga. Dad passed away when I was eight. I remember distinctly the evening that he died. He told my mother that if anything happened to him, she should return to her own family in Pangai where we would have a chance to get the best education possible. Hence, in 1928 she sent me to live with her brother

Sione Filipe and his wife 'Alisi Palauni who were members of The Church of Jesus Christ of Latter-day Saints. I attended the Mormon school in Pangai and was baptized April 6, 1930–the hundredth anniversary of the founding of the Church.

In 1932 I sailed to Tongatapu to attend the prestigious government boarding school, Tonga College. When the students and teachers found out I was a Mormon–and the only Mormon in the whole school–I became a sort of laughing stock. They seldom called me by my name. I was either "Mormon boy" or "Joseph Smith." I remember one morning we were asked to line up on the field for roll call and inspection. We were told to stand behind the signs designating the church we each belonged to. The Mormon Church sign was put right by the school garbage pit, but I marched straight for it and stood at attention. It was a solo performance.

Strangely I was never ashamed or embarrassed by my membership in the Church although I took a lot of teasing. This sort of petty harassment only increased my determination to be the best and most well-mannered student I could be. I became a prefect in the college during my final years there. The words "Mormon boy" became the ultimate compliment for me.

I was eventually to experience real religious persecution after I married Sela Pulu of Faleloa and was assigned to teach in the government primary school in Niuafo'ou. Before we departed for this, the most remote island in Tonga, President Emile C. Dunn set us apart as missionaries to assist the work of the Lord in whatever way possible. We would have the privilege of serving with Samuela and Heleine Fakatou, two of the finest leaders and missionaries in the Church.

Niuafo'ou in the pre-evacuation days before 1946 harbored a rebellious spirit in the population that could erupt on occasion in explosive primitive rage. We felt that spirit many times in threatening looks and words from certain quarters. To be sure, most of the people were very kind to us, but we knew sooner or later that there might be some Mormon blood-letting. Samuela Fakatou had already been abused.

The terrible event occurred one night in the little village of Mu'a where we were holding an open public meeting in a Tongan *fale* which was about eight by sixteen feet in size. A mob of howling men suddenly appeared and surrounded the house: "Let's kill the Mormons!" they shouted.

Almost instantly the leader of the mob rushed in the hut and struck Samuela a wicked blow on the head. When Samuela fell, the man came at me, swearing that I was the real cause of the problem and would pay with my life. In the scuffle that followed, I managed to get my right arm around the man's neck in a headlock, at the same time kicking over and extinguishing the small coconut oil lamp.

The complete darkness saved my life, for instantly a dozen men pushed their way into the tiny house flailing and punching at me. One vicious blow meant for me struck the head of my assailant who was still struggling in my headlock. Instantly he went limp and I let him fall to the floor. The whole mob, thinking it was I who had fallen, shouted in triumph and began to kick and trample their own leader. I tried to shove my way out of the house, but the place was too crowded for me to move. At least no one could see me in the blackness. The sound of the blows and groans was sickening. Equally terrifying was the murderous language and oaths of the mob. After three or four minutes, the crowd pushed its way out the front door exulting over its deed.

Caught in the press, I managed to get outside and run for my life. Samuela was guarded by Filiiku Pututau and Solomone 'Ulu'ave who took him back to Tongamama'o where he was stationed.

As I made my way in the darkness to the school compound where we lived, I could hear sounds of wailing and mourning coming from our house: *"Oiaué, Vaha'i ē, kuo ke mate"* ("My sweet Vaha'i, you are dead"). It was Sela, who was barely two weeks delivered of our second daughter. She had received word that I had been killed. In fact, people had already come to give comfort to the widow.

Well, my presence was a great relief to my wife but the cause of some alarm to the others who were now wondering about the identity of the fallen man in the *fale*. The error was soon discovered and had a profoundly sobering effect on the whole island. In fact, there was an instant and compassionate public sentiment in favor of the Mormon missionaries. The poor man who was kicked and beaten by his friends and relatives suffered three days, then passed away.

It was a sad and ironic set of circumstances which surrounded the whole unfortunate affair. The mob that had delivered death to my assailant were actually members of his extended family. This loss was not the end of their troubles. Shortly after the funeral, government officials came and auctioned off all they owned for past debts and back taxes. Everything was sold, right down to the coconut grater. All of their goods were piled in an open grassy place – the mats, clothes, tapa cloth, utensils, everything.

Seeing an opportunity to return good for evil, Samuela Fakatou and I put our heads together and decided we would buy all the family's wealth and then return it to them. This gesture not only made us feel better but made a lasting impression on the village as well.

Our congregation grew in Niuafo'ou after these incidents. When the people were later evacuated in the aftermath of the destructive volcanic eruptions, most of them eventually settled in 'Eua where the Church is now very strong.

Just before we went to Niuafo'ou, we had acquired from the Honorable Lavaka's estate an eight-acre allotment deep in the bush, far from any major village. When we returned, we discovered we had a new next-door neighbor, the Church's Liahona College, which was about to be constructed. It was to Liahona that I committed my professional life and my heart.

I know firsthand of the love of God and the power of his priesthood. I love the Lord with all my heart, might, and mind.

PART III

LIAHONA

1948–59

Abundant Gospel Fruit

President David O. McKay and Emma Ray Riggs McKay with Crown Prince Tungī, presently King Taufaʻahau Tupou IV at the palace, 1955. (Courtesy Lela Dalton)

Misitana and Meleseini Vea were early missionaries to Niuatoputapu. Misitana was a branch president in Haʻapai and counselor to two mission presidents, Fred Stone and M. Vernon Coombs (1956-60). Like her husband, Sister Meleseini Vea served selflessly in the Church, as president of Relief Societies and Primaries. (Courtesy M. Vernon Coombs family)

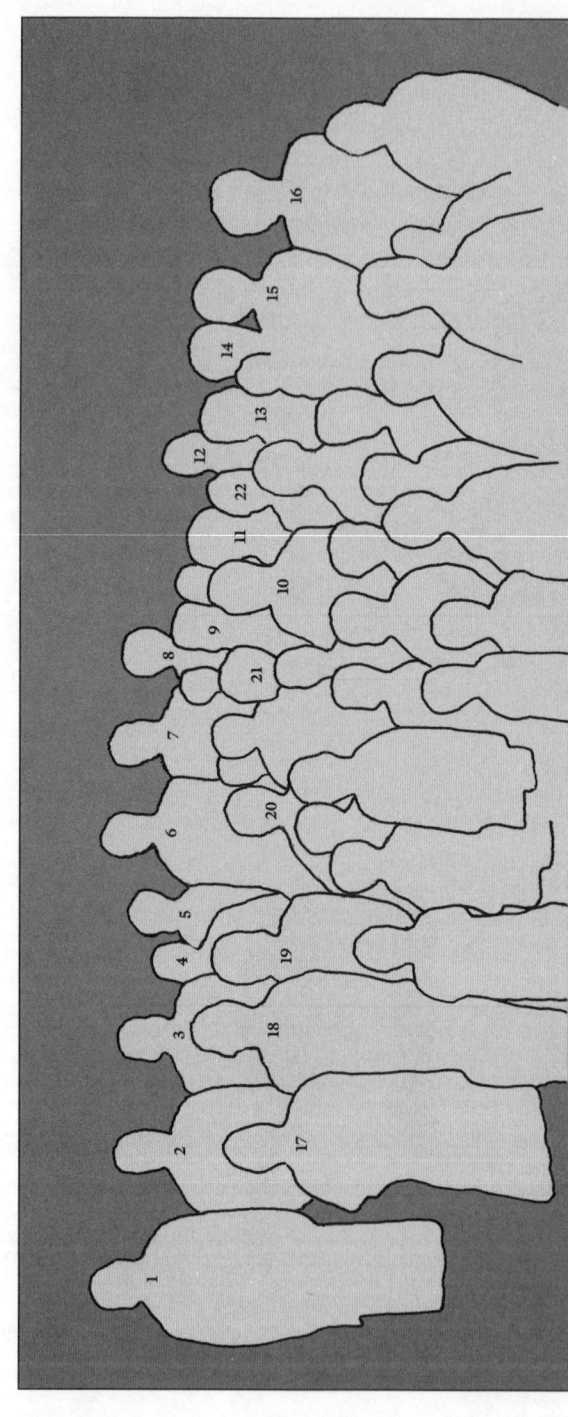

Saints in Houma in front of their chapel, a traditional Tongan fale, 1955. (1) Lupeni Fonua, (2) Tuʻivakanō Fisi, (3) unidentified, (4) Militoni Fonua, (5) unidentified, (6) Vehitau ʻEteaki, (7) Kalake Fonua, (8) Siale ʻEteaki, (9) Teiko Fonua, (10) Kaati Fonua, (11) Lilika Fonua, (12) unidentified, (13) Nola Fonua, (14) Sione ʻOlive, (16) unidentified, (17) Mele Fonua, (18) Peni Tonga, (19) unidentified, (20) Tilini Fonua, (21) Maka Fonua, and (22) Pinela Fonua. (Courtesy Ermel Morton)

Nukumovahaʻi Tonga (left) and Sela Tonga. Nukumovahaʻi, a teacher by profession, served as a missionary, branch president, and temple president (1987-89). (Courtesy Fipē Tonga Lolohea)

Viliami Sovea Kioa (right) and Mele Līvai Kioa. Sovea was a teacher at Liahona, a superior translator, and a branch and district president. He was also a lawyer and highly respected spokesman (matāpule) for Queen Sālote. Mele has been a major force in Relief Society, Primary, and MIA organizations and served a temple mission in Tonga (1987-89). (Courtesy Siua Kioa)

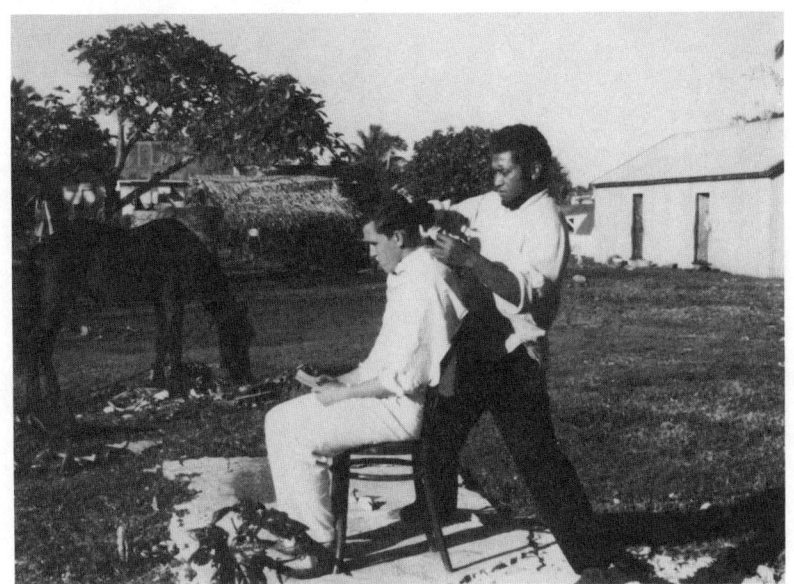
Elder Douglas Banks gets a haircut from his companion, Uatahausi Mapa, in Ha'apai, 24 July 1959. (Courtesy M. Vernon Coombs family)

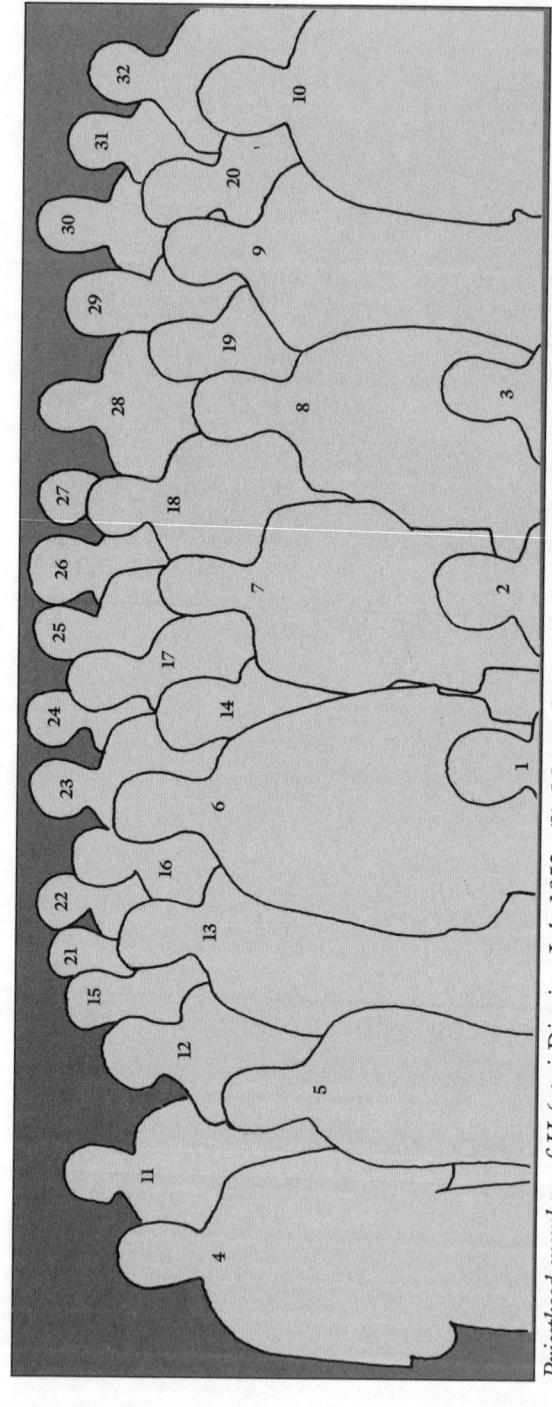

Priesthood members of Haʻapai District, July 1952. (1) Maamaloa Lātū, (2) Sāoeli Kongaika, (3) Vakapuna ʻAlatini, (4) Uai Fā, (5) Paula Tuiʻonetoa Lavulo, (6) Tēvita Finau Tafuna, (7) Lātū Makaafi, (8) Siaosi Palauni, (9) unidentified, (10) Sione Hāʻungatau, (11) Peni Tavala, (12) ʻIsileli Lolo Tuiaki, (13) Sione Filipe Pasi, (14) Mōleni Tanginoa Fonua, (15) Tumai ʻAlatini, (16) Māhanga Lavulo, (17) Kalamite Palauni, (18) Viliami Kongaika, (19) Simote Fehoko Masin, (20) Tēvita Pulu, (21) ʻInoke Vimahi, (22) Lesitelo Vaʻenoka, (23) Taufa Tuiʻone Pulotu, (24) Sione Vea, (25) ʻIufoni Langi, (26) Heamasi Kolo, (27) Viliami Fetuʻu, (28) Maʻake Mafi Kaufusi, (29) Nomani Havili, (30) Sione Pasi, (31) Kēlepi Ikatauimoana Laaʻuafi, (32) Lanipeka Tuʻileʻila. (Courtesy D'Monte Coombs)

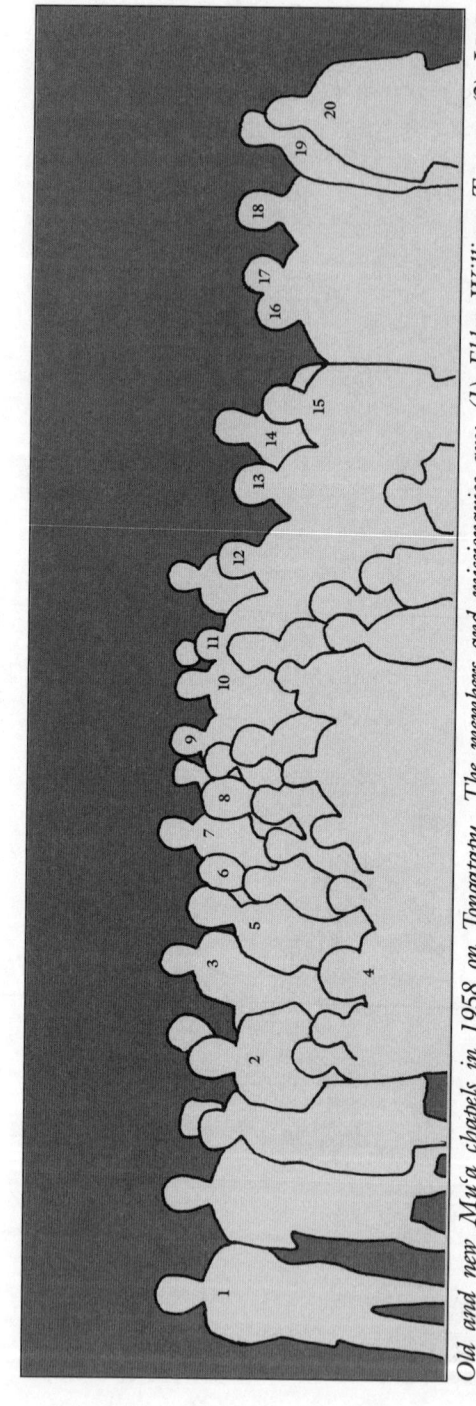

Old and new Muʻa chapels in 1958 on Tongatapu. The members and missionaries are: (1) Elder William Tenney, (2) Lātū Hopoate, (3) Sione Sākisi, (4) Mauloa Taimani, (5) Seini Tavake, (6) Kaleʻanga Taimani, (7) Semisi Moʻunga ʻOlive, (8) Ta Tapenisi ʻOlive, (9) Tavake Muʻamoholeva, (10) Sāteki Lao, (11) Māpeli Hopoate, (12) Tevita Taimani, (13) Malia Tuʻiono Toitau, (14) Sione ʻOlive, (15) Mele Māpeli Hopoate, (16) Tokilupe Taimani, (17) Mamuoso Senituli, (18) Noma Angilau, (19) Tupou Muʻamoholeva, and (20) Arlene Tyler. (Courtesy V. Lynn Tyler)

Kalo Mataele Soukop, granddaughter of pioneer Siosaia Mataele, was one of the first three native Tongans (along with Nanasi Fine Sēkona and Tupou Pulu) to enter the Church College of Hawaii in 1957 and was in the Polynesian Cultural Center's first group of dancers. A temple ordinance worker and prominent Honolulu businesswoman, she is renowned for her Polynesian shows in Hawaii. (Courtesy Kalo Mataele Soukop)

18

Lu'isa Palauni Kongaika

"SPEAKING THE TRUTH IN LOVE"
Ephesians 4:15

Lu'isa Palauni Kongaika and Viliami (Vili) Kongaika served three proselyting missions, two labor missions, and two temple missions for the Church. Lu'isa in particular represents the hundreds of Tongan LDS women who lovingly cared for the missionaries both local and foreign. Her strength is in her love and in her humility. The following account illustrates her consecration to the Lord's work and her willingness to change to do his will. Their son 'Isileli is currently president of the Tonga Nuku'alofa Mission.

My husband and I were both students at the Church's Makeke School in the early thirties but did not really become acquainted until we were back in our home town in Ha'apai. We were married at Pangai in July of 1937.

Viliami was a sweet-natured, light-hearted person who had always been obedient to his parents. I was headstrong and argumentative, tending to be pushy and dominating. But our marriage was a happy one.

In 1946 we were called on a proselyting mission to 'Eua. Taking our three children with us, we were privileged to establish the Church in 'Eua, helping to reactivate persons who later became Church stalwarts, such as Kolo Funaki. This was before the people from Niuafo'ou (Tin Can Island) had to be evacuated to 'Eua because of the devastating volcanic eruptions in that island.

It was always amazing to see how Viliami could ease his way into the friendship and trust of the people of other faiths. Even when a minister would prohibit Mormon missionaries from entering the homes of members of his congregation, Viliami would manage somehow to maintain a close relationship with them. Our own tiny congregation consisted mainly of young students who had been baptized in Makeke. Tēvita Vave was our only adult convert in 'Eua. But with the return of Kolo Funaki to activity, the Church began to prosper on the island. Brother Uai Fā and his wife Fangapulotu were also serving missions in 'Eua at that time.

In the latter part of 1946, President Emile Dunn transferred us from 'Eua to Fāhefa, on Tongatapu, where we served for the next year and a half. Even though I had our fourth child by then, I still accompanied Viliami on his visits to Kanokupolu and Ha'atafu. We preached a lot at night in the homes of the people.

Unfortunately, my habit of scolding and my angry tongue had become a burden both to my husband and to our missionary labors. I hadn't realized how bad it was until one evening I dreamed a strange dream which had an extraordinarily profound effect on me. In fact, it transformed me from a terrible nag to a humble and loving wife.

In the dream, President Dunn came to me and said he wanted me to accompany him and his wife and daughter to a special conference where the Lord himself would be present. Happily, I went with them. When we arrived at the place, I beheld a high and massive stone shaped like a door. It was made known to me that Christ was behind the door. Sister Dunn intimated that the Lord would see each one of us in a personal interview. I stayed with her little daughter while she went to wait upon the Lord. As the door opened, I remember seeing Sister Dunn kneeling with her face uplifted to the Redeemer of Mankind.

When my turn came, I walked happily and confidently forward to my interview with the Lord. When the Savior appeared, however, instead of showing a sweet countenance, he looked sternly at me and said: "O woman with the evil mouth, I don't want to see you. You are disobedient and speak such ugly words to your husband. Whatever your other fine qualities might be, your constant nagging is a disgrace. Leave my presence. I do not want you."

In shock I fell on my face before him, crying out in a loud voice, "*Oiauē*, please forgive me, Lord. I promise never to speak ugly words against my husband again. I will be obedient to his counsel and bridle my tongue forever."

The more I howled and begged, the less the Savior seemed interested in me, until finally he turned his back on me altogether and I was left alone in my grief. My sobs woke me up. My first action was to humbly beg my husband's pardon. I acknowledged my bad nature in taking advantage of his sweet disposition without taking care of him. I had been a bully, a complainer, and a combat artist. But now I pleaded for his forgiveness.

From that moment until this very day, I have been a changed person with regard to my husband, feeling much love for him and being positive and supportive.

After our mission in 1948, we returned to Pangai, Ha'apai. However, Viliami went right back to Tongatapu as a labor missionary to help build Liahona. I established a little sewing shop which took care of the needs of our family.

In 1958, Viliami and I were determined to make the trip to the New Zealand Temple. Of course we didn't have much, and our resources were already stretched to the limit in feeding the labor missionaries and preparing for the dedication of the new chapel in Pangai. Viliami's heart was set on being part of the December 1958 group; but he changed his mind when he realized that, if we were sealed without the children, we would have to make another trip with them someday.

"When we go, we are all going," he said and promptly canceled us out of the 1958 excursion.

Our plan was to sell all we possessed and take our children with us to the temple the following year. We put a "for sale" on everything we owned, large and small, our frame house, our little cook house, and all they contained. We sold things piecemeal, the roofing tin, stove, furniture—everything down to tiny household decorations. Next went the animals—pigs, horses, and cows. We sold Vili's bicycle as well as my sewing machine. Thus, we were able to secure our passage to New Zealand.

The experience at the temple was wonderful for our family, but when we finally got back to Ha'apai we were destitute, with no roof over our heads, no food, and no job. We lived for a while in the home of Simote and 'Ofa Fehoko, then in my father's home, until Vili and some priesthood brethren built us a little Tongan hut (*fale Tonga*).

In March 1961 a hurricane destroyed our new hut and nearly everything else in Ha'apai, leaving our island in a terrible state. Viliami built from scraps and debris a sort of lean-to, a shelter where we lived for a long time.

The gospel was our life and taking care of the missionaries our first love. The extreme poverty of our existence did not hinder us in our service. I became the branch Relief Society president and later the district Relief Society president. Vili was called to be counselor in the district presidency. We loved the Church with all our heart.

Note by Eric Shumway: When I was a missionary in Ha'apai (1962), Brother Vili Kongaika told me about his "strange" obsession to divest himself of all his material wealth to take his family to the temple in 1959. "It was the Lord prompting me," he said, "to get rid of my goods for a holy cause, because he was going to take them away from me anyway in the hurricane. I came back from the temple a poor man in terms of worldly goods. But after the hurricane, everyone else was just as poor as we were. The difference between us was that we were sealed as an eternal family in the Holy Temple of God."

19

Joan Winegar Coombs

"HIS SPIRIT AND HIS BREATH"[1]
Job 34:14

Joan Winegar Coombs served in Tonga with her mission president husband D'Monte Coombs from December 1951 to July 1955. The portion of her oral history included here, like the excerpts from Ada Layne Cahoon's history, typifies the many challenges of wives of mission presidents in the Tongan islands over the years. Besides bearing and caring for small children, they often presided over the mission Relief Society, taught school, became secretaries to their husbands, supervised offices, managed finances, and translated mission instructions and lesson manuals. They were both empowered and blessed by their faith.

My husband and I were both given the gift of the language when we were set apart by the First Presidency. President Stephen L Richards set me apart. He promised me that I would receive the gift of language and my husband also. And I did. I received a beautiful gift. By the end of the first year, it was just like a mantle that came over me.

Although I enjoyed the gift of language, I encountered many other problems, one of which was sickness. Unbeknownst to me, I suffered from a severe allergic reaction to the Tongan dyes used throughout the islands to make tapa cloth and other Tongan artifacts. I was pregnant at the time with my first child. When I was about eight

---

[1] Joan Yvonne Winegar Coombs, Oral History, interviewed by Vai 'Iloamanu Lātū, July 30, 1980, CRC-H22, Charles Redd Center for Western History, Oral History Project, Harold B. Lee Library, Brigham Young University, Provo, Utah. D'Monte is the son of Vernon and LaVera Coombs, who twice served Tongan missions.

months along, my lungs began to fill with fluid, and I couldn't breathe. It got very bad over a period of about a month. The doctors couldn't help me, and I didn't know what to do.

My lungs were so full of fluid, I was just gasping constantly and finally had to sit up in a chair at night because I couldn't breathe lying down. This went on for a week. We had a heavy mission schedule, and we didn't know what to do. It seemed impossible for us to leave our work and go back to America to find a doctor. But doctors in Tonga couldn't help us. Finally my husband said, "The thing for us to do is to give you a blessing."

So he got the consecrated oil out, and he blessed me. He asked the Lord to help us to know what the matter was and to clear this up. I was going to have a baby in two months and had to get rid of this problem, or I could have other complications as well.

As soon as he finished the blessing, I was able to lie down and, for the first time in a week, have four hours of uninterrupted sleep. When I woke up again and talked with him, he said, "I know now what you are to do. The cause of your trouble is an allergy to the dyes that are in this house. We must take the tapas off the bed."

We had a Tongan tapa cloth on the bed as a cover, because it was the cool part of the year. Tongan artifacts hung on the walls around the house. He said, "We must take all these things out and put them in the back room where the light is on all the time. We will keep them dry for gifts. Otherwise you won't be able to get over this sickness."

So we took everything made with Tongan dyes off the bed, and everything off the walls, plus all the instruments and handicrafts that were Tongan. We put them all in this back room and locked them away. Every time I went around them thereafter I would get this awful asthma again.

Then my husband said, "The next thing you must do is to go to the doctor and ask him for an expectorant medicine that will cause you to cough, force you to cough." So I did that. I had to take it about five times a day; and for the next four days, I coughed up the phlegm in my lungs. *This was all given to him by inspiration.* The doctor didn't prescribe it. My husband told me to get it.

So I got this medicine and took it for several days until I coughed up the phlegm and I could breath normally again. . . .

20

'Isileli Lolo Tuiaki

"HE SHALL PREPARE A WAY FOR THEM"
1 Nephi 3:7

President Tuiaki has served faithfully as a branch president, bishop, high counselor, stake president, and counselor in the temple presidency. Born in Faleloa, Ha'apai, he served missions to 'Ohonua, 'Eua; Ha'akio, Vava'u; and to Veitongo, Tongatapu. He served two labor missions to build chapels and Liahona High School.

I was born August 3, 1927, in Faleloa, Ha'apai, in a family of twelve children. I spent only five years in primary school before I bolted in favor of farming and fishing. We attended the Church of Tonga (*Hou'eiki*). When my father discovered I had joined the Mormon Church (November 21, 1947, in Pangai, Ha'apai), he chased me from the house with a hammer, declaring that I was no longer his son because no true son of his would ever believe in the likes of Joseph Smith.

So I left the home I loved and moved in with Piliote Kona'ī, the missionary who baptized me. This was the beginning of my real education as I served in the kingdom, first as a home teacher and then as a labor and proselyting missionary.

In 1949 I left Ha'apai with ten other men called as labor missionaries to build Liahona High School. I stayed in Matahau where I met and married Tangivale Kona'ī. The following year President Emile Dunn set me apart as president of Veitongo Branch with orders to work construction on the Liahona project during the day and to proselyte and teach the gospel at night. This seemed to be the pattern for many of the labor missionaries.

In 1952, we were called to be missionaries in 'Eua. I will share two stories from this era of our lives to show how the Lord moves mysteriously to bless and accommodate those he has called to serve for him.

One day in May of 1952, Sēmisi and his brother, Sione Vailiki Maile, and I, and our wives, spent the entire day going from house to house in the village of Houma, 'Eua, hoping for a chance to present our message. By late evening not one family had invited us in.

As we were approaching the home of the steward or caretaker for the Church of Tonga in the village, suddenly Sione's wife, Mele Maile, was taken with a seizure and fell to the ground very ill. She shook violently, her eyes rolling up into her head. Many people crowded around her, massaged her vigorously, and called her name. There was no response. She looked as if she were dead. The whole village rushed to the scene.

"Lolo, what shall we do?" cried Sione Maile to me.

Before I could say or do anything, the reverend steward of the Church of Tonga said graciously, "Let's take the lady into our chapel here. It's available to you!"

We carried Mele into the chapel and laid her on the table in front where the minister keeps his bible and hymnal. The curious villagers followed us into the building, the very people who had turned a deaf ear to us that day and would not allow us in their homes.

"With your permission," I said to the steward, "we would like to perform a special ordinance for this sister and offer a prayer for her. It's called administering to the sick."

The steward turned to the people, who by now had filled his chapel to overflowing, and said: "Please, everyone sit down while they say their prayer."

Sēmisi anointed Sister Maile and I sealed the anointing with a blessing. The result of this ordinance astonished everyone present as Sister Maile got up from the table and sat down again in a chair. The steward was so moved by this event he said to us: "Since the chapel is already full of people, why don't you go ahead and hold a service for us? We would love to hear you preach!"

Well, we held a wonderful meeting that night. Sister Maile led us in the opening song *"Lau 'Eni Ko e Tofi'a."* [to the tune of "I Need Thee Every Hour"]. Sēmisi offered the opening prayer, I read a hymn from the congregation's own hymn book, then all three of us elders spoke.

The Lord knew how anxiously we wanted to preach in this village and how hard we had tried, but no one had let us in. So he used a strange and interesting way to draw them to their own chapel to hear us preach the true gospel of Jesus Christ.

The next afternoon our little group of missionaries proceeded to call on families in 'Ohonua. We had no more than started our rounds when a man ordered us to leave his premises in a most threatening way, shouting obscenities and accusations against the Church and Joseph Smith. The vicious language excited the laughter of the many villagers looking on. We were shaken and embarrassed but could do nothing except remain silent and absorb the abuse.

When the man's rage was spent, I said to him, "Thank you very much. We are leaving right now! Goodbye!"

That night we heard a commotion in the center of the village. A house was on fire and people came yelling and running from every direction.

We also ran toward the fire with the intent of helping, but we were too late. The blaze had consumed the entire house and everything in it.

As we approached the fire, I heard a woman shouting something which stopped me in my tracks. She was chastising the owner of the burning home: "Your house is destroyed by fire because of your abuse of the missionaries and your malicious language against the Prophet Joseph Smith." It suddenly dawned on me that this was the very home from which we had been expelled only a few hours earlier.

21

Manase Nau

"WHETHER BY MINE OWN VOICE,
OR THE VOICE OF
MY SERVANTS"
Doctrine & Covenants 1:38

Manase Nau was a counselor to five mission presidents between 1960 and 1972. Noted for his eloquence as a speaker and his knowledge of Tongan customs, Brother Nau negotiated for large numbers of lots where chapels now stand. Like so many of the great Church leaders in Tonga, the Naus learned discipline and faith in the rigors of missionary work in the islands. He and his wife Salina have nine children.

Even though I grew up in the Church, I resented the mission call to leave my wife and four little ones to serve for eleven months in Vavaʻu, as a companion of a single elder. I well remember the night Mosese Muti, the mission secretary, brought the letter from the mission president. I was sitting in our little hut in Fuaʻamotu preparing to go torch fishing.

After I read the letter, Brother Muti asked, "What's your answer?"

I looked at my wife. Salina was a new member of the Church, the woman through whom so many of my blessings have come. She would bear the family burdens if I were to leave. "Wife, what is your answer to Brother Muti?" I asked.

"If my husband can be useful to the work," she replied quietly, "then let him go!"

No doubt many people felt that since my father was Sione Nau, a hard-working, prosperous farmer and devoted Latter-day Saint, I would have no difficulty getting enough clothes and money for the mission. In fact, my father was irritated at me and told the branch president, "Leave Manase at home. He's my son, I know him! He'll just go and embarrass the Church in Vavaʻu."

So my father did not help me at all. I got a little money by selling my shotgun to a fellow by the name of Nāpaʻa. With this amount, I began my sojourn as a missionary in Vavaʻu. My companion was Taani Pulotu. It was lonely business for me without my family but we did establish the Church in Hunga.

Frankly, I often wondered if the mission president [D'Monte Coombs 1952–55] felt any love or pity for me and my family. But as it turned out, this mission became a legacy of faith for our family. And President Coombs was like a prophet to our people.

When instructions came from the president for me to return to Tongatapu, I was the happiest man alive. I never closed my eyes or tried to sleep in the thirty-hour boat trip from Vavaʻu to Nukuʻalofa. My mind was fixed on Fuaʻamotu, on my reunion with Salina and the children. I expressed the same to President Coombs as he greeted me at the wharf.

"That's fine," he said, "but you are assigned to go to Fatai."

"But where is my family?" I asked.

"They are still in Fuaʻamotu," he said.

"Then I will go to Fuaʻamotu to see them," I declared. "We will come together to Fatai."

"No," President Coombs responded, "you will go straight to Fatai. Your family will join you later. Your new companion is Mosese Langi."

So I went to Fatai. My joy was full when finally Salina and the children arrived at Fatai to continue our mission together. Our lives were happy in the work until one day our third son, Takilisi, age four, became very ill. His condition progressed from bad to worse, and we took him to the hospital in Nukuʻalofa. After several days Dr. Peni Mapa asked me to see him.

"Manase," he said, "your little Takilisi has typhoid fever. Nothing any doctor can do will save him now. Perhaps the best thing is to take him back to your home in Fuaʻamotu and prepare for the funeral."

I am coming now to the main point of this story. I went straight to the mission president.

"Misi Timani," I cried, "my little son is dying. Please let me take him to our home in Fuaʻamotu. As soon as he is in the care of my parents, I will return to Fatai."

The president's answer stung me to the core: "No, if you want your boy to go to Fuaʻamotu, then send word to your parents to come and get him. I don't want you to leave your assigned village."

As we came out from the mission home, I said to my companion, "Mosese, do you believe that was the right answer?"

"I don't know," he muttered.

I thought of appealing to Lisiate Talanoa, the president's counselor, to intervene in our behalf. I seriously considered just packing up our little family and returning home—just leaving our mission. But by the time we got back to Fatai, I had resigned myself to another course of action. We would simply bring our little boy to Fatai and bury him there, away from our extended family. That seemed preferable to sending him to Fuaʻamotu and not being able to attend his funeral because we were forbidden to leave our "assigned" village.

A vehicle from the hospital brought our little boy to us in Fatai. He was a pitiful sight. His bones showed starkly in every part of his body. Unable to eat, he was fading fast. Mosese and I still went out every day to do our missionary visiting.

One morning Salina woke me crying and begged me to look at Takilisi. When I looked at him, so still and pale, all I knew to do was to kneel and pray.

Up from our knees, we heard a car pull up by our Tongan hut. It had to be the mission president. Our hearts were immediately joyful. No doubt he had come to see our sick child, to give us comfort, and perhaps to take us all to Fuaʻamotu in the event of Takilisi's death.

President Coombs got out of the car and walked up to our hut. *"Mālō e lelei!"* he said as we opened the door. This was our conversation as I remember it:

"Will you come in, President?" we invited.

"No, that's fine! How's the little boy?"

"He seems to be in a coma," I replied. "He doesn't know anybody or anything."

"Manase," the president said, "the boat [*Hifofua*] leaves this afternoon for Haʻapai, at 4:00 P.M. I've already purchased yours and Mosese Langi's tickets. You are transferred immediately to Haʻapai to conduct a census of Church members in all the Haʻapai Group."

"You mean today, President?" I cried.

"Yes, today. The mission car will be here in a little while to pick you up."

I came out from the house to make sure I was hearing what I was hearing and to explain again our circumstances.

"President, you want me to go *today* and leave my little boy? I was hoping to take him back to Fuaʻamotu. President, this little boy is not going to live."

The president continued, "If you decide to take him to Fuaʻamotu, that would be fine! But you must be on the boat at four this afternoon. It is urgent at this time to take a complete census of Church membership in Haʻapai. You will enter every home, and ask every family for membership information even in the smaller islands like Fotuhaʻa. It will probably take six months to accomplish the task."

Given the condition of our family, this assignment seemed very abrupt and unfeeling, but perhaps the president knew something I didn't know. After he left, I remember just sitting down on the grass with my companion and crying out: "Mosese, is the Church still true? This is strange leadership, indeed. Come and look at death in the face of my son!"

Mosese never said a word. He just stood up and walked away. At 3:00 p.m. the mission car was in front of our home. Who would want to load his luggage at such a time? My heart was full of resentment, but again my wife spoke unforgettable words to me: "Go, Manase! If Takilisi passes away, I'll be more than able to handle everything here. Go do the Lord's work."

Whether our voyage was rough or smooth, I cannot say. I just stared vacantly at the waves and the stars. I felt nothing. When we got to Pangai, we began immediately upon our task of going from house to house and asking the questions that would determine total Church membership in the islands. We started at the Shirley Baker statue outside of Pangai; and by ten o'clock that night, we had finished all of Pangai and Hihifo. We returned exhausted to our lodging in Pangai.

Fatigue and hunger had numbed my mind to my grief. But as we walked past the police station, someone yelled my name. It was Suli, the police inspector. "You have a telegram from Tongatapu," he said.

My heart sank and I couldn't control my tears. I took the telegram and handed it to my companion. We walked to the chapel where we were met by the district president, Kēlepi Laaʼiafi, who showed immediate concern for my sorrow.

"Manase has received a telegram from home," Mosese said to Kēlepi. "It appears his son has died."

We were ushered into the chapel to wait for our dinner. When we were alone, I asked Mosese to kneel with me and offer up a prayer. All my strength was spent.

As the "amen" to Mosese's prayer was uttered, he stood up and went outside, leaving me alone with my grief and the telegram. Slowly I tore open the envelope to read the dreadful words. My eyes beheld the message: "Takilisi eats, he drinks, he speaks."

After this message, can anyone imagine how long it took us to finish our six-month assignment? Exactly three weeks! I was driven by so much joy and gratitude, I inquired about Church members in every building in Ha'apai, including barns and copra sheds. Sleep fled from my eyes. I never quit to rest. Fatigue meant nothing. Poor Mosese could barely keep up. When we returned to Tonga our bags were full of membership sheets. Our labor was accomplished, and I could again behold our little Takilisi running around alive and well.

Today, Takilisi is an anchor of strength in our family. Given my wish, I would have stayed in Tongatapu and buried our son. Instead, I obeyed God's servant; and God, in turn, restored my son to life immediately. Takilisi was the miracle boy. He had been healed instantly after I had left for Pangai. Doctors who knew of his condition shook their heads in disbelief at his recovery.

Salina and I bear witness that God lives. We learned that our ideas and our opinions are feeble at best compared to his love and power. I bear testimony that President D'Monte Coombs spoke for the Lord when he called me to leave my family and go to Ha'apai.

22

Elder John H. Groberg

"THERE IS THE LIGHT"

John H. Groberg served his first mission to Tonga in the mid-fifties. He returned to the Friendly Islands with his family in 1966 to be mission president. Extremely fluent in the language and much loved by the Tongan Saints, President Groberg worked vigorously to prepare Tonga for stakehood. The first stake in Tonga was organized September 5, 1968. Later, as a General Authority, he assisted closely in the building of the Tonga Temple. Elder Groberg is currently a member of the First Quorum of the Seventy. He and his wife, Jean Sabin Groberg, are the parents of eleven children. The following excerpt from his general conference address, October 1976, communicates in spirit and content the unshakable courage and faith which have sustained the missionaries and the Saints of the Tongan Islands for a hundred years.[1]

I would like to relate an experience and make an application for our day; for even though this event happened nearly twenty years ago in the Tongan Islands, the lesson learned there has become increasingly meaningful with the passage of time and is extremely important today.

As a young missionary, I was assigned as a district president to administer the affairs of the Church and preach the gospel in a group of fifteen small, scattered islands. We traveled almost exclusively by sailboat and learned to rely not only on the winds and the currents of the usually friendly seas, but especially on the love of our Father in Heaven,

---

[1] From "There Is the Light," *The Ensign* 16 (November 1976): 44–45. Used by Elder Groberg's permission.

as we sailed week after week and month after month from island to island to island.

On one occasion, we received word that a missionary was very ill on a somewhat distant island. The weather was threatening; but, feeling responsible, and after prayer, we left to investigate the situation. Extra heavy seas slowed our progress, and it was late afternoon before we arrived. The missionary was indeed very ill. Fervent prayer was followed by administration, during which the impression came very strongly to get him back to the hospital on the main island, and to do it now!

The weather had deteriorated to the point of a small gale. The seas were heavy, the clouds were thick, the wind was fierce, the hour was late, and the sun was sinking rapidly, betokening a long black night ahead. But the impression was strong—"Get back now"—and one learns to obey the all-important promptings of the Spirit.

There was much concern expressed and much talk about the darkness, the storm, and the formidable reef with its extremely narrow opening to the harbor we were attempting to gain. Some found reason to stay behind; but soon eight persons, including an ill missionary, a very experienced captain, and a somewhat concerned district president, boarded the boat; and the spiritually prompted voyage to home base began.

No sooner had we made our commitment to the open seas than the intensity of the storm seemed to increase sevenfold. The small gale now became a major storm. As the sun sank below the horizon, bringing with it darkness and gloom, so also did my spirit seem to sink into the darkness of doubt and apprehension. The thick clouds and driving rain increased the blackness of our already dark universe—no stars, no moon, no rest—only turmoil of sea and body and mind and spirit. And as we toiled on through the fearsome night, I found my spirit communing with the spirit of the father of an afflicted child in the New Testament, as he exclaimed, "Lord I believe; help thou mine unbelief" (Mark 9:24). And he did, and he does, and he will. That I know.

As we rolled and tossed closer and closer to the reef, all eyes searched for the light that marked the opening, the only entry to our home. Where was it? The blackness of the night seemed to increase; the fierceness of the raging elements seemed to know no bounds. The rain slashed at our faces and tore at our eyes—eyes vainly searching for that life-giving light.

Then I heard the chilling sound of the waves crashing and chewing against the reef! It was close—too close. Where was that light?

Unless we hit the opening exactly, we would be smashed against the reef and ripped and torn by that thousand-toothed monster. It seemed that all the elements were savagely bent on our total destruction. Our eyes strained against the blackness, but we could not see the light.

Some began to whimper, others to moan and cry, and one or two even to scream in hysteria. At the height of this panic, when many were pleading to turn to the left or to the right, when the tumultuous elements all but forced us to abandon life and hope, I looked at the captain—and there I saw the face of calmness, the ageless face of wisdom and experience, as his eyes penetrated the darkness ahead. Quietly his weather-roughened lips parted, and without moving his fixed gaze and just perceptibly shifting the wheel, he breathed those life-giving words, *"Ko e maama ē!"* ("There is the light!").

I could not see the light, but the captain could see it. And I knew he could see it. Those eyes, long experienced in ocean travel, were not fooled by the madness of the storm nor were they influenced by the pleadings of those of lesser experience to turn to the left or to the right. And so with one last great swell, we were hurtled through the opening and into calmer waters.

The roaring of the reef was now behind us. Its infamous plan of destruction had been foiled. We were in the protected harbor. We were home. Then and only then did we see through the darkness that one small light—exactly where the captain had said it was. Had we waited until we ourselves could see the light we would have been dashed to pieces, shredded on the reef of unbelief. But trusting in those experienced eyes, we lived.

And so the great lesson: There are those who, through years of experience and training and by virtue of special divine callings, can see farther and better and more clearly—and can and will save us in those situations where serious injury or death—both spiritual and physical—would be upon us before we ourselves could see.

23

'Isileli Kongaika

CARING FOR
THE SERVANTS OF GOD

'Isileli Kongaika is currently (1989-) the president of the Tonga Nuku'alofa Mission. His parents, Viliami and Lu'isa, are typical of the hundreds of Tongan Latter-day Saints who cherished and cared for the missionaries over the years. Poor by worldly standards, they were rich in generosity and kindness. This reminiscence by President Kongaika and the following one by Taukolo Langi are living tributes not only to Viliami and Lu'isa Kongaika, but to all the Tongan Saints everywhere who have given of their own vital substance to care for the missionaries.

My parents Viliami and Lu'isa Kongaika loved the missionaries, both Caucasian and Tongan, who came to serve in Pangai, Ha'apai. They fed them, cleaned for them, nursed them when ill, and did their washing. It seemed to us children that at times they showed greater attention to the missionaries than to their own children.

The hurricane of March 1961 devastated our island and ruined what little plantation my father had. It was very painful to my parents that they were so hard up for food. What were they going to feed the missionaries?

I remember my father telling us about an incident that occurred during this time of hardship. It made a great impression on me. He said:

> While I was at the local store one day, I was called out to talk to a prisoner from the Fale'one Prison, who had come by on a horse carrying two large sacks of root crops from the prison plantation,

one of the few plantations that had survived the hurricane. The prisoner informed me that a man had just been by the prison, paid for the two bags, and asked if they could deliver them to Viliami Kongaika's home at Pangai.

I tried to find out who the generous person was, but nobody seemed to know who he was, or what he looked like, so I could identify him. This was a strange situation indeed on a poor small island where everyone knew each other.

Dad just accepted the food as a gift from an angel assigned to watch out for the missionaries. He and Mom never noticed their own poverty as long as they could care for the missionaries.

24

Taukolo Langi

GOD HONORS THOSE WHO HONOR HIS SERVANTS

Taukolo Langi, son of Saia and 'Ana Tu'ifele'unga Langi of Ha'alaufuli, has served as full-time missionary, branch president, bishop, high councilor, and temple sealer. The following remembrance illustrates again the generous commitment of Viliami and Lu'isa Kongaika in caring for the missionaries. It is not surprising that one of their posterity would some day preside over the mission.

'Isileli Kongaika's call to be president of the Tonga Nuku'alofa Mission beginning July 1989 is a fitting tribute to his parents, Lu'isa and Viliami, whose sole love in this world was to feed and care for the missionaries in Ha'apai, voluntarily and usually at their own expense.

I remember that one afternoon in 1956 they invited several of us married missionaries to their home to eat, fixing a special table for us and all of our children. During the meal 'Isileli, about six or seven years old at the time, came running in from primary school. He was famished, no doubt, and saw all the missionary children eating his mother's food.

"Mom, where's my food?" he yelled.

I'll never forget his mother's answer. Kindly but firmly, she said, "Look at our missionaries and their children! Let them eat first and you can have all you can eat in a little while."

'Isileli was not convinced and went into a pout. His mother reached down and kissed him, whispering in his ear: "Come back later and you will see. You will be the most important one at our table in a while."

We all watched this little drama, and finally Elder Groberg laughed and said: " 'Isileli, come and sit by me and share my food."

"No," said Lu'isa. "This little boy is already full. He'll eat later with the rest of the family."

Well, 'Isileli is now the mission president. I have often asked him if he realizes what his mother did for him, by putting the missionaries first and saying he would be the important one at the family table later.

So many of the Saints in Ha'apai in those days, despite their own hardships, loved and fed the missionaries: Tupou and Sione Vea, Tēvita Fīnau, Kēlepi Laa'iafi, Taufa Tui'one, Peni Tavalu, Vili and Selu Fetu'u, and Uai Fā, to name only a few.

25

Taukolo Langi

"THERE SHALL NOT
AN HAIR OF YOUR HEAD PERISH"
Luke 21:18

Taukolo Langi, son of Saia and 'Ana Tu'ifele'unga Langi of Ha'alaufuli, served a mission with his wife, Temalisi, in Ha'apai. They have nine children, seven of whom have also been on full-time missions for the Church. Brother Langi has been a branch president, bishop, high councilor, and temple sealer. The following record attests to implicit faith of the Tongan Saints, that when you are on the Lord's errand you can expect miracles.

My wife and I were scheduled to be released from our mission at the district conference and dedication of the new chapel in 'Uiha, Ha'apai, in 1958. But President Fred Stone asked me if we would extend our service to build up the branch in Felemea which had ceased to function.

Despite some private tears (we had everything packed and ready for the return to our home), we said we would accept the assignment to Felemea. According to President Stone, the first order of business would be to clean up the little chapel which had become a rooting place for the village pigs; the second would be to fill the chapel with inactive Saints.

We moved to Felemea and I became the branch president, making the regular boat trips to submit branch reports and attend district meetings in Pangai. These meetings were held on Friday so everyone could get back to their various islands by Sunday.

One Thursday afternoon in 1958, I took my son Taniela, age five, with me to the meetings in Pangai. The sea was very rough, and none of the smaller craft from the island would attempt the two-hour voyage. Fortunately we secured passage on the *Kao,* a large government boat that just happened to be on its way to Pangai.

The Friday meetings accomplished, we searched for a boat going back to Felemea or 'Uiha. None was to be had either Friday or Saturday. The Kongaikas, with whom we stayed, said we should not worry about getting back, since the absence of vessels from 'Uiha and Felemea obviously meant the ocean was too treacherous for sailing.

But I had only two things in mind—to get back for Sunday service in Felemea and to see my wife who was eight months pregnant with our second child. I told the Kongaikas I would see if we could get across the reef to Uoleva. If no opportunities to make it across the channel presented themselves, we would return. Lu'isa prepared us food to take on our journey.

Since it was low tide we crossed over the reef to Uoleva without incident. There we met Sione Moala Havili, father of Sālesi Havili, who discouraged us from even thinking about crossing the channel. The current was swift and unpredictable and the waves too high. I asked him if we could borrow a canoe to which he replied, "No boat can make it across 'Auhangamea ("place of destruction") now. If you're trying to get home today, forget it!"

Perhaps Sione thought he would be an accomplice to certain disaster if he loaned me his outrigger canoe, but I persisted in my request. He finally said, "Look, why don't you just see for yourself what the ocean is like, then come back and stay with us tonight? Tomorrow we'll help you get back to Pangai."

My son and I just sat down on the sand. Of course he was too young to understand the situation. I was determined to attempt the crossing and felt that, since I was on the Lord's errand, we would be protected.

I asked Taniela to kneel with me by Sione Moala's outrigger canoe and beg Heavenly Father to bless our crossing. We offered the prayer as huge waves crashed and rolled into shore. Taniela held tightly to his lunch which he said he would not eat until we arrived home in Felemea.

Putting two large melons and our clothes sack in the front section of the canoe, I shoved off in the ocean with five-year-old Taniela seated just in front of me. Although my faith was strong, I was not expecting a smooth journey over these, the roughest waters in Tonga, especially in a Tongan outrigger that lies so low in the water. But not one wave broke over the bow during the whole journey. We might just as well have been skimming across a becalmed surface. We hardly got wet. Nor did we have to bail water.

As we approached 'Uiha, many villagers lined up along the beach wondering who this fool was crossing the 'Auhangamea Channel in such weather. As we got closer to shore, I began to recognize many of these spectators as former rugby buddies of mine, acquaintances of former days. All the outrigger canoes of the village had been dragged up from the beach and secured on high ground. Even there the heavy surf very nearly reached them with each surging wave.

We landed easily through the surf. Securing the canoe, I gathered up my son, the melons, and our clothes bag and walked the distance to Felemea. With every step, I felt deep gratitude for the obvious blessing from the Lord in saving us from disaster. The Saints in Felemea, Lītani, Vili Tau, Tukuafu, Toʻa, and my wife were astounded at our appearance and said that not one boat had left the shores of Felemea for three days because the sea had been so rough. We were pressed with questions by the people, "How could you possibly make it in an outrigger? Did your little boy do the bailing, etc.?"

Our answer was: "We bailed no water, because no waves broke over us and no ocean spilled in over the sides."

As I contemplate today that "foolish" journey, perhaps we were spared because of little Taniela who later served a worthy mission for the Church and is now a bishop.

26

Lela Jesperson Dalton

"IN VISION . . . A TEMPLE IN THESE ISLANDS"

Patrick and Lela Dalton are on their third mission in Tonga for the Church. They first served as teaching missionaries at Liahona High School (1955–58), then in 1963 Patrick was called to be president of the Tongan Mission. In 1989 they were called as president and matron of the Nukuʻalofa Tonga Temple. During President Dalton's tenure as mission president (1963–66), an increasing number of young single Tongan men and women were set apart as full-time missionaries, easing the burden of proselytizing which had been carried for decades by married couples. This shift of missionary responsibility to the Tongan youth had a major positive impact on the annual number of convert baptisms and the growth of the Church in Tonga. The Daltons also played a major role in organizing annual excursions of Tongan Saints to the New Zealand Temple. In the following excerpt from an address in Tonga, Sister Dalton verifies what came to be known among the Tongan Saints as the "McKay prophecy" regarding a temple in Tonga.

As most of you know, President Dalton and I have been in Tonga two other times—first as missionaries teaching at Liahona, and then as mission president. We feel comfortable here and are happy to be working now in the temple with such committed people.

I would like to relate a little story that happened in 1955 when President David O. McKay visited Tonga. He was the first president of the Church to come here. He was on his way to New Zealand to dedicate the ground for the building of the temple there. Since it was difficult to record electronically the talks of President McKay, our mission president, D'Monte Coombs, asked me to do it in shorthand. We accompanied the Prophet on the ship as it passed through Vava'u, Niue, Samoa, and Fiji.

When we reached Vava'u we were able to have a meeting there with the members of the Church. During his talk, President McKay said, "Last night in vision I saw a temple in these islands."

I was very surprised at his statement and thought to myself, "He must be talking about the temple in New Zealand. Surely he cannot mean these small islands of Tonga."

And so, when many years later the temple for Tonga was announced, I saw that it would be true, and I was very happy for the people of these islands. I knew they would no longer have to sacrifice by making the long trip to the temple in New Zealand.

I have told this story many times—and also how many of the Tongan people have given all they owned, even to the selling of their homes, in order to go to the temple and have the blessings of the holy House of the Lord.

27

Mosese Lui Muti

"FAITHFUL . . . OVER MANY THINGS"
Matthew 25:21

Born in 'Uiha, Ha'apai, on August 6, 1911, Mosese Muti first attended the LDS school in Pangai, Ha'apai, in 1924. He was baptized the following September 13, 1925. He married Salavia Hautau in 1933. They are the parents of ten children.

In his nearly sixty-five years of service in the Church, Mosese Muti's testimony and faithfulness have become legend, as a proselyting missionary, teacher, radio preacher, labor missionary, and branch and stake leader. Besides his several missions in Tonga, Patriarch Muti also served two missions to Niue, where he became as fluent in Niuean as in his native tongue. Thousands of Church members have been taught, blessed, and encouraged by this remarkable and articulate man.

Since my baptism at fourteen years of age in 1925, the more faithfully I have kept the Lord's commandments the more I can testify with a perfect knowledge that God our Father lives, and so does his son Jesus Christ. This knowledge is as much a part of me as my right hand and my left hand, even as my whole body. . . .

In March 1936 I completed a short-term mission to Makeke where I cared for the rather extensive plantation of the Church school there. Receiving my release from President [Reuben] Wiberg, I returned to my wife and family in 'Uiha, Ha'apai, where the branch president made me secretary to the Sunday School and clerk for the whole branch.

I cherished these assignments in our little branch and performed them with care and attention. Even when I got a painting job with Burns Philp, Ltd., and took Salavia with me to Pangai during the week, we would always catch a boat back to 'Uiha on Saturday afternoon and spend Sunday there. I simply could not neglect my calling. I was still a priest in the Aaronic Priesthood.

One Saturday we could not find a way to 'Uiha, which is about two hours distance from Pangai by boat in good weather. Night fell and still no boat. In my anxiety, I told Salavia I would go out again, this time to Niu'ui, to see if anyone were going to 'Uiha that night or early the next morning.

I started out in the pitch-black night just as the clock at the police station struck nine. My thought was to cross over (wading or swiming, depending on the tide) to Uoleva island and from there swim across the channel to Tatafa island, then swim on to 'Uiha.

Now I had never before crossed over from Lifuka to Uoleva and in the darkness could not see even an outline of Uoleva at all, a distance of several hundred yards. The ocean was rough and the current strong as it rushed over the reef between the two islands. Foolish as it appeared to some later, I felt confident that I could make it since I was on the Lord's errand and was on my way to do his work.

The crossing to Uoleva was dangerous, but I did not feel danger. And when my feet finally touched the sands of Uoleva, I proceeded to the side of the island looking out on one of the most treacherous channels in Tonga, 'Auhangamea Channel and Tatafa island. With hardly a second thought, I waded in and started to swim across the dark, deep water.

I had not gone forty yards when a voice spoke to my mind to look back. I looked and beheld a light in the thick vegetation back on Uoleva island. The voice urged me to turn around and go back to where the light was shining. I did. There in the bush, I discovered the hull of a canoe. Now the hull was useless to me without the boom or the outrigger itself. But at that very moment, the light which had guided me to the canoe moved away into the bush. I followed it about ten yards; and lo, I beheld a fine, unattached outrigger with sennit rope to bind it to the canoe. Dragging the canoe down to the shore, I lashed the outrigger to it, then went in search of something I could use as a paddle. I had gone no more than a few yards when I literally stumbled over the lower stalk of a large coconut palm frond. Fumbling in the darkness, I picked it up to discover that it had already been cut and shaped into a paddle.

Despite the heavy sea and the blackness of night, I launched straight for Tatafa island across the 'Auhangamea Channel. My direction was accurate, and I came straight on to the reef connecting Tatafa and 'Uiha island. I paddled on through to the landing at 'Uiha village.

As I hauled the outrigger up high on shore, I felt the strength of the Lord within me as well as deep gratitude for the miraculous way he had brought me to 'Uiha for his sake. Pausing under a tree, I offered a prayer of thanksgiving and proceeded to my family's home. It was after 4:00 A.M. when I entered the house.

Salavia's adopted father greeted me in amazement. "How did you come?" he asked.

"I swam across to Uoleva, and crossed over by outrigger." I replied.

To which he responded, "Muti, true religion is not so very stupid as that."

I did not answer him but lay down and slept. After services the next day with all my duties accomplished, I returned as I had come, this time in broad daylight and with a Sunday meal for Salavia. I paddled across the channel, put the canoe back exactly where I had found it on Uoleva, and crossed over the reef to Lifuka. I was home by 9:00 P.M.

I have since contemplated this experience many times and have marveled that I should have taken such risks. I have thought of the blackness of the night, the roughness of the ocean, the strange concentrated light that guided me to the canoe—a light I have not seen before or since—my lack of fear, and my love for my Church assignment. To be a secretary in the kingdom of God was more important to me than nearly anything else. This I do know: since this experience I have never doubted. I have never been fearful nor fainthearted, no matter what the task or mission the Lord has called us to perform in his Church....

We have served many missions for the Church. Our call to serve on Niue island came in an interesting fashion. Sometime in July 1956, I was on my way back from Liahona on my bicycle, having visited our daughter Meleseini there. I had met 'Atonio 'Amasio on the road in his horse-drawn cart and was holding on to one of the side boards, letting the cart pull me along. Suddenly, the mission car passed by and came to a stop up ahead of us.

"Muti," said 'Atonio, "someone in the car is beckoning to us."

I rode up to the car. It was the mission president, President Fred Stone. His first words were, "Muti, do you know anyone who would like to go on a mission?"

"No sir, I don't know anyone right now who is anxious to go," I replied.

"I suspect you must know someone," the president insisted. "You are acquainted with everyone in the Tonga Mission. How about someone in your branch?"

"No, I really don't know of anyone," I said.

"How about you, Muti?"

"If it's a call from the Lord I'll go gladly. If it's just your idea, I will not go at all."

"Do you have any money, any savings?" the president inquired.

"That's why I gave you the answer I did. If it's a call from the Lord, he knows how poor we are and what he would have to bless us with for us to make it on a mission."

"How many children do you have?" continued the president.

"Four at home."

"Could you support them if you all went? When you get home, ask your wife if she would agree to such a mission call."

"President," I said, "could you tell me where we would be serving? I can tell you right now what my wife will say."

"Niue!" answered the president.

"Then," said I, "even though we don't have a penny in our hands now, we gladly accept the call. In fact, we have talked about Niue at home, because of a recent dream I had. I saw her and me in the dream strolling through an island foreign to Tonga. It was a place where all the villages are located around the island along the seashore. Every village had a view of the ocean. I had never seen such an island before. It must be Niue! My wife and family will be happy to go, for it is a call from the Lord."

"Good," said the president. "You have two and one half weeks to prepare before the boat [the *Tōfua*] comes to take you to Niue."

That evening Salavia and I rejoiced exceedingly over the call and thanked Heavenly Father for adding this blessing to our family legacy of missionary work.

But the fact was that we had very little money. Just four days before we were to depart, our visa to Niue had not yet been approved, so we could not buy passage to our mission field. Our efforts to sell our goods to raise funds had resulted in a total sum of nineteen pounds Tongan money [*sovaleni'e taha hiva*]. President Stone had offered to pay for our passage but was not on Tongatapu when our visa was approved. I decided we would pay for it ourselves. An acquaintance of mine named Sēmisi worked in the travel office. While he was figuring out our passage I said to him: "May you follow the impression of the Holy Ghost as you do our tickets, Sēmisi."

After several minutes of calculating, he said, "Nineteen pounds for everything!" I reached in my pocket and gave him every cent we had, which covered our deck passage exactly.

Our happiness and our faith could not have been greater. Again our attitude was that the Lord knew how poor we were and that we were going with small children to a strange land. He would prepare the way. The way he blessed us with money or opportunities to make money was both fascinating and humbling. When we arrived in Vava'u, for example, on our way to Niue, the children of the Church primary schools made us a gift of eleven pounds. We were so careful with this money that after four months in Niue we had spent only four pounds of it.

We did not tell our fellow missionaries from America about our financial problems, even when Elder Chuck Woodworth told me I needed to buy a bicycle so I could preach with them from village to village. He said it would probably cost twelve pounds.

With only seven pounds in my pocket, it seemed impossible for me to afford one; but when Elder Woodworth announced we were all going the next day to the village of Ha'akupu, ten miles distance, and could I please get a bicycle, I said I would have one by nine o'clock the next morning.

That night while the other missionaries were out enjoying an activity together, I stayed home and read scriptures and prayed for a bicycle I could afford. At about 9:30 P.M. a knock came at our door. It was a white man named Jackson, a New Zealander, who said: "I'm returning home next week. Would you be interested in buying my bicycle?"

"I would be very interested if the price is right," said I.

"It's a year old," he said, "and in perfect condition. Is seven pounds too much?"

"No!" I cried. "It's exactly right for me."

So I got the bicycle, like the boat passage, for precisely the amount I had in my pocket. I thanked Heavenly Father for his answer to my prayers. However, we were left again with no money at all and no idea how we would sustain ourselves.

Heavenly Father was not finished blessing us. Just a day or two after the bicycle purchase, Salavia baked a big traditional Tongan pudding (*puteni*) for our midday meal. Our daughter Sini took a portion of the pudding and gave it to her friend who had a little store just opposite the church building. This friend sent word back to us that she would like a whole pudding the next day to sell in her store. We accommodated her request, and that evening she brought us seven pounds New Zealand money. By selling the pudding in portions, she made a good profit and now asked if we could provide her with one or two good-sized Tongan puddings every day ongoing. Well, that little arrangement turned out to be the most amazing blessing of all. Some months we earned as much as £140, enough to feed us and all the missionaries including some labor missionaries. . . .

Our labor in Niue was to preach and to build chapels. We hauled coral rocks by hand and crushed them with eight-pound sledge hammers. We loaded and unloaded sand with hand shovels. We carried crushed rocks in old burlap bags. Our crew included older women whose names I revere: Eia, Tauia, Kolikoli, Tuiolo, Fei, Favini, Foini, Tanita, Sitela, and Sifahenga. Each had her old sugar sack with which to haul the crushed rock. Elder Archie Cottle was the construction supervisor.

Whenever I wanted to lie down on the job or give up, I would only have to consider the swollen and blistered hands of the missionaries. They were a constant blessing to us. In fact, our greatest blessing as a family came literally at the hands of Elder Chuck Woodworth, who was a wonderful servant of the living God, leading well our little zone of seven missionaries.

At the conclusion of his mission, Elder Woodworth fought and beat the All-Pacific boxing champion, Kitione Lave, in a much-celebrated match, the proceeds of which paid our way as a family to be sealed in the New Zealand Temple. I consider this remarkable gift and blessing a fulfillment of the promise bestowed upon me by Apostle George Albert Smith when he ordained me an elder in 1938. He said in his blessing that if I always served mightily and faithfully as a missionary in the Church, the day would come when I would go with my family to the temple without the loss of a single cent of our own money. Our family would never suffer from poverty. He also promised we would have opportunities to serve and bless others in numbers we could not even imagine at that time.

28

Charles ("Chuck") J. Woodworth

FIGHTING FOR SALVATION

by R. Lanier Britsch

Charles J. Woodworth, former missionary in Niue Island and later president of the Tonga Mission, had a unique experience as a missionary. Written by Dr. Lanier Britsch, the story reconstitutes unforgettable moments cherished by the Tongan Saints. It also illustrates faithfulness, love, obedience to principle, hard work, and prayer.

Chuck Woodworth's untanned body made him look smaller than he really was as he entered the ring with his bronzed opponent. The opening bell sounded and both men sprang from their corners. Victory is but a few moments away, thought Kitione Lave, his rock-solid body seething with power.

Woodworth was thinking more serious thoughts. After all, he had not been in the ring for over two and a half years. Then before many seconds had passed—almost before they had felt each other out and settled into a pattern—Chuck threw a left jab. Lave countered with a left hook that knocked Chuck flat. It should have been all over, but. . . .

What was it that led Chuck into the ring with this big Tongan champion, anyway? Most men are satisfied to put in their full mission term and then just go home and get back into a normal existence.

But Chuck wasn't like most men. He had been doing things a little bit differently for years. While his friends were pushing brooms or pulling weeds to put themselves through college, Charles J. Woodworth, a Missouri boy, was making his way by boxing. Almost every month he found himself matched with some fighter for a bout at the Utah State Fairgrounds. "I got paid fifty dollars for each fight whether I won or lost. All I had to do was train, which I did anyway, fight in a match once each month, and I could make ends meet."

Costs for a college education at BYU in the mid-1950s were a great deal lower than they are now. Over the years he had fought several men who were nationally ranked. Scheduled fights pitted Chuck against Rex Lane and Ezzard Charles. To pick up some needed cash he had even sparred with light-heavyweight champion Joey Maxim.

Chuck loved boxing but it was not the center of his life. It was simply a means to a much bigger end. He wanted an education. He also loved the Lord and the Church and wanted to serve a mission. During the summer of 1955, he received a call to the Tongan Mission and arrived there in August. Mission President D'Monte Coombs assigned him to work on the distant island of Niue.

Niue is not part of Tonga, but it was a part of the Tonga Mission. This hot little island is located several hundred miles northeast of the Tongan islands. In those days a mission to Niue lasted two and a half years.

Life on this coral island is difficult. Everyone works. The elders there learned to work very hard too. During Elder Woodworth's time there, a chapel was being built by volunteer labor. The missionaries, it turned out, were the most important volunteers.

Two of the most vibrant missionaries in Niue at this time were a couple from Tonga, Mosese and Salavia Muti, with their five children. The Mutis had served three different missions previously for the Church. They were a poor but very devout family and exceptionally gifted in the Niuean language.

As the months passed and long hours of work were accomplished, a warm fraternal love developed among Elder Woodworth, his companions, and the Mutis. The people of Niue were also friendly and kind but not enthusiastic about the message of the missionaries. The fact that there were only five thousand people on the island did not make matters easier.

While these missionaries were working together to build a chapel, another important Church structure was under construction in New Zealand—the temple. As work progressed there, news of its near completion was sent to all the Pacific area missions. Mosese and Salavia

Muti wanted more than anything else to attend the dedication of the temple and then receive their own endowments and sealing.

As the end of Elder Woodworth's mission approached, he had feelings of disappointment. He had been faithful, he had worked hard, he had taught the truth to the best of his ability, but he wanted to do something more. His labors did not seem complete. Then it all came together in his mind. He knew how much the Mutis wanted to go to the temple. There was the answer. He would send them to the temple, and he would do it by fighting in one big boxing match.

Elder Woodworth had many details to arrange. He needed permission from the mission president to go to New Zealand and arrange the bout. When permission was granted, he contacted Don Meister, a boxing promoter he had actually met and taught the missionary discussions to in Niue. The fact that Elder Woodworth had fought such men as Ezzard Charles and Rex Lane made it possible for Meister to arrange a fight with the Australasian heavy-weight champion, Kitione (Gideon) Lave, later ranked eighth in the world. The contract for the match was signed in February 1958, to be held in Auckland.

When he was released from his mission in January, Elder Woodworth traveled to Auckland and, with permission, moved in with the missionaries living near the Queen Street Chapel. They considered him one of their own.

He took his training very seriously. He adhered to every principle of body conditioning for a good fight. All of this was not so difficult as it might have been if he had not been doing hard physical labor on his mission. Even during those years Elder Woodworth had kept himself in shape through regular exercise.

There was plenty of excitement in New Zealand as the boxing match approached. Very few people thought Elder Woodworth had a chance. Kitione Lave was a great fighter. After defeating everyone in Tonga, he had moved to New Zealand to fight. As one observer put it, "He went through the Australian and New Zealand boxers like a knife through butter."

William Harris, who saw the fight from Woodworth's corner, described Lave in these words: "He was just an ideal heavy-weight. Potentially he was a world leader. He had the size. He had the strength. He had eye quickness and body speed. He went to England and fought Don Cockle, who was ranked third in the world, and knocked him out in three rounds. Kitione was a natural fighter. He was just beautiful."

Unfortunately, when Kitione returned to New Zealand he had an overdose of confidence. Training for this match was taken lightly. He would handle this "sparrow," as he called Elder Woodworth, with little trouble.

Kitione Lave was a very popular fighter in New Zealand; so when the night for the fight arrived, the stands at Carlow Park were full. Those who had seen Lave and Woodworth in training didn't give the Mormon elder much of a chance. In New Zealand, betting odds were heavy against him.

But out on Niue island there was much faith that he would win. On the night of the fight, Mosese Muti sent Elder Woodworth a telegram wishing him good luck. The man operating the wireless asked Muti why he thought Chuck would be lucky. He said that he had seen Lave fight before and did not think the American had a chance; Lave would knock Woodworth out!

Muti then told the telegraph operator that he had a special feeling about the fight. Elder Woodworth was not going to lose.

The opening bell sounded, and both men rushed from their corners. Only seconds passed before Chuck was on the mat. One onlooker said Lave threw the hardest punch he had ever seen. "Chuck just went up in the air and down he went."

No one expected him to get up. But on the count of eight, with superhuman strength and as much determination, Elder Woodworth staggered to his feet. The count ended and the fight continued. He spent the rest of the round back-peddling, dodging, and evading. The bell finally rescued him from sure destruction. The rest period was like a moment of heaven, but the bell sounded again—almost too soon, he thought.

Rounds two and three were a study in survival. Elder Woodworth kept dancing out of the way of those sledgehammer fists. As the minutes dragged on, his head began to clear and his perception became less foggy. Before round four sounded he was feeling good. The effects of the killer punch were gone. His confidence was boosted and his manager carefully instructed him to "take the offense, but be careful."

Lave was beginning to tire. He seemed to have spent his strength chasing the elusive American in the first four rounds. Elder Woodworth went to war. In round five more and more of his punches found their mark. By round eight Kitione, the "sparrow killer," was himself being pecked to death. By round eleven his fate was sealed.

Lave never gave up. He tried to make up for lost points with a twelfth-round flurry, hoping for a knock-out. But it was too late. The Mormon elder had endured Lave's worst punch and had proven to the whole crowd and the judges that he was an excellent boxer, good enough to be the champion that night, good enough to win the decision.

The morning following the bout, Muti and his wife received a telegram from New Zealand. In it Elder Woodworth told them that with the prize money he had purchased tickets for the two of them to go to the temple dedication. Until that time they did not know why he had been anxious to fight the Tongan champion.

Two wonderful things happened that night in Auckland. A missionary proved his love for a beloved Tongan family. And a poor Tongan missionary couple suddenly had a way to be part of a great historical event, the dedication of the New Zealand Temple, and to receive their own temple blessings.

A fitting sequel to this story was that during the summer of 1972 Charles J. Woodworth (now a Ph.D. in marriage and family counseling) was called to be president of the Tonga Mission, a position he held until the spring of 1974, when the mantle of leadership in the mission was given to local Tongan brethren. He will always be remembered for his kindness and for his integrity, and for his magnificent bout with Kitione Lave. It was a fight for life, the eternal life of a family he loved so well.

29

Enoch LaVell Manwaring

THE SAVIOR'S BLEEDING HANDS

Enoch LaVell Manwaring was a prominent building missionary in Tonga and served as the president of the Liahona Branch from 1956 to 1958. Known for his loving nature and his spiritual stature, Brother Manwaring had a profound influence on many of the future Tongan leaders of the Church such as Sovea Kioa and Tonga Toutai Pāletuʻa.

I was asked by the building supervisor, Brother Franklin Knowlton, to take some of the Tongan building missionaries and go to the island of ʻUiha, about a hundred miles from Tongatapu, to lay up the bricks for a chapel there. We loaded our supplies, tools, bricks, and a cement mixer onto the Church launch. It was towed by another boat which we rode on, and we started for ʻUiha. On the way we had to cross some of the deepest water of the Pacific Ocean.

We arrived at the small island and had to wade and float the supplies ashore because there was no dock.

In ʻUiha there was a small elderly lady named Vaikato Tāvutu. She was not certain of her age but thought she might be 102 or so. She was on the work site the next morning helping to fill the barrels with water with which to mix the mortar; she was also carrying the coral bricks to the builders.

I spoke to her through an interpreter and told her not to carry the water. The buckets were too heavy for her and the men could do it. I also asked her to please only carry one brick at a time, as they were about the size of our cinder blocks. However, as soon as I was out of sight, she started carrying two bricks at a time again. One of the Tongan builders came to me and asked for some gloves for Vaikato because her hands were bleeding from the rough blocks. I got down from the scaffold and went to the lady, admonishing her again through the interpreter to only carry one brick at a time. I took off my gloves and gave them to her.

The tears started running down Vaikato's cheeks, and I thought I had wounded her feelings. Then I noticed the tears rolling down the interpreter's face. He told me, "The little lady said that the Savior's hands had bled for her and that she was not ashamed to have her hands bleed for the Savior's work."

Not long after we had arrived and the work was progressing on the building, some of the Tongan building missionaries came to me and asked if I had talked to Vaikato about the chapel. I told them no. They asked me if she had seen the blueprints to the building or, if she had, would she be able to read them. Again I told them no.

The men told me that she was telling all of the workers just where the classrooms would be, where the pulpit would stand, and just how the chapel would look when it was finished. It was amazing what she knew. Through an interpreter, I learned that, twenty years before the building program was started in the South Pacific, she was the Relief Society president on her island. Her health was not good, and she thought she might have to be released. At that time Apostle George Albert Smith was visiting the Tongan Islands. When he arrived at 'Uiha, she asked him for a special blessing. She told us that while Elder Smith was blessing her, she could understand everything he said in her own language. He told her that if she would be faithful, she would live to see a beautiful chapel erected on her island. In fact, during the blessing she could see in vision the chapel and how it would look and that it had a gold steeple that shone in the sunlight.

She told her people of the beautiful chapel to be built on their island, but the years passed and nothing happened. The people began to laugh at her and call her "the big liar."

One day she became very ill. Her brother went to her and told her she had better repent of her sins and confess her lies. He told her she knew that she had told lies all those years, and now she was going to die with that on her conscience. Well, Vaikato recovered; and after many years, her vision was fulfilled.

I saw Vaikato raise her hands in prayer many times to thank Heavenly Father for letting her live to see the chapel being built. Tears of gratitude ran down her face. I have never known anyone who could put the working spirit into a group of young men like Vaikato. She was the first one on the job in the morning, getting things ready for work. When it got hot during the day and the labor missionaries started to slow down, she would call out to them in Tongan, and they would take new heart.

When we got word that a silver steeple was being shipped to us, I began to worry. Vaikato had already told the labor missionaries that she had seen a gold steeple in her vision. I did not worry long, because word came that the silver steeple was being diverted to a chapel in Tongatapu about to be dedicated by President Marion G. Romney. When our steeple finally arrived we were delighted to see it was bronze, which shone like gold in the sun.

The day the builders left the island, Vaikato waded out in the ocean as far as she could to tell us goodbye and to thank us for coming to her island to build such a beautiful building. I could see her waving a white handkerchief for a long ways as we went out to sea.

After the chapel was dedicated, President Fred Stone told me that Vaikato brought out the bedding of fine mats and tapa cloth George Albert Smith had slept on many years before and gave it all to him as a gift. She had kept the bed in good condition all those years, airing the tapa cloth frequently, so she could give it to whoever dedicated the chapel. He also told me how she danced and sang praises on the day of the dedication.

30

'Uiha and Senivia Tu'ikolovatu

"RECEIVE YOUR BLESSING"

'Uiha and Senivia Tu'ikolovatu are both converts to the Church and have served generously in many Church assignments. 'Uiha has been a bishop and is now serving as president of the Nuku'alofa Tonga Stake. Senivia served as ward president of both her Relief Society and Primary. They have eight children. 'Uiha's story speaks for thousands of Tongans who learned the gospel and gained a testimony at Liahona High School. Like many Tongan women who marry into another faith, Senivia joined the Church just to please her husband. Her real conversion came at a moment when she tried to resist it the most.

'Uiha

It was a set of strange circumstances that led me to Liahona High School and eventual membership in the Church. I was a boarding student at another private institution when Liahona was opened for students in 1948. I had become very disenchanted with my school because of no decent meals. I was hungry most of the time, especially on Sunday. I told my parents I was through with education if it entailed that kind of forced fasting.

Some young people from my village had attended classes in Makeke and were planning to enroll in Liahona. When their families took them out to the new school, I went along for the ride just to see the beautiful grounds and buildings. After registration the students went into orientation activities and we, the onlookers and family members, went back to our vehicles to return to Nuku'alofa. I was sitting in the truck when Luti Wolfgramm, the principal, walked up to us, looked at me, the only school-age person in the group, and said, "Young man, don't you want to go to school?"

"Yes, I do," I said. "But I'm not prepared. I have no clothes, bedding, money, or materials."

"If you want to attend," said he, "you can stay right here and enroll now. Your parents can bring those things later."

Well, he was very persuasive; and I stayed at Liahona and enrolled with nothing to my name except the clothes on my back and a few cents in my pocket. It was six weeks before I received from home my bedding, clothes, and money for fees and materials. In the meantime, I borrowed a sheet of paper a day from a friend in the dormitory to write my lessons on.

By the following year, as a result of the Sunday evening missionary devotionals (*pō malanga*), I gained an understanding and testimony of the gospel and was baptized in October of 1949. Although I left Liahona in 1950 to look for full-time employment with the government, I continued to grow spiritually, receiving the Melchizedek Priesthood in due time and finding a permanent position with the Board of Electricity where I have been ever since.

My life since Liahona has been full of blessings and opportunities to serve, as bishop and now as a stake president. In the Book of Mormon, I am impressed that Nephi constrained Zoram to stay with Lehi and his family and go with them to the promised land. It was Luti Wolfgramm who constrained me and persuaded me to stay and study in Liahona, which brought both the testimony and the joy of the gospel to my life.

Senivia

I married 'Uiha Tu'ikolovatu in 1955 and was baptized a member of the Church in 1956. I was baptized out of love for my husband, not from any understanding or feeling I had about the Church. 'Uiha never forced the Church on me, and I attended services or stayed home as I pleased. In fact, there were times when we would attend my old church together or just not go anywhere at all on Sundays.

My real conversion occurred after six years of marriage, when I was pregnant with our fourth child. 'Uiha had gone to priesthood meeting one Sunday morning when I began to feel severe labor pains. I sent word for him to hurry home and take me to the hospital. As he came into the house he said, "Senivia, I've asked the branch president to come give you a blessing before I take you to the hospital."

This statement offended me greatly, and I told him I wanted no part of it. He stood at the window watching for the arrival of President Tovi Lavulo and his counselor Simote Fieʻeiki. When they appeared at the entrance of our yard under the *tava* tree, I said to my husband: "If they come in with the intention of laying hands on me, I am very sorry but they are not going to do it to me."

I spoke out of my true feelings, but my husband quietly ignored me because of his faith in priesthood blessings. My grandmother was present in the room with us.

Despite my negative attitude and my resistance to these two servants of the Lord, the moment they came up the steps into the house, a profoundly moving spiritual sensation came over me. My whole body tingled. Grandma felt it too and wept.

"Senivia," said my loving husband, "come and receive your blessing."

Perhaps President Lavulo sensed my reluctance at first because he asked me if I really wanted them to bless me. "Yes," I said, "very much!" Brother Simote Fieʻeiki then anointed me with the consecrated oil, and President Lavulo pronounced the blessing, promising that the delivery would be "fast, easy, and safe."

At the hospital Dr. ʻAlo ʻEvakihakau examined me and said I wasn't close to delivering and for me to take a long walk and come back and rest. The baby would not be born until the next morning (Monday). It was then 11:30 Sunday morning. According to him, I was in for a long labor. The words of the blessing, "fast, easy, and safe," kept coming back to me, and I believed them with all my heart.

I sat down on the hospital bed, telling the nurse I couldn't walk around as the doctor instructed because I was about to give birth any second. The nurse slapped me on the back and said to get up and walk around and quit pretending to be in pain. Instead I lay down. Moments later I asked the lady who accompanied me to the hospital to bring the nurse quickly, for the baby was coming.

Well, the baby came just as the promise was made, "fast and safe," so fast that everyone else missed it, even the nurse. Since that wonderful experience I had with the priesthood in 1961, my testimony and joy in the Church have multiplied.

31

Mosese Naeata

RICHNESS IN POVERTY

A graduate of BYU–Hawaii, Mosese Naeata is currently the president of Nuku'alofa Liahona Stake. He and his wife 'Akanesi Hikilā have five children. This short history offers a typical picture of life in Tonga in the 1940s and 1950s. His story could be the story of many, particularly those who are lured to leave their homeland and seek their fortunes abroad.

I often thought growing up that nothing in this world could be worse than the poverty my family was subjected to. In my early teens especially, I felt crushed by it and by the strain of living in a large family with an invalid father. It was not until much later I realized that in those formative years I gained through dogged work and strict obedience to righteous parents the strength and stamina to be a leader today.

I was born February 8, 1940, in Tongatapu while Dad and Mom were serving as missionaries in Fo'ui, Tongatapu. Mom often went with Dad to district meetings, leaving me with Mē Mataele who had her own tiny baby named Teisa. If Mom got home late, Mē generously let me nurse along with her own baby. These were my blessings as a missionary baby.

The Naeata family is well known in the Church in Tonga, particularly in Vava'u. My grandfather, Siosifa Naeata, was baptized in the Church on January 31, 1915, in Ha'alaufuli. A devoted man, he was, I believe, the first Tongan to receive the Melchizedek Priesthood which was conferred on him that same year or the next. Grandpa outlived four successive wives and is the head of a large posterity in the Church.

He served faithfully on seven different missions for the Church, laboring in Pangai, Makeke, Houma (Tongatapu), Matahau, and Koloa.

My own father, Viliami Naeata, continued the missionary commitment of our family. He and Mom married in Pangai, Ha'apai, on August 27, 1934. The next year they accepted a mission call to Tongatapu, to work in the Church school at Makeke for six months and then to be a branch president in Fo'ui. Two years later, we were all back in Vava'u where Dad was called to be a counselor in the district presidency.

My earliest recollections are of riding on a horse through the bush with my father as he made his Church visits to various villages. I would stand on the horse's back behind him and cling tightly to him with my arms around his neck. We rode this way everywhere, to Ngā'unoho, 'Utui, Makave, etc., preaching and gathering genealogy. He even took me along to a conference in Niuatoputapu on the old government boat, the *Aoniu*.

As a young man, Dad was a good farmer with substantial garden crops of taro, yam, and plantains. He also kept pigs, horses, and a small dairy herd which I learned very young how to milk. He ran a licensed butcher shop where he sold salt-cured beef and pork.

Our family troubles began in March of 1952 when Dad was stricken with the illness that would finally kill him on November 15, 1956. The two older children were boarding at Liahona at the time, making me, at age twelve, the oldest child at home.

The received Tongan wisdom, of course, was for my older brother Tomasi, the heir to Dad's goods and property, to come home and assume his rightful position and care for the family. But Dad rejected the idea, insisting that Tomasi continue his high school education. For him none of us should be without education. Thus I was "elected" to be man of the house.

The doctors who treated Dad recommended that he move to a place by the sea where the air was fresh and clean. 'Otualea beach seemed ideal for this purpose, except that it was a considerable distance from Ha'alaufuli and was located at the bottom of one of the precipitous cliffs for which Vava'u is famous. The path winding down the cliff was long and arduous. One either walked or rode a horse on the trail.

Notwithstanding the inconvenience, our entire family relocated to 'Otualea beach where I was to assume a key role in winning our family's livelihood—fishing, growing, gathering, hauling, and cutting. I was also responsible for the family's cattle, which had to be watered and moved to new pasture nearly every day.

We arranged for a forty-four-gallon drum of fresh water to be brought from town to the cliff in a horse cart. This was our back-up system. My sister Vika and I would fill our buckets and bottles each day after school from the village and carry the water down the trail to our camp.

Dad was soon a complete invalid, resting most of the time. Food became scarce. Mom often sent me with a pudding to relatives I didn't even know to ask for taro and other food. Sometimes, begging a ride on an old quarry dump truck, I would venture as far as Leimātu'a. Back again I would struggle with the baskets of food down the trail to our beach home.

Money was more scarce than our food, coming mainly from our copra-making. Mom kept me out of school sometimes to gather dry coconuts for this purpose. She would remind me that the small profit from our effort would buy bread and butter, softer food for Dad in his sickness.

When we lacked meat, Mom simply ordered me and my sister Vika to make a torch and set out at low tide to catch fish at night. Bush knife in hand, we would wander barefooted over the coral, peering in tidal pools and overturning rocks to expose the sleeping fish. If I struck and merely wounded a fish, we gave chase, ignoring the pain of the sharp rocks on our bare feet, until we captured our prize. Back at the camp, Mom would boil the fish for Dad. As Dad ate, we sipped the fish broth. When the sea was too rough for torch fishing, we gathered, boiled, and ate *hihi* (snails).

The responsibilities of the family continued to weigh heavily on my twelve-year-old mind. Life seemed pretty miserable. Every day was drudgery, and I longed for escape. In fact, the idea of escape so preoccupied my mind that I vowed I would never be poor again and, if I ever got out of Tonga, would never come back. I remember climbing the ironwood tree growing by the cliff path and looking out on the expanse of water to where the ocean met the sky. "Which would be faster," I thought, "if I were to float out on a log toward the horizon—death or rescue by a foreign ship which would take me away forever?"

My pain would ease a bit in the evenings when we gathered for family prayer with Mom and Dad. But faced with the same heavy chores, the next day my feelings of frustration and self-pity would return. Added to these feelings was the pressure of getting ready for the government exams for entrance into a college [high school]. Group study for these exams was held after school and in the evenings in Haʻalaufuli. My parents still expected me to perform every daily chore, attend the group study, and then come back to ʻOtualea to sleep with the family at night.

In retrospect, I am certain my biggest source of unhappiness at this time was the fear of ghosts and demons. The evening study groups in Haʻalaufuli meant that I was obliged to walk a mile or so from Haʻalaufuli to ʻOtualea in the dark of the night through heavy bush country. This journey filled me with terror because, like many Tongans, I was sure evil spirits and demons lurked in the shadows of the forest.

It was this fear that often prompted a hasty return to ʻOtualea without caring first for the animals. I often lied to my father when he asked about my chores. As our group study let out at night between nine and ten o'clock, I would linger at the house of Kalisi and ʻAlisi Maʻasi on the edge of the village, looking as pitiful as possible, asking for a torch to light my way, and hoping someone would say, "Wait there, son, and we will walk you back to the beach."

No such offer ever came. I remember one evening standing in front of Maʻasi's place and peering down the dark path through the bush. My hair stood on end and my body tingled with a fear perhaps only a Tongan can understand: "Should I stay in Haʻalaufuli for the night or walk through this sinister forest?"

The debate ended when I finally decided I would rather face the evil spirits of the Vavaʻu forests than my own mother if I failed to go home that night. So I lighted my torch made from dried coconut leaves and started my journey to ʻOtualea. Tense all the way, I did not breathe freely until I entered our hut and crawled into bed.

On another occasion I arrived home at ʻOtualea just at dusk. Father asked if I had watered and relocated the cattle. He now suspected I had lied to him several times before on this matter. I couldn't lie this time. No, I hadn't cared for the cattle because I was terrified of the walk through the forest in the dark. The fear of demons was too powerful in me. I wanted to get home before nightfall.

Well, Dad was not impressed and I got a good spanking that night. This overt discipline was the last straw for me. "I work myself to death," I argued to myself, "and still get punished. I'm finished with this place and this family."

I made immediate plans to run away from home. Secretly gathering up my personal belongings, I smuggled them out of the house, hid them under the massive ironwood tree by the path up the cliff, and returned to the hut to contemplate where in Tonga or anywhere else I could flee.

In this dark mood, I sat sullenly waiting to make my escape. Suddenly my baby sister, Fakaola, crawled over to me and begged to be held. Fakaola was only one year old, born about the time Dad had become ill. She had been weaned early so Mom could spend her time and energy caring for Dad. Fakaola nosed right up to me and cried: "Mama, Mama." I reached down to pick her up, at which instant all thoughts of running away disappeared. With Fakaola in my arms, I walked outside to the ironwood tree, retrieved my bundle of personal belongings, and put them back in the house. So much for running away.

There was never any let-up in my chores. Our family's condition, it seemed to me, was desperate. Little food, less money, and no help from anyone else. But Mother lost no opportunity to praise me, either publicly or privately, for my assistance to the family. "Mosese is working to take his father's place someday," she would say. "His time is coming."

The day in February 1954 when I boarded the boat in Neiafu to sail to Tongatapu to attend high school at Liahona, I said to my father, "When I leave, how will you all get by?"

"You will put it all behind you," he said. "The thing that is wanted now is your education."

Dad passed away two and a half years later while the three of us were at Liahona. When we heard the news, we sailed immediately for Vava'u. Unfortunately, fierce winds and heavy seas forced us to stay in Ha'apai for nearly two weeks. We missed the funeral entirely. Dad's insistence that we work hard and his desire for us to get as much education as possible have been a living tribute to his memory.

In 1960 I graduated from Liahona with an obsession stronger than ever to leave Tonga and seek my fortune abroad. I was determined not to live in the squalor I had endured as a child. The chance to attend Church College of Hawaii was going to be my escape and, as I promised Mother, the rescue of our whole family from material hardship.

However, the very day I received word from the principal to return to Liahona and prepare to go to Hawaii on CCH sponsorship, I received a call from President Vernon Coombs to serve a full-time, two-year mission for the Church in Tonga. Mother was overjoyed with the call. I was upset. Frankly, I did not want to serve a mission. My plan was firm. The opportunity was here. I remember telling Mother: "Please let's look realistically at our condition. We are miserably poor. My plan is to find a way for our family to rise out of our poverty. My education abroad is our chance."

Mom's words were unforgettable. "You will not go to college at this time but will serve your mission first. Then you may go to Hawaii for your education."

In December of 1960, I entered the mission field with four shillings from my mother in my pocket. Missionaries in those days, largely dependent on the generosity of members and the people at large, lived in relative poverty anyway, so my condition was not unusual. Assigned to Talihau as a companion to a married missionary, 'Otiti Fungavaka, I spent almost all my mission time in the outer islands of Vava'u.

After the hurricane of March 1961 which devastated so much of the island (every building in Talihau had been destroyed), nearly everyone in Vava'u was reduced to a desperate course of just surviving. Food became scarce. Many lost everything they had. Although scarcity of food or goods was not a heavy adjustment for me, I was often touched by the kindness and generosity of the most unlikely people during the months of hardship after the hurricane.

One day I and another companion, Sinipata Fonua (from Fo'ui), were on our way back to 'Otea after a two-day preaching tour through Talihau, Kapa, Falevai, and 'Otea. We had not eaten for those two days. Usually very kind to missionaries with their food, none of the people offered us a meal simply because they had nothing to give. But as we were coming through Falevai, a widow lady by the name of Teu Puta called us to please come in to her home and eat. She put before us a tin of fish and a plate of *'uto*, the soft center of a sprouting coconut, a magnificent feast to our eyes.

The next week, we followed the same route through the same villages. Again, only Teu Puta invited us to turn aside into her hut and eat, this time dried coconut meat and a piece of root from the *sī* plant. We ate enthusiastically of this meager fare, saving half of it for the next day.

Leaving Teu's home, we were still so moved by her generosity that we knelt down in the bush outside of Falevai and petitioned Heavenly Father to bless her for her kindness. We thanked him again for the most excellent food she gave us.

Unlike my experiences growing up in Ha'alaufuli, I seriously did not feel poor or hungry as a missionary, although I was without money or food much of the time. I learned wisdom and obedience. Most of all, I acquired a burning confidence in the Lord's love and how his servants are miraculously cared for. During my service, Mother's gift of four shillings was all the money I received the whole two years. Yet things worked out. We taught and baptized many people, including Manukia Tupou, who later became a bishop in the Church.

Returning home from the mission in December 1962, I began immediate preparations to go to Hawaii. Thanks to the generosity of many people I was able to secure the funds for the venture of going to America and seeking a university education. My brother Tomasi willingly took out a six-month advance on his salary to pay for my airfare, which meant that for those six months he must struggle as best he could to support his new family. . . .

The years at the Church College of Hawaii were glorious. My work habits and skill in sports gave me an edge. I played on the 1967 National Championship Rugby team, served as president of the Tongan Club on campus, maintained an acceptable academic record, and graduated with a B.A. in physical education.

On August 8, 1970, I married 'Akanesi Hikilā who continued in school while I worked full-time in Honolulu as a construction foreman. Life in Hawaii was sweet and full of promise for us. At no time did we ever consider going back to Tonga. Why go back to the hardship and poverty I had experienced as a youth? I was rid of that kind of misery for good. Now was our opportunity to achieve the comforts and prosperity of America, to pursue the American dream.

All was well with us—a good job, apartment, and a savings account—when one day in 1972, Alton Wade, then an administrator for the Church Educational System and currently president of BYU–Hawaii Campus, contacted me for an interview. He said very simply: "The Lord wants you back in Tonga."

I said just as simply and directly, "No!"

Brother Wade begged me to reconsider, using again the "will of the Lord" as a means of stirring my conscience. He said he was going to New Zealand for a visit and would return for our final answer.

When I told 'Akanesi of Brother Wade's request, she wouldn't even hear me to the end of my report. "If you want to go back to Tonga," she said, "that's fine with me, but you will go alone. I and the children are staying here."

Both of us resisted the thought of returning to Tonga, but we finally agreed that perhaps we should fast and pray to learn the Lord's will in the matter. I kept saying to myself: "I don't want my children to go through what I went through."

After the fast, however, the feeling came to us both that we should go back to our homeland, come what may. When Brother Wade came back through Hawaii from New Zealand, we gave him our answer, with this comment: "If, as you say, it is the Lord's will that we return, then fine. But if it's just your ploy to get us back to Liahona, then may the Lord punish you for even suggesting the idea to us in the first place."

If there was any doubt before about the Lord's will regarding our return home, there was no question once we got back to Tonga. The opportunities for service have multiplied constantly, as teacher and as director of the sports program at Liahona, later as president of the Sports Committee coordinating the competition of all the secondary schools in Tonga, as bishop, as counselor in the mission presidency, and now as stake president. As we have served the Lord, material prosperity has come with nearly everything else we could have possibly had in America and much more—a happy family, health, a righteous, beautiful wife, a fine marriage, and a burning testimony of the gospel of Jesus Christ.

32

Tēvita Folau Mahuʻinga

PROMPTINGS, PROMISES, AND PRIESTHOOD BLESSINGS

Tēvita Folau Mahuʻinga represents faithfulness in high places. For years, while serving his country as a police inspector and district officer, he has also served in the Church as a branch president, district president, bishop, stake president, and patriarch.

Brother Mahuʻinga attributes his rise to a top position on the Tongan Police Force and, since retirement from the force, his continuous reelection as district officer to specific blessings bestowed by David O. McKay, Marion G. Romney, and Spencer W. Kimball. These positions have given his family security and allowed him to serve generously both the Church and his country.

I became branch president in Nukuʻalofa in May of 1956, while I was still a sergeant on the police force. My father, Tēvita Mahuʻinga, was the branch president in Pea at the same time. The members and I had been preoccupied with raising money for the construction of a new chapel in Latai, in Nukuʻalofa. The construction completed, we looked forward to its dedication by the visiting apostle, Marion G. Romney.

I and my wife ʻOnita accompanied President Fred Stone to the wharf to greet the apostle and escort him to the mission home. Apparently President Stone had told him of our sacrifices and hard work in the Church as well as our scanty means. President Romney said to me, "President Stone has told me of your work and sacrifice in your Church calling. For this devotion there will be a blessing in your life that will allow you to take your family to the temple."

I took these words to heart; but the distance to the temple in New Zealand, the expense, the time requirements of my daily job, and our relative poverty made it impossible to imagine such a blessing.

After the dedications of the Latai and Matahau chapels and all the attendant activities, I took Elder Romney back to his boat, at which time he more specifically said I would be promoted on the police force to a position that would "take" me and my family to the temple.

Elder Romney sailed away on Tuesday afternoon. On Wednesday, the queen's cabinet met and approved my very unlikely promotion from sergeant to inspector, bypassing the standard promotion to sergeant major. This meant that I had been promoted to a top-level government position which, after three years' service, would give me six months' leave with pay to a foreign country of my choice within the commonwealth. Suddenly the impossible seemed possible. My wife and I wept for joy, for we were very poor at the time with a large family.

The vacation benefit in my promotion solved only one problem in our quest to go to the temple. To save money in a ceremonial society that demanded so much from one's private resources for the purposes of the extended family and the chiefs, etc., putting aside money from my salary alone was again next to impossible.

The next month I was transferred to the Ha'apai Group to be police inspector there. My first church assignment was as second counselor to Taufa Tui'one Pulotu in the branch presidency. We were happy in Ha'apai, but my father, Tēvita, kept writing and insisting we take him to the temple. Of course, for us it was a difficult matter of money and time off from work. Further, I wouldn't be eligible for foreign leave until 1961, the year I had targeted to make the trip to New Zealand.

In 1959 I was called to be the district president in Ha'apai, which increased my responsibilities dramatically. The closer the time came for the temple trip, the less prepared financially we were to make the trip. Ha'apai did not offer many opportunities for earning large amounts of extra money.

One Saturday night, having made preparation to sail to Hā'ano island early Sunday morning on a church visit, I slept and dreamed a strange dream. I saw myself in a small boat making my way toward Hā'ano. As we approached the northern end of Lifuka, we came to the beacon light on the reef just out from the village of Koulo. Suddenly, I could see huge schools of fish swarming everywhere along the reef, and the powerful thought occurred to me that I must build a fish trap in this area, catch the fish, and sell them for our temple money.

I awoke at 4:00 A.M. and took my journey with other leaders in the district and Kouli Tautuaʻā, our captain. As we approached the place I had seen in my dream, I had the urge to just take a good look. The sea was calm. I asked Kouli to run over to the beacon light on the reef and tie up there so I could survey the area for fish. I felt instantly the shock of recognition as huge schools of fish appeared in the crystal-clear ocean below us. I was actually seeing what had come to me in the dream the night before. My mind was clear about what I should do.

The next afternoon I went to Koulo to investigate building a trap, running a small-mesh chicken-wire fence straight out from the beach to where I had seen the fish. The fishermen experienced in this area tried to discourage me from building a trap in any proximity to the beacon light. There had never been a trap there before because of the depth of the area at low tide, the danger of sharks, and the swiftness of the tidal currents. They argued that the trap enclosures, to which the long mesh fences would lead the fish, should be in shallower water at low tide. Here I was proposing to run the fences into a deeper spot without the protection of the reef, which meant that at low tide a shark could still attack a fisherman who waded out to harvest the fish trapped in the enclosures.

But with a clear vision of where the traps should be, I was insistent. I invested over a thousand dollars in building the entire trap which I knew would last at the longest only six months.

With the help of dozens of villagers, racing during low tide to dig the post holes in the coral sand, stretch the wire, and put the four trap enclosures in place, we completed much of our task in a single afternoon. Our first harvest at the next low tide produced seventeen burlap sacks full of fish for market. And even though the trap sustained the full force of the ocean, it caught thousands of fish in those six months before the wire rotted and the posts gave away. After expenses, our profit was well over two thousand dollars, more than enough to book passage to New Zealand for our family and my parents, Tēvita Mahuʻinga and Mele. We were sealed in the New Zealand temple in 1961.

In May of 1963 my father, a long-time faithful missionary and leader in the Church, became ill at our home in Pea. I was still inspector of police in Haʻapai and district president in the Church. Dr. Siaosi Niumeitolu called to say father was paralyzed and was not likely to live longer than five days. My wife, ʻŌnita, preceded me to Tonga to watch over Dad in the hospital. When my boat finally arrived at Tongatapu, we were all relieved that I could see him before he passed on.

As I contemplated my father's illness, I remembered a promise to me in my patriarchal blessing that I would have the gift of healing, to restore life to the dying, give sight to the blind, and make well the sick and the crippled. I blessed my father to live and asked boldly for Heavenly Father to extend his life ten years. My father miraculously recovered. Dr. ʻAlo ʻEvakihakau, for many years the chief surgeon in Tonga and my second cousin, told me he had never seen a recovery like that from such a severe stroke. He also told me he had prepared to take charge of Dad's funeral if I arrived too late.

Heavenly Father honored the blessing of my father exactly. Dad died precisely ten years later, to the very month. But just before his death on May 17, 1973, he seemed concerned about whether the Church was planning to build a temple in Tonga. As I was preparing to attend the 1973 April General Conference, he spoke to me and said, "I will not die while you are away but will await your return. Please inquire about a temple to be built in Tonga."

I returned from conference on April 16, 1973. His first question to me was about the temple. I told him there was no mention at all of a temple for Tonga, to which he said, "There will be a temple built in Tonga someday; and our five-acre piece just next to Liahona I have reserved for the temple site. You will give it to the Church at the appropriate time."

That was in 1973. Several years later, long after Dad was gone, the Brethren in Salt Lake City announced a temple for Tonga. The leaders here searched and negotiated for prime land on the west side of the Matangiake Chapel (called Nauvoo), but to no avail. They looked at land in Makeke, ʻAtele, and Tatakamotonga, even Nakolo. No parcel seemed completely right anywhere. Meanwhile I said nothing, until finally Sione Tuʻalau Lātū, the Director of Temporal Affairs in Tonga, approached me about our property by Liahona, the very piece my father had declared would be the site of the temple someday.

I cherish my father's vision of the temple in Tonga. It is wonderful to me that he should consecrate his land as its building site long before the leaders of the Church decided to build it. The edifice was dedicated in August of 1983, just over ten years after the death of my father, Tēvita Mahuʻinga.

PART IV

STAKEHOOD

1960–73

Deep Roots, Wide-Spreading Branches

Liahona faculty, 1960. Front row left: Emma Nielsen, Mary Trueblood, Marsha Woodworth, Adele French, Pauline Langi, and Jean Tyson. Second row left: Albert Pope, Ronald Mortensen, David Butler, Principal Kenneth P. Lindsay, Edwin Higbee, Duane Handy, and V. Lynn Tyler. Third row left: Sione Takapautolo Kinikini, Viliami Pasi, Tonga Toutai Pāletuʻa, Sēmisi Nukumovahaʻi Tonga, Reed Garfield, Helu ʻAlatini, and Viliami Sovea Kioa. Top row left: Misitana Vea, Sēmisi Taumoepeau, Dean Harmon, Duane Skinner, Charles "Chuck" Woodworth, ʻAlikisānita Vīmahi, and ʻAtonio Tuʻiʻāsoa. (Courtesy V. Lynn Tyler)

Saints in Haʻakio, Vavaʻu, after the 1961 hurricane, standing in front of the huts they have patched together for shelter. (Courtesy Eric B. Shumway)

Elder David Murdock, Manase Nau, second counselor in the mission presidency, and Tolu'ia Fungavaka, wife of the missionary in Tefisi, Vava'u, stand on the floor of the chapel. The devastating hurricane simply peeled the walls and roof off, leaving the floor. Members built makeshift huts out of corrugated tin for living quarters (right). (Courtesy Kākolosi Tui'one Pulotu)

This one-dense tropical forest near Tefisi with many plantations was devastated by the 1961 hurricane on Vavaʻu. The violent wind threw down most of the trees and stripped the fronds from those still standing. Most were dead. Copra, the chief export of the area, was severely set back for years. (Courtesy Eric B. Shumway)

Mission Relief Society Board, 1966. The Tongan sisters are still wearing mourning for the death of Queen Sālote. Front row left: Finehika Palauni Pulotu, secretary; Salavia Muti, second counselor; Lela Dalton, supervisor; Tuʻavavaʻu Mataele Mapa, president, and Sūlia Tuʻiketei Pule, first counselor. Back row left: Siu Tuʻifua Angilau, Katalina Laomakeʻi, Lili Taufa Wolfgramm, Liahona Taufa Fifita, Seini Lola Afu, and Alaimaluloa Taimani. (Courtesy Lela Dalton)

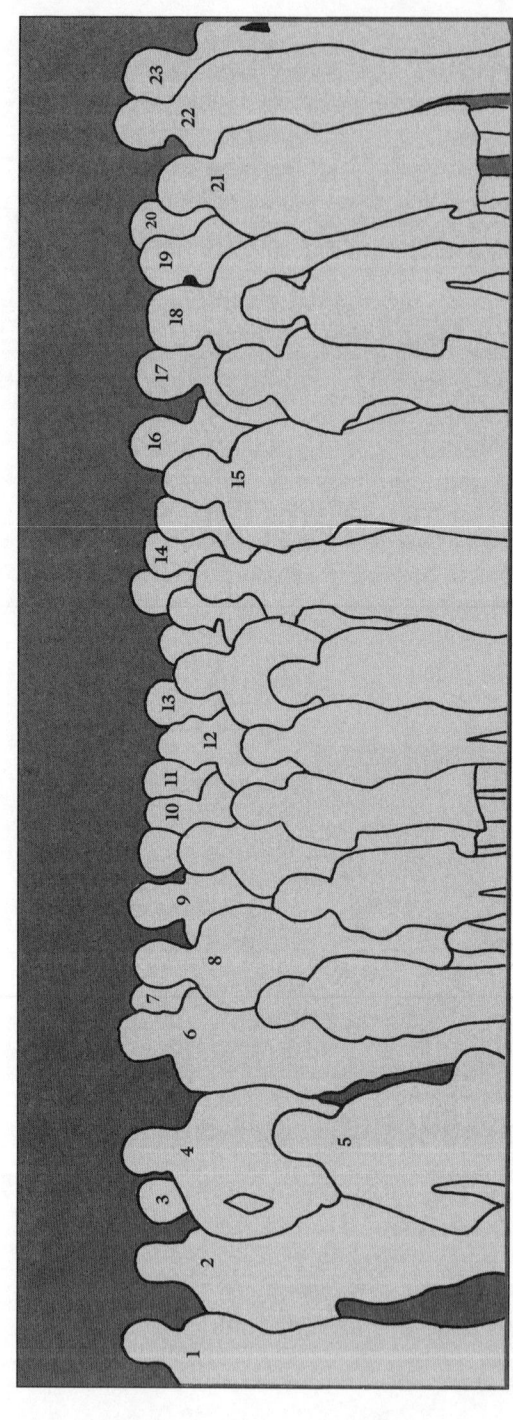

Hofoa Saints with district and mission leaders in front of their first chapel, 1961. With twenty-two members, it was the newest branch in the mission then. (1) Elder Boyd Helquist, (2) Tevita Muli Kinikini, (3) Maile Mataele, (4) Elder Eric B. Shumway, (5) Kupu Ha'alaufia, (6) Manase Nau, second counselor in the mission presidency, (7) Noa Folau, (8) Mele Mafi, (9) Filimone Mafi, (10) 'Asi Lolohea Folau, branch president, (11) Kalisi Mafi, (12) Lesieli Fie'eiki, (13) 'Aisake Tu'ihalangingie, (14) Salelei Tukuafu, (15) Losimani Mafi (Tukuafu), (16) Taufu'i Mafi, (17) Siaosi Loiti Talakai, (18) Tu'ipulotu Mafi, (19) Tevita Mafi, (20) Hale Vete, (21) LaVern Coombs, (22) Motulalo Tonga, (23) Sione Po'uha. (Courtesy Eric B. Shumway)

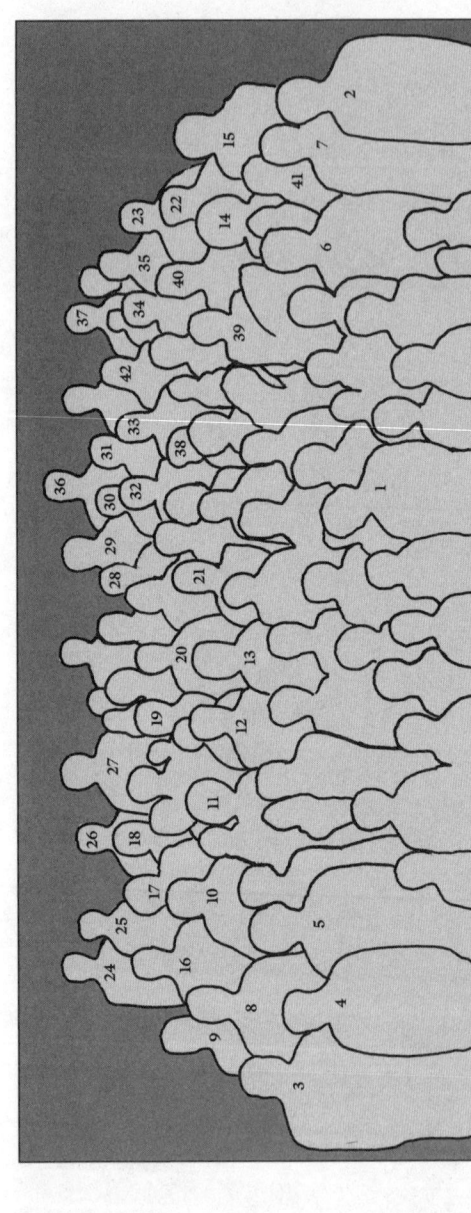

Tongan Saints at the New Zealand Temple, 1971. Thousands of Tongan Saints made this sacred pilgrimage before their own temple was dedicated in 1983. (1) Unidentified, (2) Percy Harris, (3) Fred W. Schwendiman, temple president, (4) Semisi 'Tongi, (5) Lillian A. Schwendiman, matron, (6) Tupou Harris, (7) Norman Harris, (8) Nukumovah'i Tonga, (9) Sefanaia Lotulelei, (10) Sione Ma'ake, (11) Tiu Ma'ake, (12) Siua Moala, (13) Ma'ata Hafoka Moala, (14) Manu Mahu'inga Kivalu, (15) Kelikupa Kivalu, (16) Sione Ma'afu, (17) Same Ma'afu, (18) Kēlepi Laa'uafi, (19) Sione Saafi, (20) Taisia Saafi, (21) Senitila Folau, (22) 'Akesa Langi, (23) Mosese Langi, (24) Sione 'Tongi, (25) Musie 'Tongi, (26) Fipē Tonga, (27) Sela Tonga, (28) 'Ofa Vakena Kinikini, (29) Vaiokema Kinikini, (30) Nola Iketau, (31) Sioeli Iketau, (32) Mele Talanoa, (33) Sione Talanoa, (34) Heu'ifanga Kaumatule, (35) Veuki Kaumatule, (36) Filiuku Pututau, (37) Sione Fakavā, (38) 'Alisi Pahvlu Masiu, (39) Nola Lātū 'Otuafi, (40) Fe'ofa'aki 'Otuafi, (42) Stella Lavaki, (43) Fatai Tovo. (Courtesy V. Lynn Tyler)

Tongan sister missionaries in mid-1970s waiting to board the ferry. Women began serving missions in large numbers after 1964 when all Liahona graduates of the appropriate age were called on missions. (Courtesy Kākolosi Tuʻone Puloru)

Elder Ma'asi Mataele stands before his fale, *typical missionary living quarters, May 1973. (Courtesy Glen Pickeral)*

In Laie, Hawaii, James P. Christensen, right, Polynesian Cultural Center president and general manager, and his wife, Metta, welcome Manase Nau as the new chief of the Center's Tongan Village. The Christensens presided over the Tonga Mission from 1969 to 1972. (Courtesy Polynesian Cultural Center)

Mōleni Fonua (center, hands on gunwales) of Faleloa, Ha'apai, delivers Elder Talikavili Toluta'u (holding basket) to the "outer" islands. An expert sailor and an eloquent speaker, he has served as a branch and district president in Ha'apai and is currently president of Ha'apai Tonga Stake. He is also the elected Foa-Kauvai district officer. (Courtesy Kākolosi Tui'one Pulotu)

Zone leaders in Lulunga islands in Ha'apai, Elders Tēvita Likiliki (left) and Moeaki Fifita, about 1980. (Courtesy Kākolosi Tui'one Pulotu)

33

Tonga Toutai Pāletuʻa

"THESE I WILL MAKE MY RULERS"
Abraham 3:23

Tonga Toutai Pāletuʻa and his wife Luʻisa Hēhea Konaʻi have had a profound influence for good upon the Church in the last four decades. Equally gifted as a leader and a teacher, President Pāletuʻa was the first Tongan to hold an impressive number of callings: patriarch, stake president, mission president, regional representative of the Twelve, and temple president. He is currently president of the missionary training center at Liahona. President and Sister Pāletuʻa have two children and twenty grandchildren. The following highlights are taken from their oral history.

I grew up in Pangai, Haʻapai, the sixth child out of ten born to Viliami Pāletuʻa and Milika Mafi. Father was a Free Church of Tonga minister and Mother held the conferred title of teacher. The friends of my early youth were Sione Siolaʻā, Sitani Niupalau, Tūfui, Manase Tonga, and Viliami Pasi, to name a few.

In 1929 at age six, I started primary school. These were the days of no paper and pencil, only hard slates and hard chalk. The head teacher was Tēvita Fīnau Tafuna assisted by Kesaia Funaki and Fifita ʻOkoa. Other teachers were Sione Huʻakau, Malakai Lomu Tuiono, and Lupeni Fakahua.

Tēvita Fīnau Tafuna was a prominent Latter-day Saint in Haʻapai with a booming voice and personality. He preached about the Church even in school, so by the time I entered Tonga College in 1939 I had an understanding about the LDS Church, especially the need to be baptized by immersion.

At Tonga College I was bunk mates with Teiko Fonua, a Mormon boy from Houma. He and my friend, Vili Pasi from Pangai, would often take me to Church in Matavaimo'ui (Kolomotu'a) where I was inspired by the teaching of Sūlia Tu'iketei Pule and another sister named Hola Fangupō. Other Sundays I attended church in Houma with Teiko Fonua.

With the threat of war in the Pacific, Tonga College was moved inland to its present site at 'Atele. The curriculum was mainly in areas of agriculture. There was not much intellectual training at the time. Rather we learned how to plant and grow nearly everything, including peanuts. My teachers in the college were Matei Taumoepeau, Tēvita Kilisimasi 'Aho, and Nikolasi Fonua–to whom I became a house boy.

When I returned to Ha'apai in December of 1941, I had determined to join the Church. The baptismal ceremony was held at the wharf in the presence of many people, mostly curious onlookers. Taufa Tui'one performed the baptism. Kēlepi Ikatau'imoana Laa'iafi, the branch president, confirmed me a member.

Despite the catcalls and shouts of "Drown him!", I had a truly spiritual experience as I went down into the water. My soul was filled with joy and with the knowledge that I was following Christ into the strait and narrow gate. Joining the Church meant that I could no longer stay in the home of my birth and with parents I loved. I was no longer welcome there. So I moved in with my maternal uncle who was a member of the Church, Sione 'Iufoni Langi.

In 1943 I returned to Tonga College to continue my schooling. It was at this time I made acquaintance with Mosese Muti, the branch president in Ha'ateiho and a much loved leader in the Church. In 1944 I was selected to be a member of the first class of the newly established Teacher Training College with Reverend Cecil F. Gribble of the Wesleyan Church as the headmaster. My first teaching assignment after graduation was in the primary school in Faleloa, Ha'apai. The head teacher there at that time was Tupou 'Ahofaiva Malekamu, an active Latter-day Saint. 'Inoke Mataele was the resident Mormon missionary. Piliote and Uiketolu Kona'ī and Tēvita and Mele Mahu'inga were also part of the congregation.

The fledgling branch of the Church in Faleloa in 1945 was sustained largely by the faith and force of four women, Lupe Teutau, Taina Fonua, Pesi Hafoka, and Moala Makaafi.

I remember that Lātū Makaafi made a lot of fun of his wife and the other ladies for their faithfulness in the Church. In fact, he had heard about their weekly fasts and would often follow them secretly into the bush where they met to pray. Then he and Tupou Malekamu would retreat and wait for them to come back from their devotions, at which time he would jeer at them and say, "We know what you are up to. You're fasting for us to join the Church. We will never join, so spare yourselves the hunger."

Well, the first thing you know, Tupou Malekamu was baptized in the Church. It was a beautiful service at the little harbor in Faleloa. Lātū Makaafi was there announcing that no way was he ever going to follow his wife into the Church. To make his point, he raised his right hand and swore to heaven it would never happen. He then raised his left hand and made the same "solemn" gesture, while repeating his announcement. Then, as if this oath wasn't convincing enough, he sat down and lifted both his feet up (in ridicule, no doubt) and swore a covenant that he would never, never join the Church. Well, he was baptized a few days later and has become a significant leader in the Church.

The great people in the Church in Ha'apai in those days, whom I was privileged to work with and learn from, were Vili Fetu'u, the district president, and his wife Selu, Siaosi and Soko Palauni, Tupou 'Ahofaiva Malekamu , Kēlepi Saile, Sione and Mele Kongaika, Simote and 'Ofa Fehoko, Tēvita and Mele Lavaka, Taufa and Ane Tui'one, Kēlepi Laa'iafi, Tēvita Fīnau and 'Olotomu Tafuna, Ma'ake and Seini Mafi, Sione and Fine Filipe, to name a few.

I taught school in Pangai and Faleloa. In December of 1948, I accepted a two-month call to be a labor missionary in Liahona and soon became an expert at shoveling sand. My sand-loading partner, 'Aisake Likiliki, was also my preaching partner, as the building missionaries were expected to proselyte at night. It was also a time of joy and socializing with people my age and soon I had my eye on a beautiful young lady from Matahau, Lu'isa Hēhea Kona'ī. We were married in Matavaimo'ui just a few weeks before I was to leave for my new teaching assignment in the island of Matuku. After the ceremony, President Emile Dunn ordained me to the Melchizedek Priesthood and set me and Hēhea apart as missionaries in every village in Tonga where I might be assigned to teach.

My service as a primary school head teacher for the Tongan Department of Education allowed me to preach the full gospel of Jesus Christ in many villages and islands in the Kingdom of Tonga: Hā'ano, Mo'unga'one, Hōfoa, Fāhefa, Talafo'ou, Nomuka, Faleloa, and Fatai. In each of these places I was able to nourish friendships and plant the seeds of faith in hundreds of people. My school children I would encourage to attend Liahona. Many of these students eventually came to Liahona, were baptized, and have since become stalwarts in the Church.

In 1954 I became head teacher in the primary school in Fatai. Malakai Mokofisi, Pesi Bloomfield, and Lilieta Bloomfield were my fellow teachers. It was in Fatai that I accepted a mission call from President D'Monte Coombs and Principal Ermel Morton to teach at the Liahona College. It was to be a labor of love. When I notified the Department of Education of my intentions, the reply came: "If you leave your position and move to Liahona, that's the end of your service with the DOE."

I was pleased to go and be part of this exciting educational venture in Liahona. Thus began a long association with students and leaders, which has become so very precious to us today.

In 1959, I represented the Church and Tonga at the World Scout Jamboree in Melbourne, Australia. Back in Tonga I became the Scout leader for both the Church and the government, working together with the high noble, Kalaniuvalu. In Liahona, besides teaching, I became the chief correction officer (judge in Israel) for the students, as well as the supervisor of the milking crew which included Mosese Naeata, Hāmani Wolfgramm, and Sione T. Vīmahi—all later to be district and stake presidents and top administrators in their professions. In 1957 I became a counselor (along with Fakatou Vaitai) to Bishop LaVell Manwaring. A man of deep spirituality, Bishop Manwaring taught us much about true welfare principles, really caring for the unfortunate, the widows, and orphans.

As I think of the great men who groomed and prepared me for my many responsibilities in the Church, I realize my heavy debt to them all. From Sovea Kioa I learned skill and poise, both in public and in personal relations and especially in ceremonial settings with royalty and the nobility. From Misitana Vea I learned serenity, how a great leader should love his wife and family, and how to rebuke the Saints with love. From President Emile Dunn I learned the value of consistent hard work and straight talk to the members. He understood and loved Tongans as well as anyone.

I remember a conference in Vava'u, which I attended with mission president Patrick Dalton, when we were invited to the village of Koloa for a meal. A severe drought had scourged the land for a long time, and water was very scarce. As we sat down to the dinner, the branch president leaned over to President Dalton and said, "There is something I would like to ask the person who prays. We desperately need rain. There is no water in the land."

Of course this was long before community water pumps came into being. President Dalton looked searchingly around at the crowd. Finally he said, "Tonga Toutai, stand and pray for us, and ask the Lord to send rain."

The noonday sun was beating down hard on the congregation. I was given an order to bring rain, to open the doors of heaven and bless all of Vavaʻu, the land and the people. After my very fervent prayer, I sat down to the meal. Suddenly (and very obviously) clouds began to gather over the land, lightly shading us at first, then transforming themselves into a thick dark covering. The meal had not finished when the first drops of rain in many months began to fall. By the end of the meal everything was wet. When we went back to our meetings in Haʻalaufuli, the rain was still falling. This moisture was the greatest blessing of the conference. It was not just my faith, but the power of the command of authority for me to pray that made the difference.

My call in 1974 to be the first native Tongan mission president in Tonga was a shock to some people; but many forces, opportunities, and leaders had prepared me over the years for such a call. I had been a branch president, a district president, a patriarch, and a stake president. Beyond that I had really never been separated from active missionary teaching since I joined the Church.

From 1962 to 1968, I had preached regularly for the Church on national radio. . . .

The call to be mission president actually came by telephone from President Spencer W. Kimball, on May 5, 1974. The tender sweetness and tone of his voice will stay with me for as long as I live.

After the conference in which I was sustained, I accompanied Elder Thomas S. Monson and John H. Groberg, then regional representative of the Quorum of the Twelve, to the palace where I was introduced to the king as the first Tongan mission president for the Church. I sensed His Majesty's pleasure in the progress among his people that a Tongan should be called to such a position.

An all-Church fast throughout Tonga was called on May 22, 1974, for the purpose of uniting all members, particularly the priesthood leaders, behind the great missionary program of the Church and in building the kingdom of God here in Tonga. The Saints were to break their fast in their own wards and stakes.

At the appointed time, the priesthood leaders on Tongatapu met in Havelu to break our fast. After a hymn, Elder John Groberg led us in prayer. The Spirit descended mightily on that assembly as Elder Groberg struggled through his tears to call upon the Lord. He could barely utter the words of his prayer. No one could resist the overpowering presence which bound us together that day. I was as a "prophet in his own country," but I could sense now they all accepted and sustained me as the mission president.

One of the greatest moments in our missionary service occurred at a special openhouse in the mission home on April 27, 1975. By design the missionaries brought all of their golden contacts with the understanding that there would be a baptism at the conclusion of the program. The place was teeming with people, and we had to use every room. The openhouse extended almost until midnight, but the end result was forty-four baptisms in one night.

As a mission president (1974–77), I became obsessed with the idea of teaching the gospel from the Book of Mormon. Most Tongan members over the years have been uncomfortable teaching from a book not commonly accepted by other Christians. In fact, they have been afraid to use it or to even mention it in the presence of nonmembers. I believe during our tenure presiding in the mission, we were able to change that attitude among the Saints.

I organized and encouraged our missionaries to read the Book of Mormon with member families as well as nonmember families. The standing rule for every missionary was to be teaching every night in some home, if not with a nonmember family, then with members, in a family home evening setting. But they must read the Book of Mormon with the family and teach from the Book of Mormon.

I remember in one meeting I held with the missionary leaders, I instructed them to read the Book of Mormon again. I had done it in four nights of intense reading. They were to read it again and to make sure when they ever spoke in Church to preach from the Book of Mormon. Well, one of my zone leaders did not take my instructions seriously since his time as a missionary was concluded. When I released him at the scheduled time, somehow word mistakenly got out to the missionaries that his release was a disciplinary action for not reading and teaching from the Book of Mormon. From then on there wasn't one missionary who failed to study the Book of Mormon faithfully.

We launched a program called the "Year of the Lamanites and the Book of Mormon." Each zone was named after a Book of Mormon prophet. Songs were composed by the missionaries from each zone, featuring themes and testimonies from the Book of Mormon. These songs are still popular to this very day. The spirit of the program took over the whole mission so that not one missionary, whether in Vava'u, Ha'apai, Tongatapu, or 'Eua, failed to read and teach from the Book of Mormon.

The ideas for all of this came from my own love for this great book, for the great generation of Lamanites in the islands, and for Joseph Smith, as well as the great prophets of the Book of Mormon. I longed to possess the qualities of Moroni, Nephi, and Lehi in their work. While Amalickiah armed his people with weapons of war, Moroni armed his people with righteousness and truth, and thus overcame the enemy. That concept had taken root deep within me, and I longed for every one of our missionaries to be thus armed. I wanted our young missionaries to become as the great missionaries of the Book of Mormon who baptized thousands. And we did.

On April 2, 1980, I was invited by the First Presidency of the Church to gather with selected leaders from the South Pacific to their office in Salt Lake City for a special meeting. At that time, I was regional representative for Tonga and for Tahiti. Present were President Kimball, President Tanner, President Romney, and members of the Quorum of the Twelve Apostles. We sat in a circle and received instruction from Elder Boyd K. Packer, after which President Kimball made the historic announcement: "There will be more temples built in the South Pacific, in Tonga, Tahiti, Western Samoa, and Australia."

Silence! No one spoke. Warmth and joy filled our hearts and tears flowed freely, impossible to control. The regional representatives were asked to respond to the announcement. I stood representing Tonga and told the group how long the Tongan people had been praying and fasting for a temple. I reminded them how we had supported with prayers and money the temple to be built in Samoa. And now we will obey in every way their requests regarding the temple in Tonga, whatever the money or labor to be required of us. However great the work, we will do it! I also stood and spoke for Tahiti in the same terms.

After the meeting, Elder Packer came and took me in his arms and embraced me saying, "You're the best!", an expression I felt was directed to the Polynesian Saints everywhere.

34

Sifa and Sela Tāfisi

"THOUGH I WALK
THROUGH THE VALLEY OF THE
SHADOW OF DEATH"
Psalms 23:4

Sifa and Sela Tāfisi have been pillars of the Church in Kolomotu'a, Tongatapu, since 1960. Sifa has been branch president and is currently a counselor in the bishopric of Nuku'alofa Third Ward. Sela served many years as Relief Society president. The initial animosity ignited by their conversion and their Church activity was typical, though more extreme, of much public reaction to new converts. Bad feeling was usually very short-lived, however.

Sela

My conversion to the Church, my faith, and my testimony, came years after Sifa and I married. I grew up in Mu'a a good Wesleyan, attended the Wesleyan primary school, went a year to the Catholic College then spent four years in Queen Sālote College, from 1941 to 1944. Sifa and I were married in 1944 while he was still a soldier. We have had ten children; nine of them are still alive today.

Frankly, I hated the Mormon Church at that time, and I was more than happy to chase the missionaries away when they came visiting. They were absolutely forbidden to enter our home.

Then in 1959 I was afflicted with a disease which seemed certain to take my life. Many doctors treated me, including the Tongan bush doctors or medicine men. No one had any hope for me. They were just waiting for me to die. I had stopped eating entirely, and no longer had the use of my eyes. However, I still prayed earnestly in my heart to be healed and clung to a thread of hope. My thoughts were on my poor husband and our eight small children.

In my extremity one afternoon, my husband whispered in my ear that two Mormon missionaries, Muli Kinikini and Vili Fakataha, had come to call. I gave permission for them to enter but told Sifa to inform them I was gravely ill. When they asked about my illness, I told them I was dying, to which they replied:

"Sela, have faith that we can heal you by the gift and power of God, and we will bestow a blessing, and you will be healed immediately."

I yielded completely to the two missionaries, feeling no more resistance to them whatever. They laid hands on me and blessed me; and in that very instant, my sickness left me and I felt my strength return. When the missionaries rose to leave, I asked them to come back, to please not forget about me.

They came back many times and taught our family the gospel. On August 6, 1960, Sifa and I and six children were baptized.

Sifa

Our joining the Church was a happy but traumatic time for our family. It was difficult also for some people at our village. We experienced persecution from many sides but felt and still feel a fullness of joy in our membership in the Church.

The bitterness of our friends and acquaintances increased. One night Sela and I accompanied the missionaries to Hōfoa to preach. There was no branch of the Church in Hōfoa at that time. On our way, when we were crossing the swampy area in Sopu, we heard hissing sounds as if someone were letting others hidden to us know we were coming, but we continued our journey. I had a premonition that trouble was brewing for us.

The service was held in the home of Palei and Sisīlia. It was well attended, but the guests seemed a bit noisy, perhaps even rowdy, as if they were agitated about something. After the sermon, several men entered the home and began to ask questions of the missionaries. I noticed several former army buddies among them.

The question and answer session went badly, and there was a commotion. I stood up to make a show of leaving. Suddenly someone grabbed me from behind and pinned my arms to my side, holding me tight. In rushed several men and started hitting me. I yelled at Sela to grab the gas lantern and hold it aloft. I squirmed and ducked but several punches landed solidly, one squarely on my nose, which spewed blood everywhere.

After a moment, the assailants backed off; and I recognized not only my former army buddies but also members of my extended family. My wife and the missionaries stood at my side, and a young boy named Taufu'i, a student at Liahona, clung to me crying. I assured him that I was just fine. At the same time I addressed all the people present saying:

"If there is anyone else who would like to take a punch at me, please come forward at this time. I'll not resist nor retaliate. But know this: My blood spilt here tonight is a testimony that the Church will be established in Hōfoa. Christ's blood was shed on the cross, Joseph Smith's blood poured out from a fatal gunshot wound, and now you have the blood of Sifa Tāfisi as a third testimony of the truth of this Church."

Shortly after this incident, we took several members of the Church and built a Tongan hut in Hōfoa, the first meeting place for the few members in that village. [The branch was established under the direction of President Vernon Coombs the following year, with Lolohea Folau as the first branch president.]

By now the people in our section of Kolomotu'a were becoming alarmed at the presence of the Church and the vigor of our missionary work. When we baptized a young boy named Maea and brought him to church meetings, they became openly angry. Our family was hated, I most of all.

Sela

The pressure from this animosity made us all a little jumpy. It seemed we had no more friends. We talked a lot about the possibilities of what else might happen to us.

One night in February of 1961, I dreamed a strange dream, arising probably from our fears about the threats from people of the village. In the dream, I saw massive waves sweeping to engulf our little house. To my shock it was not ocean water but blood.

My heart sank as I witnessed our home disappear under these waves of blood. The thought occurred to me: "We've joined the wrong Church. We are going to be killed."

But then when I looked again, our hut was still intact, being elevated above the flood by four corner posts. When I looked even closer, they were not wooden posts at all holding up our home, but four men, the very four missionaries who had taught us the gospel, Muli Kinikini, Vili Fakataha, Eric Shumway, and Samu Vehikite.

When I awoke and related the dream to Sifa, he simply said, "Don't worry. If the blood represents some scheme to murder us, the holy priesthood of God will save us."

Two weeks later, on the second Sunday, I think, of March 1961 an attempt was made to take our lives.

Sifa

On that Sunday evening about nine o'clock, just after we got home from Church in Latai, our oldest daughter told us our dogs had been barking furiously for a long time as if someone had come into the yard. The children were nervous and frightened especially when Viliami, our number three child, told me he had actually overheard two men talking at the beach across the road about blowing the Tāfisi family to bits.

I assured them there was nothing to worry about, that the Lord would protect those who believed and were baptized in his Church. At that very instant, our dogs began to bark wildly again and a crude home-made bomb—two sticks of dynamite packed into a large cocoa tin—fell into our doorway.

Acting reflexively, I pushed Sela and my oldest daughter to the floor just as the bomb exploded. It reduced the door to dust and shattered the glass bottles Sela used to decorate the front of our home. The force of the blast and the flying glass passed just over our heads as we lay on the floor, ripping to shreds the clothes hanging on the wall.

As we struggled to recover from the shock and the smoke, a second bomb was thrown into the room. Fortunately, I had the presence of mind to grab it and throw it back out the door before it exploded.

The second explosion rocked all of Nuku'alofa, but by now I was out of the house and on the trail of the two fleeing culprits. Following them in the dark was easy because one of the men still carried the burning piece of tapa cloth with which they had lighted the fuses.

I pursued them deliberately from a distance until finally the burning tapa fragment fell to the earth and the men disappeared. It was still aglow when I picked it up.

Interestingly the tapa fragment had been cut from the end of a larger piece of tapa with the name of its maker still visible on the unburned portion. As it turned out, Sēla's brother was the would-be assassin.

I took this piece of evidence and returned home, feeling calm and thankful. We didn't have to call the police. They came to us, and so did everyone else. I think the people were filled with awe that such a powerful blast had not hurt any one of us. One woman by the name of Sātua was so moved by this miracle she said she knew the Church was true. In fact, we baptized her shortly afterward.

The two persons were arrested that night and charged with attempted murder. The young boy served one year, the man seven years in prison. Upon his release, he came back to the community where to this day we greet each other in friendship. There is no outward animosity between us, and we never bring up the past.

The Church in Kolomotu'a has grown since that time from a little Sunday School held in our hut to three wards and hundreds of Saints. We cherish our testimony and our membership in the only true and living Church on the face of the earth. The dynamite incident only increased our courage and magnified our faith.

35

Vaikalafi Lutui and Mele Tafuna Lutui

"OUT OF OUR WILDERNESS"

Vaikalafi and Mele Tafuna Lutui grew mightily in the gospel as a result of the Church labor missionary program. As a painter, Vaikalafi helped build chapels and schools in Tonga, Hawaii, and New Zealand. He has been a bishop, stake president, temple sealer, and regional representative of the Quorum of the Twelve. The following account provides another glimpse into what it meant to be a labor missionary and the multiple blessings this program was in the lives of the missionaries.

Mele

I was number five in a family of twelve children born to Fehoko Vāvasa Tafuna and 'Ilaise Ma'ukavaongo from 'Uiha, Ha'apai. Mother and Father were converted to The Church of Jesus Christ of Latter-day Saints in 1940 and, like many stalwart new converts, were soon deeply committed to the work of the Church. The family moved to Veitongo, Tongatapu, so they could be close to the older children attending the Church's Makeke College. In 1947 when the school was moved to Liahona, Father was appointed to take care of the Makeke property. He also became a branch president.

In 1950 the family was called on a mission to 'Eua where Dad labored among the immigrants from Niuafo'ou (Tin Can Island) and served as branch president in Tongamama'o. It was on this mission to a strange island that I felt the struggle and experienced the hardships of missionary life. Of course, as the oldest child at home, I bore much of the burden of running the household and caring for the younger children. Day and night, Father and Mother were gone on their missionary assignments and I was stuck at home.

I complained bitterly to my parents that my life was not going anywhere and begged them to let me attend school at Liahona. Their reply was simply, "Mele, please be comforted. Don't fret. Know that we are on the Lord's errand and are doing his work."

But it got no better for me. In 1952 Dad was called to be branch president in Felemea, and then in 'Uiha in 1954. He and Mom both were frequently off-island "doing the Lord's work." I pleaded again and again with them to let me go to school, to send me to Liahona. I hated being the homebody, the family servant confined to our little island. Their response was the same. "Mele, this is the Lord's work. We need you to watch over the little ones while we are gone."

Besides my responsibilities at home, I was asked to do the laundry of the proselyting missionaries in our island twice a week. I enjoyed this, but I suffered anguish again whenever the Liahona students from our village came home for vacation. Seeing them caused me to hide my face in shame because I was now over twenty without any schooling beyond primary school. I felt so foolish and stupid around them.

One day Elder John H. Groberg came to 'Uiha to confer with my father. Two missionaries on Lifuka were stricken with typhoid fever and needed someone to care for them full-time at the hospital. [Families and relatives were required in those days to be physically present at the hospital to feed and care for their sick.] I immediately volunteered to get away from home and was overjoyed that both Dad and Mom were happy to let me go perform this service.

For six months I watched over these two missionaries, lying in beds next to each other, until they were completely well. Returning to 'Uiha in November of 1955, I resumed my former work of caring for the family. In January of 1956, however, I received an invitation from Elder Groberg, then supervising elder in Ha'apai, to attend Liahona High School as a special student. I'll never forget his words to me: "Mele, there is an excellent education program at Liahona in cooking, sewing, English, and religion. If you want to go, I'll make arrangements for you."

No one can imagine my joy. Being twenty-two years old, I had long given up any thoughts of an education. My parents also softened, giving their blessing; two weeks later, I was on the boat to Tongatapu. The doors to my future were miraculously opened.

I studied in Liahona for two years and worked in the cafeteria to support my little sister in school. Most importantly, I met a wonderful priesthood holder, a labor missionary who asked me to marry him. Vaikalafi Lutui was released from his mission June 30, 1959, and we were married by Sovea Kioa, the Hihifo District President, on July 2, 1959.

At the wedding party, the mission president, Vernon Coombs, stood to address all the guests. He said, "Last Tuesday I released the groom from his labor mission. Today I now call him on another labor mission together with his bride. His assignment will be with the painting crew to paint all of our chapels in Tonga."

Well, we commenced that mission the following day; and for the next five months, Vaikalafi worked on the chapels in Foʻui, Fāhefa, Houma, Veitongo, Nakolo, and Haʻatuʻa, ʻEua. What a delight to return to ʻEua where my father and mother had served as missionaries with us children. Vaikalafi painted the very wooden chapel in Tongamamaʻo where my family and I had worshipped years before.

In November we were released to go home. Vaikalafi had received another call to go to Hawaii to work on the Church College of Hawaii. I was pregnant with our first child. Unfortunately I could not accompany him as did the wives of other labor missionaries, because there was evidence in my blood of filaria. So I waited a full eighteen months for him to return.

Vaikalafi

I was one of the thirty-one Tongan labor missionaries called to Hawaii in 1961 as part of the building program of the Church. Illness plagued me during my mission in Hawaii, causing me to spend many days in the hospital at Kahuku and finally requiring stomach surgery.

My main problem, though, was being away from Mele so long. When it became obvious that she would not be able to join me in Hawaii, the brethren sent me back to Tonga, only to call me again to go to New Zealand on another labor mission. That was a joy to me, especially when I discovered I could take Mele and our little boy Samisoni with us. For three years I served in the Church building program in New Zealand. Each year we were there we gave birth to a new child. Edith, Whitikei, and Mele Kafoʻatu were all born in Hamilton, New Zealand.

The frequency and the stress of having children so fast caused us to consider limiting the number of our children. We even received from the doctor the paraphernalia to keep Mele from ever bearing children again. At first we were delighted with the idea of a small manageable family; but when we got back to Tonga, doubts began to swarm in our minds. And it soon became clear to us that there were other children the Lord meant to send us. Together we took all the medicines, pills, and devices, dug a hole, and dumped them in. The Lord gave us six more beautiful children.

Mele

Our last child caused a lot of anxiety for us because I was deathly sick during the pregnancy. In the first month, it was as if I had polio. By the third month three different doctors feared for my life and encouraged me to terminate the pregnancy. "Mele," they said, "the only way to be sure your own life is saved is to remove the baby now. Chances of the baby surviving are slim; and even if it comes to term, it will likely be retarded."

Vaikalafi

Despite Mele's suffering and extreme weakness (as well as the advice of the doctors), we decided together not to abort our baby. We gathered our other children around us and asked them to fast and pray for their mother and the baby. Mele also received a priesthood blessing and was promised she would live and the baby would be healthy.

One of the blessings during this difficult pregnancy was that Mele read faithfully in the Book of Mormon. This book became her companion, and she clung to the prophet Moroni's words, "For if there be no faith among the children of men God can do no miracle among them; wherefore, he showed not himself until after their faith" (Ether 12:12).

The doctors were still very skeptical about the birth and kept telling us that if the baby lived it would likely be seriously damaged mentally. The signs were not good. So you can imagine our joy when our little girl was born alive. She was weak at first but grew to health. She was our tenth child. We were ready to give her back as our tithing to the Lord. But God did not take her; and as you all can see, she is now a bright, lively student at Liahona High School.

When this gift child was delivered, I asked my wife: "Mele, what will the name of our daughter be?"

Mele picked up the Book of Mormon, turned to 1 Nephi 16:10–14 and read out loud the account of Lehi's discovery of the Liahona, that divine compass which worked according to the faith of the user. After traveling four more grueling days in the wilderness Lehi's party came to a beautiful, fertile place which he named Shazer. There they rested from their journey and restored their provisions.

"We shall call the baby Shazer (Seisela)" Mele declared. "I love the name, because it will remind us that no matter what wilderness journey we endure in life God will provide an oasis of hope and love, just as this miracle child is to us."

One year after Shazer was born, we took her to the doctors who had feared so much for Mele's life. They were good men and members of another faith.

"This is the child you suggested should be aborted," Mele said.

"Yes, we know," one of them replied. "Was the special healing ordinance in your Church administered to this child?"

We told them of our family's fasting and the many priesthood blessings.

Mele

When I consider my obscure upbringing and lack of education, I realize God will open doors for his children. I was not taught in the ways or the language of the world, but I have been blessed to get by sufficiently because of the callings which have come to my husband. I know that all true education begins at home. My testimony of the gospel and the Church is deep and strong. God lives and loves us no matter how smart, educated, or isolated we might be. He will bring us out of our wilderness.

36

Tonga Pōteki Mālohifoʻou & ʻAna Toki Mālohifoʻou

"HE AROSE, AND REBUKED THE WINDS"
Matthew 8:26

Tonga Pōteki Mālohifoʻou and ʻAna Toki Mālohifoʻou are known for their kindness and devotion to the Lord's work. ʻAna has served faithfully in every Church auxiliary. Tonga has twice been both a branch president and a proselyting missionary. He is currently an ordinance worker and sealer in the Salt Lake Temple. This account has been frequently told by others, but here Tonga and ʻAna tell it themselves. Those who have had any experience with tropical hurricanes will recognize the significance of their experience.

Tonga

When I first met ʻAna, I asked her to marry me. I smoked and drank at the time and knew nothing about things religious or what it meant to go to church. ʻAna told me, "I like you but I don't love you, because we are not of the same faith. You would forsake instantly the church you belong to if a threat were made on your life. As for me, nothing could make me deny my church. If someone were to command me to leave it, I would say, 'Never! Better that I should die first!'"

When I married ʻAna and joined the Church, I was twenty-five years old. I came to consider her as a mother as well as a wife. She taught me how to pray, at mealtime and in family prayer. She insisted I be worthy to receive the Melchizedek Priesthood. Indeed, that became my life's principal goal, to have the power and the privilege to bless others in their affliction.

Long before the hurricane of 1961, I had come to honor and respect the holy Melchizedek Priesthood I held and had used it in blessings and in the healing the sick. 'Ana and I were not necessarily holy people, but the authority of the priesthood and the name of Jesus Christ became the source of great power to save us and others from the hardships of this world.

'Ana

When the hurricane struck Vava'u on March 16, 1961, our little wooden frame home became a haven for many people whose houses had already been destroyed. Our youngest child, Peni, clung to me in fear and wouldn't let me go. Looking into my face he asked me if this were the last day of the world. I remember holding him and assuring him this wasn't the end of the world, but if we should die all would be well for us. Tonga heard his little boy's questions and saw my tears.

Stepping up onto the bed in our room and reaching up toward the rafters, he bestowed a blessing upon the house. The roof had been shaking terribly, bouncing up and down as if the storm would blow it off. After the blessing, although the wind was still violent outside, the roof settled down in its right position.

Tonga

The storm descended in force at break of day. Just after a most earnest family prayer for divine help, we heard cries from outside: "Tonga, 'Ana, save us!" Opening the door, we ushered in several women and their little children. Their homes were destroyed, and they had no place to go.

The wind continued to rage with ever-increasing fury. Its velocity eventually exceeded 115 miles per hour. Some estimates ran as high as 150 miles per hour. From our living room window, we witnessed widespread destruction—houses and trees torn up and flung across the face of the land. One frame home was lifted right off its foundation and disintegrated in the air. Parts of a house from another village landed on our property. The new Tonga Free Church chapel across the road from us also crumbled into a heap before our eyes. Fortunately no one was hurt.

By nightfall, there was still no let up. We had heard that the Wesleyan chapel in Neiafu had collapsed, killing a man named Viliami

Tatafu. And by now the roof and the walls of our own fragile house were groaning and heaving in a terrifying manner. 'Ana touched me and said, "Tonga, it is clear we are in for real hardship tonight. Perhaps our home will be torn apart in the storm. What is your plan for us?"

We had already offered our evening prayer, so I tried to comfort her again by reminding her the Lord would not forsake us. But as I thought about our circumstances and the destruction around us, a strange idea came to my mind: "If I can heal the sick with a priesthood blessing, why can't I bless this house and stop the wind from destroying it?"

'Ana was cuddling our little son Peni, who kept asking if this were the last day of the world. "No, Peni," we replied, "not until the gospel is preached to the world will we be close to the final day."

At that very moment there was a loud banging on the roof as if the roofing tin would be torn off. I stood on the bed, reached upward toward the roof, and said: "By virtue of the holy Melchizedek Priesthood vested in me and in the name of Jesus Christ, I command this roof to stay exactly where you are! Do not move even one degree. Also to the roof over the kitchen, to every piece of lumber and sheet of tin in this house and to the unfallen trees outside in the yard, I command you to stand solidly where you are!"

I pleaded with the Lord to honor my words, answer our prayers, and save us. From that very moment on, the house quit shaking and the roof stopped trembling. There was perfect calm throughout the night. The next morning the destruction was unbelievable across the island, as if a giant bulldozer had ripped and torn the landscape.

'Ana

Later the next morning, Elder Shumway and Vili Pele Folau made it to our home. They were shocked to see it still intact and asked Tonga why he would foolishly remain in our little house. We could have been killed. Tonga tried to explain to them that if we had run for shelter elsewhere our house *would* have been destroyed.

The two missionaries then asked Tonga to go to the chapel to supervise the hundreds of people from many churches who had taken refuge there. As for me, I remained in our house with the other people and our children until the hurricane was over.

37

Sela Feinga

"THROW THE BABY!"

Hāʻunga and Sela Feinga were among the first couple missionaries called to the western islands of the Haʻapai Group. Despite their inexperience and youth, they willingly assumed the burden and the expense of the most compelling enterprise in the Church in Tonga—missionary work, ngāue fakafaifekau. The following is condensed from an account by Sela, now living in Laie, Hawaii. Hāʻunga passed away in 1986.

The idea of serving a mission for the Church with my husband and five-month-old daughter was overwhelming to me. To be assigned to labor on the remote island of Fotuhaʻa filled me with terror. I was relatively new at the time both to the Church and to motherhood; but like so many others, when the call came from the mission president, July 11, 1965, we sold everything we had (our little Tongan house and all our farm produce brought us a total of thirty-six Tongan dollars) and gathered for pre-service training at Vainī on Tongatapu.

When the mission president announced to our group that the Hāʻunga Feinga family was assigned to Fotuhaʻa, they all turned to look at us and chuckle, which only increased my fears. I took comfort, however, in the setting-apart blessing by the mission presidency. They promised us that, despite severe hardships, the Lord would strengthen and preserve us as we served him faithfully. That promise and subsequent blessings still live in our hearts to this day.

Because of bad weather and rough seas, it took many weeks to get to Fotuhaʻa. As we waited on the island of Haʻafeva for good weather, we learned more about why Fotuhaʻa is so talked about. The inhabitants are good people, but one puts one's life at risk to even get there. There is no safe approach to the island, no secure anchorage, only deep ocean pounding on rocky cliffs. The seas around the island are almost always rough, making it impossible to moor a boat for unloading. The procedure is to transfer from the motor launch to an outrigger. The person manning the outrigger paddles to a rocky ledge jutting out into deep water, where citizens of the island stand to catch the goods that are heaved from the canoe. Passengers who can't swim simply jump toward their outstretched hands.

Such landings can be treacherous indeed, since their execution requires perfect timing with the waves which rise to the level of the rock landing and fall ten to fifteen feet below it. The trick is to select the right wave so the canoe can get as close to the rock landing as possible without crashing into it or being sucked under it.

Hearing the lore of this island frightened me beyond anything I had felt before, since I had little experience as a sailor and could not swim. To make matters worse, just three days before we were to sail, our baby daughter came down with a 105 degree fever. I too became ill, partly no doubt out of terror at what was ahead of us. The missionary couple in Haʻafeva insisted that our trip be postponed for the baby's sake, but Hāʻunga said that we would go together. He gave the baby a blessing and declared she would be just fine.

On the morning of our departure, the fever was still high. Little pustules began to appear all over her body from head to toe. She had measles. No amount of pleading, however, would change my husband's mind, even when the "captain" of our little boat suggested that the baby and I stay in Haʻafeva until we were well.

I wrapped our little one in a blanket and boarded the small open boat that would take us to Fotuhaʻa. There was no shelter. A light drizzle accompanied us all the way. As we approached the island from a distance, I looked longingly for houses and trees or a friendly sandy beach. Only formidable cliffs and rocky coasts loomed in front of us. We circled the island twice. Apparently our captain wanted to see if another landing spot was better than the usual one. The waves around us were huge.

As we contemplated the landing point, I think for the first time I sensed fear in my husband. A few of the island citizens had already begun to congregate on the rocky ledge, waiting to receive us and our goods.

When the canoe came out to get us, we got into it without incident. It was a small outrigger paddled by a young schoolteacher on the island. When we got close to the rock, he said, "We will count the waves. When one big enough comes in to lift us up even with the top of the ledge, you must jump on to the rock or throw your goods to people standing there. They will give the orders at the precise moment."

The rain continued to fall. Hāʻunga held our sick baby, still wrapped in her blanket. I was nearly numb with fear. As we got closer to the treacherous landing, the schoolteacher said to my husband, "Prepare the baby! They will give the orders for her first."

The order came to my husband almost instantly from the man on the ledge. "Hey, you, sir, holding the baby. Take off the blanket and remove all its clothes."

"How can that be?" I cried. "The baby is sick with measles. You should not take off her clothes."

Our paddler spoke sternly to Hāʻunga, "You must take off everything, because you are going to have to throw the baby ashore. You can't risk the man dropping it on the rocks or in the ocean because of the blanket or any loose covering."

The command from the ledge came again. "Hurry up. Remove the baby's clothes entirely." But my poor husband simply could not do it. Perhaps by now he was as terrified as I.

Instantly the young schoolteacher reached for Hāʻunga and wrenched the baby from his arms. In a second he had removed every speck of her clothing except her little diaper. The voice from the ledge yelled again. "OK, when I say *throw*, then throw the baby. I'll tell you which is the right wave."

In rushed a wave and lifted the canoe up, but not quite high enough. Down we went out of sight as the ocean retreated. Up again we came on the back of another wave. Not high enough still. Down again out of sight. As we rose on the next wave, I heard the command, "Throw the baby." I screamed, then held my breath. I could not bear to see it. The next words were my husband's, "Worry no more. The baby is safe ashore."

I had no time to be grateful. "You are next, woman," shouted the man on the ledge.

How I was to be transported ashore I had no idea, since I couldn't be thrown. "You will jump at the exact moment I tell you," he instructed.

By now I was hysterical with fear. Four times the "right" wave came, with the school teacher expertly maneuvering the canoe close to the ledge and the man commanding me to jump. I could not do it. I simply clung to my husband trembling. Finally, in anger the man said, "Woman, do you want to see your baby again or not? Now when I tell you to jump, jump with all your strength."

For a moment then I seemed to have my right mind. I prayed again and said, "Oh Lord, please show thy love and help me now for my poor baby's sake."

"One, two, three, jump!" shouted the man. With my eyes closed, I jumped as best I could. My next sensation was that of being pulled up onto the ledge. From here many hands pushed and pulled and guided me up the steep path to the top where I fell to the ground, drained of energy. Someone put a sweet green coconut in my hands to drink. Another came up and said, "Don't worry. Your baby is fine. Our young women are taking care of her."

That was the beginning of an exciting mission full of hardship and joy. The Lord did not only strengthen us as we served, but our fears he dispelled and our weaknesses he made into strengths. We have taught our children the power of faith and the glory of the Lord's work. Our testimony of the gospel and the Church is precious and sacred to us.

38

Saia Paongo

"TAKE NO THOUGHT FOR YOUR LIFE"
Matthew 6:25

Saia Paongo, an administrator at Liahona High School, is first counselor in the stake presidency of Nuku'alofa South Stake. President Paongo's story illustrates what thousands of young local Tongan missionaries have experienced when they are stationed in remote and sometimes primitive settings. Humility, obedience, and hard work are rewarded by innumerable evidences that a caring Heavenly Father watches over them.

In August 1964 I was in charge of the missionaries in the remote island of Niuatoputapu, living in Falehau with my companion Elder Saia Fonua. There were six of us missionaries on the island, and we were not always sure where our next meal was coming from.

Our plan this particular day was to all come to Falehau fasting, visit and preach in the homes in Falehau, then break our fast in the afternoon at five. We worked diligently that day; but unfortunately there was no food to be had when we finished our visits. The mother in the family we stayed with was pregnant and sick; the father had been gone all day.

The idea of breaking a fast without a morsel of food for six hungry missionaries seemed a bit depressing to us. But according to plan, we met back at our little missionary hut and, after scripture study, knelt in prayer and broke our fast.

As we came out of the hut, I felt an impression, as if someone said to me, "Take your missionaries to the beach on the back side of the island" ("*Mou ō ki liku*"). I told my companion to bring a fishing spear and we all headed for the rocky coast of Niuatoputapu.

Unfortunately, when we got there we discovered the ocean was already at full tide. There was no way we were going to do any spear fishing on the reef. Disappointed, we sat down to rest and chat, except for Elder Fonua who wandered off along the beach, maybe fifty yards from the rest of us.

Suddenly Elder Fonua yelled for us to come and look. We scrambled over to him, and there we saw a wonderful sight—a large, fat *menenga*, or deep ocean parrot fish, which had almost beached itself. Incredibly it had swum right up to the sand. Its dorsal fin and back were showing above the water. I judged the fish to be nearly three feet long and a foot thick.

We stared at it for a long time. The fish just lay there looking back at us, as if it were a willing sacrifice to feed the missionaries. It made no effort to swim away. Finally, Elder Fonua ran back and got the spear, and, while we watched, walked right up to the fish and speared it. It died with hardly a struggle and made a wonderful feast for us.

Now you can make of this story what you want, but I know that this fish was prepared for us, that Heavenly Father loves hungry young missionaries even in tiny remote islands, that he honors those who serve him, and takes care of those who are close to him in fasting and prayer.

39

Samuela 'Iloa

"AND HATH COMPASSION ON THEE"
Mark 5:19

Samuela and Silivia 'Iloa live in Vainī, Tongatapu, where Samuela serves as president of the Nuku'alofa Vainī Stake. Son of Church stalwarts Sione Fūnaki 'Iloa and Sela 'Iloa, President 'Iloa has served as a proselyting missionary twice and as a bishop, in addition to his present calling. He is also director of the Church welfare farm in Tonga.

Despite some occasional animosities among the various denominations toward The Church of Jesus Christ of Latter-day Saints, I found out as a missionary that most people are very kind to our missionaries. In 1964 I received my first mission call to serve in Lulunga, with Tōfua 'Iongi as my companion. There were six of us (three companionships) set apart to serve in 'O'ua, Ha'afeva, and Tungua. No members of the Church lived on these islands at that time. The instructions from the mission president were for each companionship to go to an island, find our own lodging as best we could, and preach the gospel from home to home.

We arrived as complete strangers in Ha'afeva but were instantly befriended by a sweet elderly lady named Soana, mother of Sione Tu'alau Lātū, who invited us to stay with her. Before long we were accepted as citizens of the community, beloved of the chief (*matāpule*) Havealeta, and invited to participate in the activities of the village. During our stay in Ha'afeva, we helped establish the first branch of the Church in the Lulunga District. The first missionary couple to serve as branch president were Sēmisi Kioa and his wife, Sālote, from 'Uiha.

We were transferred the following year to another island known for the friendliness of its people, people who were always happy to feed the missionaries as long as we did not bring up the subject of the gospel. We made the mistake one day of giving a missionary discussion to a lady whose husband was away. He arrived back from the bush during our visit and became very upset at us. He showed his anger by repeatedly striking the washtub by the side of the house with his bush knife. Then rushing into the house, he grabbed us both by the throats and unceremoniously threw us out.

We were embarrassed and frightened by this behavior, but the villagers were even more upset that we would be treated thus. There was an immediate compassion towards us that didn't exist before. The result was that nearly every home in the island invited us in and asked us to share our message with them. We took it as the Lord's way of preparing an opportunity for us to preach the gospel. . . .

Shortly after our marriage, Sister 'Iloa and I were called as missionaries to preside over the branch of the Church in Longomapu, Vava'u. We arrived at the village during a time of food shortage which had a severe effect on the members of the tiny branch there. Of course, since we were new to the area, we did not have our own garden to depend on. Members in Neiafu had raised our hopes about a reportedly productive banana plantation between Longomapu and Tu'anuku, which would serve us for a while. Disappointingly, there were no bananas fit for eating in that stand of banana trees.

One windy and rainy morning, my wife announced to me: "There is absolutely no food at all in the house, and I don't have the slightest idea where we are going to get any."

Our situation seemed desperate! My only answer to my wife was that the Lord would feed us that day. We knelt down together in prayer and asked Heavenly Father to send us food or let us know what we should do. Only moments after our prayer, we heard the hoofbeats of a horse coming down the path to our hut. Opening the door, we saw a rider balancing a large burlap sack stuffed full of taro in front of him. "Here is food for you," he called out.

We barely had time to thank him before he departed. It was several weeks later that we discovered he was a prominent member of the Wesleyan congregation in Longomapu. We will always be grateful that his kindness was an answer to our prayers. Hundreds of Mormon missionaries over the years have been blessed by the Lord through the generosity of people of other faiths.

40

Irene Clare Holmes Tukuafu

"AND SENT HIS SERVANT"
Luke 14:17

Irene Clare Holmes Tukuafu and her husband Tomasi Tukuafu from Hōfoa, Tonga, are the parents of fourteen children. Irene and Tomasi met as students at Church College of Hawaii and were married in the Hawaii Temple, July 30, 1964. A native of California, Irene was one of the first Caucasian wives to accompany her husband back to Tonga to teach for the Church schools there and had the experience that she wrote for inclusion in this volume. Lacking knowledge of the language and culture of Tonga, she looked to the Lord for comfort and guidance. The Tukuafu family now live in Green Valley on Oahu in Hawaii.

We were hired to teach in Tonga for the Church School on Lifuka, Haʻapai, Tonga, and moved there in August 1967.

On the night of September 27, 1967, I was seated in our little house in Pangai, writing in my journal, when suddenly the door flew open and two of my husband's fishing companions (Pōsesi Talanoa and Kisione Taukolo) came in, supporting my poor stricken husband. He could hardly stand. They had been out spear-fishing on the reef. Tomasi had speared a beautiful, but lethal butterfly cod (*houhau*) and had strung it on his tow line. He said he wanted to bring it home to show me because it was so beautiful.

Unfortunately, his line was too short; and as he swam, his leg brushed against the poisonous spines of this deadly fish. Immediately Tomasi felt the pulsating fire go up his leg. He pulled off his T-shirt and made a tourniquet to stop the poison from spreading throughout his body. He called his companions, and they swam ashore and walked the two miles back to our village. Pōsesi and Kisione gave Tomasi a priesthood blessing and returned to their homes.

All I knew to do was to put coconut oil and hot water on the wound, since this is what my home medical book prescribed for a black widow spider bite. We went to sleep about 12:00 midnight, but soon Tomasi woke up in terrible pain and delirium. He told me to find Feleti, a near neighbor who had one of the few vehicles on this island, a rambling old truck. Feleti would take him to the Pangai hospital.

I picked up Tomasi's flashlight and stepped out of our back door into total darkness. There was no electricity on the island at that time. Even the kerosene lamps were out in the few homes that had them. The instant I began walking down the path from our home, a pack of dogs began to bark and howl. I was pregnant, terrified of dogs, and totally unable to speak Tongan. Yet I must get help; my husband was deathly ill.

I turned off the flashlight and dropped to my knees in tearful prayer for guidance. Arising from my prayer, I began walking in the hoped-for direction of Feleti's house. All was pitch black. Then to my surprise a calm, reassuring voice spoke out of the darkness and asked in perfect English, "May I help you?"

I shone my flashlight into the face of a man I had never seen before. He said his name was 'Anitoni and repeated his offer to help. I tearfully told him my story. 'Anitoni walked with me to several houses, but we had no luck in finding Feleti. I asked him to use Tomasi's bike and flashlight to find Feleti at whatever kava party he might be engaged.

Feleti finally came and rushed Tomasi to the hospital about a mile away. The medical practitioner said that if Tomasi's heart had not been strong, he would have died. Fortunately, the appropriate antidote was available at the hospital.

Tomasi was unable to walk for two weeks. He lost his equilibrium completely and his leg swelled to a grotesque size. Nevertheless he finally recovered.

When 'Anitoni returned the bike, I asked him what brought him to Ha'apai. He lived mostly on Tongatapu and only came to Pangai once in three or four years. He didn't know exactly why he was still there and was returning to Nuku'alofa the following day.

Truly, I am thankful for this heaven-sent "coincidence," this "chance" encounter in Pangai with a man from Nuku'alofa, who just happened to be walking by our house at midnight and who spoke fluent English and who just happened to hear my desperate prayer for help. I know God sends people into our lives as immediate answers to prayer.

41

Tonu Naeata

"FLED FROM THE PRESENCE OF THE LORD"
Jonah 1:10

Tonu Naeata has been a bishop, stake high councilor, and is now a member of Neiafu North Stake presidency. A graduate of BYU–Hawaii, he is presently director of Physical Plant at Sainehā High School in Neiafu, Vavaʻu. Brother Naeata is typical of the many bright Latter-day Saints who chose after their university study to come back to their homeland and serve their people. He and his wife, Lenisī Vea Naeata, have eleven children.

I was born while my father and mother were serving as labor missionaries to build Liahona High School in 1951. We were very poor in material things but immensely rich in the things that matter.

Our home was always full of cheer, the children being taught to honor our father for his many Church assignments, heating water for his bath and preparing his clothes for his visits to the various branches.

As for me, I owe all my joy to the gospel and to leaders who encouraged and lifted me when I could have easily drifted and become a nothing.

One such time was just before my final term at Liahona High School in 1968. I had earned a part of my school expenses but was notified along with the other children that I must come back to school with the money my parents had promised as their portion for my fees.

Well, my parents were in New Zealand at the time, getting medical help for Mom. There was simply no money for us. Embarrassed to ask for help or explain our circumstances to the principal, Albert

Pope, I simply stayed home in Vava'u, thinking it was the end of my education.

When Brother Pope saw I had not come back to school, he wrote and promised me a job to pay for my schooling if I would return. I have often thought what might have happened to my life if this conscientious principal had not extended himself to contact me. I believe he rescued me from a life of unemployment or subsistence farming.

By disposition I was quiet and backward, fearful of being accused of putting on airs or aspiring to leadership positions. I was a back-row person who stayed close to the shadows. But my great desire to achieve competence in my chosen field (industrial education and technology) and the need for local Tongan leadership in the Church schools led me into positions of authority much faster than I was ready. I graduated from Liahona High School in 1970 and in 1972 was appointed teacher in the industrial education section of the school.

In 1974 I was able to enter BYU–Hawaii. By this time I was married with two small children. My wife's family had long before immigrated to America and were anxious to file our papers for permanent residency and eventual citizenship. My resistance to this "invitation to prosperity" was rooted in my love for Tonga, in a driving sense of duty toward the Church, and a sense of obligation for Brother Pope's extraordinary kindness to me. Our sojourn at BYU–Hawaii was perhaps typical of many married Polynesian students. We were already used to austere living back home. Experts at survival, we sustained ourselves on my part-time student employment and an occasional yard job on the weekends. Turkey tails were the only meat we could afford for Sunday dinner. Depending on how fortunate I was in getting a weekend job somewhere, our meat (*kiki*) might last until Tuesday. From Wednesday to Saturday it was straight rice, sweetened or unsweetened for variety. Three more children were born to us while at BYU–Hawaii.

Occasionally my wife and children complained about the straight rice diet and wondered why I even stayed in school at all. If we just settled in America as her family wanted, I could easily get a good job and support them nicely without a college degree. At such times I just begged them to trust me in my quest for the degree.

My main Church assignment at BYU–Hawaii was that of sacrament coordinator in the student branch. It fit perfectly with my natural aversion to "front row" leadership positions. Our branch president, Charles Goo, Sr., affected us greatly for good, teaching me the importance of constant spiritual nourishment. He made me understand that this nourishment was to prepare me for leadership in the kingdom.

Still it seemed impossible for me to put myself forward as a leader or to consider myself worthy. Perhaps it was my upbringing, our material poverty, or the low social status of my family in a very caste-conscious society. Even years after returning with my family to Tonga and serving as bishop in Haʻalaufuli, I could not overcome the discomfort of assuming high Church responsibility and risking the displeasure and criticism of the people.

Thus, when the time came to reorganize the Neiafu North Stake presidency, realizing that as bishop I would probably be part of the interview process, I decided simply not to be available for an interview. Without confiding in anyone, I left early that day to get out of the village and wander down on the seashore. But I could not suppress thoughts of Jonah running away from the Lord's call to Ninevah. I walked back to a friend's home on the village outskirts and "hid" there.

Suddenly a young boy came running up to my friend's home with the news that my little daughter, Maʻata had been killed. Frantic, I ran home to find only crying and confusion. She had already been taken to President Hāmani Wolfgramm's home. Just arriving back from Neiafu, President Wolfgramm had met the two full-time missionaries on the road, carrying the unconscious child and searching for a vehicle so they could rush her to the hospital. He brought them into his home, saying they would administer to her first.

I came into the room just as the president and the two missionaries were giving my daughter a priesthood blessing. I looked down at her lifeless body and spoke her name. Miraculously, she opened her eyes and began to cry. She was fine now.

Maʻata had been electrocuted by trying to yank a fan cord out of the electrical outlet while she was standing knee-deep in a tub of bath water. Somehow she had grabbed bare wires and couldn't let go. Considerable time elapsed before anyone had the presence of mind to turn off the electrical switch to the house, so the girl could be retrieved from the tub.

Shock, gratitude, and my own guilty conscience seemed to reinforce in my mind the Jonah parallel in my life. Was this the miracle that would finally get my attention and persuade me not to run away from Church responsibility? I went to the interview. The following Sunday I was sustained as second counselor in the Neiafu North Stake presidency.

42

Sione Moala Fineanganofo

"THE FAST THAT I HAVE CHOSEN"
Isaiah 58:6

Sione Moala Fineanganofo and Falaetau Mahu'inga Fineanganofo have both served full-time missions and teach in the Church Education System in Tonga. Sione has served as bishop of Nuku'alofa Ward and is currently president of Nuku'alofa Tonga North Stake.

I received most of my early schooling in the government primary school in Nuku'alofa, transferring to the Tonga Free Church primary school for my final year in class six. At this school, every Friday was a work or cleaning day (all day) for the children, which got to be a real pain for me. One Friday I noticed a government bulletin that announced entrance examinations for admission to Liahona High School would be held that day.

Applying to the Mormon high school was definitely frowned on, if not forbidden, at our primary school, but I would do anything to get out of scrubbing and cleaning. So on this Friday I persuaded two of my buddies to sneak away from our work detail and go with me to Liahona to take the entrance examination. We were on a lark. President Viliami Pasi was our examiner.

Of course, my first and only choice of colleges [high schools] was Toloa, sponsored by my church, the Free Wesleyan Church of Tonga. I had no desire whatsoever to attend Liahona. Although I knew nothing about the Mormon Church, I had heard plenty of negative stories about it and generally hated it as part of the emotional environment I grew up in. Liahona was also considered an inferior educational institution in those days.

My life was shattered when word came that I was not selected to attend Toloa but that Liahona had accepted me. The entrance exam to Liahona, which I had taken on a lark, was now my only serious option for an education beyond primary school. It was either Liahona or nothing, but I was adamant against going to high school at all if I had to attend Liahona. My parents and the older children of our family had to exert extreme force to make me enroll in the lowly Mormon school. I finally agreed to attend on the promise and understanding that I would transfer to Toloa the following year (1958).

When this plan didn't materialize and I was not permitted to go to Toloa the next year, I was very upset. But by the end of my second year at Liahona I had adjusted happily to the place and to my new friends. More importantly I had begun to acquire a faith and testimony in the Church and the full gospel of Jesus Christ. There were no more thoughts of Toloa.

In 1961 I was baptized; and in 1963, at graduation, I was part of the famous first group of Liahona graduates who all got their mission call along with their diploma. My family, who had more or less accepted my "Mormon" baptism, were now gravely concerned and angry that I should go on a mission for the Church. They had already made arrangements (they claimed) for me to continue on to university overseas. But by then I was so full of the spirit of the gospel and missionary work that no one could persuade me to give up my call. Emotions ran high in my family against me and the Church. The unfortunate conclusion was the solemn declaration that I would "no longer be considered a member of the family."

So I moved out of the house and went back to Liahona where I found odd jobs as a house boy, saving my money for clothes, books, and other materials for my mission. The person who helped me most in this quest was Brother Vaughn Neilsen, a faculty member at the school. On November 5, 1963, I entered missionary training in Matahau.

Vava'u was my field of labor for most of my mission. Through many trials of faith, I grew spiritually, witnessing the miracles of priesthood blessings and the value of obedience to eternal principles. Early one fast Sunday morning in the little island of Matamaka, there was a cry throughout the village that a large deepwater fish had been landed at the beach and everyone should come and get his or her portion. We came back from the beach with the liver of the great fish. In our fasting state, we were sorely tempted to fall to and devour this delicious morsel immediately. However our branch president, Tēvita Taufa, stopped any debate on the matter, declaring that we would complete our fasting and our church services as planned, then break our fast in the proper way.

In the late afternoon before we had our meal, cries were heard from around the village that the flesh of the fish was poisonous. There was much sickness in Matamaka that day which we were spared because we had obeyed an important principle. . . .

I wrote my family faithfully without a reply from them for two years; but when I returned home from the mission in 1965, they were overjoyed to see me. All animosity was gone and our former happy relations were restored. I think my parents could see a big difference in their clean-cut youngest son just off a mission. . . .

I was taught another great principle by Tu'iketei Pule on the eve of my departure for university training at Church College of Hawaii: "Young man, you tithe every penny you earn and you will be able to complete your education." That counsel made such an impression on me that my tithing to the Church was precise and exact during the six years I was in America, completing my degree. That was a miracle.

And miracles have never ceased as we have seen the growth and progress of the Church in Tonga. I add my testimony to all the others which have been borne of the power of faith, and the truthfulness of the gospel of Jesus Christ.

PART V

TEMPLE

1974–91

*Gracing the
Lord's Garden*

Left: Sione Fineanganofo, now president of the Nukuʻalofa Tonga North Stake, with his arms around his sons, Mahuʻinga and Sione, Jr.; Folau Moehau, and Kākolosi Tuiʻone Pulotu. The occasion was clearing land for the construction of the Nukuʻalofa Tonga Temple (Courtesy Kākolosi Tuiʻone Pulotu)

Right: Luʻisa Hēhea Pāletuʻa and Tonga Toutai Pāletuʻa, 2 November 1975 at the national service commemorating the centennial of the Tongan Constitution. Tonga has been bishop, stake president, patriarch, regional representative of the Quorum of the Twelve, Tonga Mission president, Nukuʻalofa Tonga Temple president, and Missionary Training Center president. Hēhea has been prominent not only in support of her husband, but as a Relief Society president, missionary, temple matron, and missionary trainer. (Courtesy Tonga Toutai Pāletuʻa)

King Taufaʻahau Tupou IV accepts an honorary Doctor of Humanities at BYU–Hawaii, 1976. (Courtesy BYU–Hawaii Archives)

ʻUiha Tuʻikolovatu, currently president of Nukuʻalofa Tonga Stake, greets Church President Spencer W. Kimball, February 1981, present for temple ground-breaking ceremonies. (Courtesy Kākolosi Tuiʻone Pulotu)

King Tāufa'āhau Tupou IV turns a ceremonial shovelful of earth at the groundbreaking ceremonies for the Nuku'alofoa Tonga Temple February 18, 1981, flanked on the right by Elder Adney Y. Komatsu of the First Quorum of the Seventy and President Spencer W. Kimball. (Courtesy Kākolosi Tui'one Pulotu)

Sione Tuʻalau Lātū (left) and Tēvita Kaʻili, two Tongan regional representatives of the Quorum of the Twelve, discuss the construction of the Tonga Temple. (Courtesy Kākolosi Tuiʻone Pulotu)

Vili Pele Folau (center), former president of Nukuʻalofa Tonga East Stake, rests with his work crew while clearing the temple site, 1980. (Courtesy Kākolosi Tuiʻone Pulotu)

The Nuku'alofa Tonga Temple, dedicated in 1983. The design for the facade includes the form of one of Tonga's most famous architectural landmarks, the prehistoric trilithon called the Ha'amonga. A massive stone beam resting upon two equally massive notched pillars, the Ha'amonga was probably the entrance way to an ancient royal compound. Copyright by The Church of Jesus Christ of Latter-day Saints. Used by permission.

A young Ha'apai man stands outside his new home, a makeshift hut cobbled together from corrugated tin in the aftermath of Hurricane Isaac, that devastated Ha'apai and Tongatapu in 1982. (Courtesy Kākolosi Tui'one Pulotu)

The Church provided much relief throughout Tonga after Hurricane Isaac, 1982. Here men unload supplies to be distributed among the smaller islands of Ha'apai. (Courtesy Kākolosi Tui'one Pulotu)

Viliami (right) and Lu'isa Palauni Kongaika, missionaries and temple ordinance workers, renowned for their care of the missionaries. Viliami was a branch and district president in Ha'apai. (Courtesy Viliami F. Kongaika)

Tonga Pōteki Mālohifo'ou (right) and 'Ana Toki Mālohifo'ou. Tonga was a missionary, branch president, Vava'u District president, and temple sealer. 'Ana has been president of several different branch and district Relief Societies and Primary presidencies. (Courtesy Lakalaka Mālohifo'ou Ka'ili)

Three stalwart families at the designated temple site on Tongatapu in 1980. Left: Kelikupa Kīvalu and Manu Mahu'inga Kīvalu. He has been a bishop and a counselor in the Tonga Mission presidency. Center: Vaikalafi and Mele Lutui and their children. Vaikalafi has been a stake president and is now a regional representative. Right: 'Asaeli and Selu Ika. 'Asaeli is Ha'akame's town officer and patriarch of Liahona Stake. All three women have been ward Relief Society presidents and served missions with their husbands. (Courtesy Kākolosi Tui'one Pulotu)

'Alifeleti Malupō from Vainī, Tongatapu, graduated from BYU–Hawaii (B.A.) and BYU, Provo (M.A.) and is now director of Church Social Services in Hawaii and president of Waipahu Stake on Oahu.

Sione Feinga from Haʻalaufuli, Vavaʻu, and currently president of the Laie Hawaii Stake, came to Hawaii from Tonga as a labor missionary in 1960 and is now associate director of physical plant at BYU–Hawaii. He represents the many Tongan Saints who have become trusted Church leaders outside Tonga.

Tonga priesthood leadership, 1983. Front row left: ʻAisea Pikula Sāteki, Fanongonongo Vaitai, ʻUluʻamū Tuʻifua, ʻIsileli Lolo Tuiaki, Viliami Pasi, Tēvita Kaʻili, Tonga Toutai Pāletuʻa, Elder John H. Groberg of the First Quorum of the Seventy, Sione Tuʻalau Lātū, Pita Foliaki Hopoate, Vaikalafi Latui, Penisimani Muti, Samisoni Uasilaʻā, and Samuela ʻIloa. Second row left: Siaosi Moleni, Maʻake Muti, Kepueli Pakalani, Veuki Kaumatule, Suliasi ʻUasikē, ʻAsaeli Ika, Viliami Mākoni, Richard Westover of the Presiding Bishop's Area Office, Nukumovahaʻi Tonga, Filimone Fieʻeiki, Norman Harris, Simeni Tuʻivai, Sione Schaumkel, Sione Fineʻanganofo, Taliaʻuli Tongaʻonevai, ʻUiha Tuʻikolovatu, and Kelikupa Kīvalu. Top row, left: Mosese Naeata, Kākolosi Tuʻone Pulotu, Taipe Vaka, Timani Tonga, and ʻIteni Helu. (Courtesy Tēvita Kaʻili)

43

Leni Tuʻihalangingie

"THE TRIAL OF YOUR FAITH"
1 Peter 1:7

Leni and Losaline Tuʻihalangingie are the parents of twelve children living in Nukuʻalofa where Leni serves as bishop of the Nukuʻalofa Eighth Ward.

I was born on November 15, 1935, in Nukuʻalofa. My mother was Nanisi Hafoka Tuʻihalangingie, and my father was Siosaia Lātū Tuʻihalangingie. I was the eleventh of nineteen children. Descending from the great paramount chief Aleamotuʻa, who helped establish Christianity in Tonga, we belonged to the Wesleyan Church. My family loved that church. It was the center of our lives, for we thought it was true in every respect.

But on May 4, 1961, something very important happened. At eight o'clock in the evening, as I was walking along the road in Kolomotuʻa, my friend Sēmisi Motuliki called to me invitingly: "Leni, the Mormons are holding a missionary meeting at the home of Sitīveni Koloa. Let's go over there and throw rocks at the house."

I was game for the fun; but when we reached the house and looked inside, I beheld something remarkable. A young Caucasian man, clean and handsome and wearing a white coat, was speaking in Tongan, telling about the time he was first called as a missionary to the Tongan Islands. His mother had been very worried, wondering what kind of a place Tonga was. Perhaps they were still cannibals. The missionary had told his mother, "I will go to Tonga and I will become a Tongan man. I will love the Tongan people as my own."

As he said those words, my desire to disturb the meeting faded. Instead of wanting to stone the house, I experienced a surge of love and a desire to listen. The missionary continued his sermon on service without pay in the true church.

On the night of May 6, 1961, I went again to another Mormon meeting with the missionaries, this time at the large hall *Tali 'Eva*, owned by Hale Vete. I heard for the second time the preaching of this loving missionary in Tonga. My friend Sēmisi Motuliki wanted nothing more to do with the Mormons (although he was later baptized), so I went by myself.

Vili Fakataha preached the first sermon, after which the missionary from America gave the closing sermon on the apostasy. He also spoke out against infant baptism. Small children should be blessed not baptized. Older children and adults should receive baptism because of their faith.

I truly believed this "new" doctrine. When I went home that night I explained it to my wife, but she became angry and rebuked me for accepting Mormon doctrines so quickly. This was the first time we ever had such a conflict in our relationship. I deferred to her anger; but from that time forth, I had no peace of mind. I knew that there was another truth which was more consistent with the Bible, according to the words of the missionary. I could not get his testimony out of my mind.

As my faith increased, I took my oldest son to the local LDS branch president to be blessed. Returning home I encountered the collective rage of my wife's family and was chased out of the house. Still determined to uphold my new-found faith, I was baptized on the first day of July, 1961.

Unfortunately, this action complicated my problems with my wife's family. They persuaded her to reject me entirely. It was a heart-breaking moment in which I was compelled to choose between my testimony of the gospel and my wife and her family. I very nearly denied the truth. But I kept faith with the promise that, if I would endure all difficulties well and pray fervently, I would be blessed and be restored as head of my little family. You can imagine my pain when, in August of 1962, my wife sent me money to get a divorce, then sailed away to New Zealand. I had lost my loved one because of my testimony of the gospel of Christ and his Church.

Despite these hardships, my faith drove me to be more and more active in the Church, especially in missionary work. By February the following year, I was serving a full-time mission and began preaching the gospel to my family. Ironically, those in my family who were most upset at my own baptism were the first to be baptized into the Church. During my mission, both of my parents were baptized and sixteen of their children.

At the conclusion of my missionary service, my joy and gratitude were full. My whole family were now members. But the rewards of our activity did not end there. Within two years I was married to a beautiful young lady in the Church with a plan to be sealed in the New Zealand Temple as soon as possible. I also promised my parents I would take them with us to the temple.

In October 1968 a baby girl was born to us. We named her Taina (Dinah). I got a job at Liahona working as a baker for which I received a salary of eighteen dollars every two weeks.

The fare to New Zealand was $675 round trip per person and I had to raise enough money to take four adults and our two children. I needed $3500. Day and night I yearned and prayed that somehow I would be able to fulfill the promise I had made to my wife and parents. From each pay check, I took out two dollars for tithing and deposited sixteen dollars in our temple account with the bishop. We bought no food, eating only what I could grow on the land or gather from the ocean.

Our family was listed with the temple group leaving on November 1, 1972; but by October, we had raised only $800. The bishop needed to verify who was actually going to be able to make it. I begged him to leave our names on the list, although my family was feeling dismay at what appeared to be an impossibility. My wife and mother both scolded me, saying it was a great embarrassment to the family because I had kept saying we were going, yet we had not sufficient money. "We will be the laughing stock of Tonga," they said, "and our children will be humiliated."

Even the bishop suggested I put our names on the list for the following year. I begged for just fifteen more days to try to raise the rest of the money. Day and night I yearned and prayed to find means to make the trip that year.

Well, on October 15, 1971, we received news from heaven, as it were. A large French passenger liner just happened to be sailing from Tahiti to New Zealand and, by popular request of the passengers, wanted to stop briefly in Tonga. I understand the passengers actually paid for this detour to our island. The mission president was contacted about anyone in the Church interested in going by boat to New Zealand at very little expense. Thus, though we could not afford to fly, our little family and my parents were able to sail to the temple on November 1, 1972.

We arrived on November 5th. On November 7th, I clasped the hand of my wife across the temple altar to be sealed together for time and eternity. With our children also we covered the sacred altar with our tears as we were sealed as a family forever.

We stayed for two glorious months serving in the temple of God. Despite the infirmity of my eighty-year-old father, he attended the temple sessions nearly every morning at five o'clock. Since he was unable to walk up the hill to the temple, I carried him on my back. He was a large man (over six feet tall) and heavy, and I am small; but he felt light to me, as if I were carrying a little child. Such love and appreciation for God and each other were the source of our constant happiness.

But then there was the problem of returning home! We did not have enough money to book a flight home, and we had no extended family in New Zealand to help us. Again the Lord answered the prayer of one forsaken, humble, and poor. It was announced one day that those unable to get a flight back to Tonga might get passage on the ocean liner *Oriana* coming from Australia and making its first voyage to Tonga. Accordingly, we were able to get nearly free passage on a once-only opportunity for Tongans to sail on this large passenger ship.

Blessings continued to be poured out on our family since our trip to the temple. On May 23, 1974, I was called to be a bishop in the Nuku'alofa Eighth Ward.

In 1980 our family experienced one of the greatest trials of our lives and, as it turned out, one of the most sacred moments in our family history. It was our oldest daughter Taina's twelfth year, and I noticed one day that she was walking strangely. Her right foot seemed to be dragging somewhat behind the other. When I asked her about it, she said her foot was just that way. After a week, although she did not feel pain, her condition was clearly getting worse. The dragging had increased, and her leg seemed to show signs of atrophy.

We took Taina to the hospital. The doctors prescribed a medication which did not help. Two months later, I remember coming home after the temple grounds dedication (February 18, 1981) where President Kimball had presided and had bestowed such a profound blessing on Tonga. Taina was in extreme pain and nothing could give her relief. That very afternoon I took her back to the hospital where she was admitted for ten days of X-rays and tests. These tests were sent to New Zealand for interpretation and diagnosis. On Saturday February 29, Dr. Senili Moala came to me and said, "Bishop, Taina has bone cancer; and with your consent, we feel her leg should be amputated."

I asked to speak to Dr. Sālesi Havili, the LDS doctor, to which Dr. Senili Moala replied, "Dr. Havili asked me to break the bad news to you because he has such deep feelings for you."

My next request was to take Taina home for a while. On March 1, I invited my two counselors, Sēmisi Uhi and Tautuaʻā Kavapalu, and the high priest group leader, Paula Vakalahi, to join me in administering to Taina. It was the first time I had ever blessed my daughter. I had fasted for forty-eight hours. Paula Vakalahi anointed Taina with the oil and I sealed the anointing with a blessing and promise that she be completely healed. As I lay my hands on Taina's head, the same sensation came over me that I felt on those mornings when I carried my father weighing more than two hundred pounds up the hill to the temple.

Although my heart was extremely troubled and I well knew that where there is cancer, death follows, at the moment I pronounced the blessing all troubled feelings and doubts were swept away. I knew Heavenly Father had heard my cry and honored my promises to Taina. It was a happy day in my life.

Two weeks later, Dr. Sālesi Havili, my friend and fellow bishop, came to ask us to come back to the hospital for more tests and treatment. By this time Taina was walking perfectly normally. Further tests showed no sign of cancer, her leg returned to its proper size and shape, and now Taina is grown and well educated. She studied overseas and is currently serving the Lord in the Salt Lake City North Mission.

I know for a certainty that the windows of heaven are opened through sincere prayer. I trust in the Lord's love and rejoice that he attends to and honors the humble and obscure like myself. We now have twelve children plus four adopted ones. Our lands and cattle are sufficient to sustain us. Most of all we express the deepest gratitude for Heavenly Father's holy plan which brings happiness in this world and full hope in the life after this life.

44

Sione Tuʻalau Lātū

"I GO TO DO HIS BIDDING"

Sione Lātū has made significant contributions in Tonga as an ecclesiastical leader and as a Church employee. He has served as a bishop, stake president, mission president, and regional representative. He taught at Liahona before assuming the directorship of Church translation in Tonga. For several years he was employed as the regional area director in Tonga for the Presiding Bishop's Office of the Church. He and his wife, Helen Kaleialoha Kaneakua Lātū, have six children.

My mother, Soana Hafoka Lātū Sikalu, was a strong Methodist from her childhood. Daughter of a Methodist minister, Selivenusi Hafoka, she both devoted herself to her church and resisted strenuously all our efforts to teach her and bring her into The Church of Jesus Christ of Latter-day Saints. I was the youngest of her children, born just after Father passed away suddenly in 1938. Although she was proud of me for my work in the LDS Church, she listened to me least of all since I was her "baby." We fasted for her, prayed for her, begged her to join her children in the true Church of Jesus Christ, even brought her to live with us. Nothing influenced her. She would not be baptized. She enjoyed immense respect and honor in her own congregation; but mainly, I think, she simply could not feel anything for the Church.

In the summer of 1977, I became the president of the Tonga Nukuʻalofa Mission. Mom and my stepfather Tēvita Sikalu had since returned to our ancestral island, Haʻafeva. We kept in touch, but she was as resistant as ever to the Church.

Sione Tuʻalau Lātū

On June 8, 1978, however, I received a strange letter from Mom, insisting I come to Haʻafeva as soon as possible. She must see me. That very day Helen gave birth to our fourth child, Kahealani; but I explained that I must leave for Haʻafeva immediately. After all, Mother was seventy-nine years old, and I sensed there was something momentous about to happen to her. Perhaps she was ready to join the Church.

I flew to Pangai and rented a boat to Haʻafeva, arriving at the island on Saturday evening, June 10. I carried with me my white baptismal clothes. Mom was astonished and overjoyed to see me. I had no more than seated myself in front of her and Tēvita when she said simply: "The reason I asked you to come is that I want to be baptized, now."

Despite my hopes, I was not quite prepared for this blunt announcement especially in front of her husband, who was not overly fond of the Church. The shock, I suppose, was in her resolve, her forthrightness.

"Are you really ready?" I asked.

Reaching for a small hand basket, she showed me the white baptismal clothes she had carefully prepared for the occasion.

"But, Mother, why this sudden change of heart?" I pressed. "What has happened to make you want to be baptized now?"

This was her story:

"Two weeks ago I slept and saw my father Silivenusi Hafoka. In all these many years since his death, I have never dreamed about him or seen him. But here he was standing before me, dressed completely in white. His countenance had not changed from when I knew him before. As I looked at him, he spoke to me and I could see that he was standing in front of the LDS chapel in Latai. 'Soana, come and join. This is the true Church.'

"When I heard these words I rushed forward to embrace my father. But as I moved toward him the vision retreated from me. The more I tried to reach out to him, the farther away he appeared to be, until I woke up to discover that in my reaching out I had actually pushed open the front door of our house.

"I slept no more that night but pondered the words of my father, who died still a minister in the Methodist Church. The next day I spoke to my husband and said, 'Sikalu, I'll not wait any longer, no matter what you think or say. I believe the Church and I'm going to be baptized.'"

The next day at nine o'clock we proceeded down to the beach, actually walking past Soana's former ministers who were in front of their chapel waiting to begin their service. Without hesitation or embarrassment, Soana spoke to the chief minister. "Reverend sir, thank you for being an excellent shepherd in the past. But I am telling you now so you will know. Today I truly believe in the Lord Jesus Christ and I go to do his bidding."

The minister politely acknowledged Mom's announcement. And the whole village looked on as this aged but revered lady went down into the water and was baptized.

45

Sālesi Falefoʻou Havili

"ASK IN FAITH, NOTHING WAVERING"
James 1:6

Dr. Sālesi Havili was ordained a bishop in February 1982. He has also presided over branches of the Church in Pangai, Haʻapai; Sydney, Australia; and Port Moresby, Papua New Guinea. Subsequently, he completed an M.D. (1987) in Australia and is now practicing medicine in the United States.

I had not been a member of the Church a year when I learned in a very desperate moment what it means to pray with *real* intent, nothing wavering. The experience occurred in the operating room of the Vavaʻu Hospital during surgery on Mafi Vakaloa, an elderly gentleman living in Neiafu.

My wife, Selu, and I had joined the Church the year previous in Tonga, April 30, 1977. Our baptism came just fifteen months after I had returned from my medical studies in Fiji and had begun work at the Vaiola Hospital on Tongatapu.

By the time I was transferred to the Vavaʻu Hospital, we were both on fire in the Church and preparing to go to the temple. Every experience in the Lord's kingdom was a moment of truth and growth for me, but nothing had made as profound an impact in my spiritual life as what happened during Mafi Vakaloa's surgery. I was both tested and taught.

Suffering from ulcers and a perforated intestine, Mafi was very weak and in great pain. Because of his age and deteriorating health, we feared he might not withstand the trauma of surgery. But we really had no choice. Drs. Viliami Tangi and Malakai Ake were the surgeons and I the anesthesiologist.

I had administered the ether, and surgery had begun. Given the limitations of our island hospital, all seemed to be in order. But then the nurse assisting me whispered that she could no longer feel Mafi's pulse. I checked for a pulse and could not get one either. Fearing an outcry from the nurse I said, "It's okay. I'll take care of it," and she left for other business. I grabbed my stethoscope and listened to Mafi's heart. There was no beat whatsoever. Standing at Mafi's head I could see into the incision in which Drs. Tangi and Ake were working. There seemed to be no blood flowing anywhere at all. I kept feeling for a pulse and listening to his chest. Nothing!

Desperately, I rehearsed in my mind every procedure I had followed in administering the anesthesia, the injections, and medications—kind and amount. There were no mistakes that I could think of, but the man had died on the operating table.

Admittedly, I should have informed the two surgeons immediately of the crisis; but in my consternation and self-recrimination, I kept asking why this was happening. What had I done? Was Mafi just too old and weak for such an operation? Would people accuse me of his death? In my confusion, precious minutes elapsed.

I knew that without blood flow in the head, brain damage was imminent. But still I kept checking and rechecking, trying to discover what had gone wrong! Five minutes had gone by. My attention was fixed on the blood transfusion bottle. The dripping through the transfusion tube had ceased entirely.

Reinserting the tube in another vein, I checked for blockage. It was all right. The I.V. just would not flow, which I took as more evidence that poor Mafi had passed way.

By now a long time had passed since Mafi's heart stopped beating—over ten minutes. Drs. Tangi and Ake were preoccupied with the repair of the intestine and did not seem to notice. I was in a panic. And that's when I began to pray. It was a desperate but shallow prayer at first, as if I were speaking words without feeling or conviction. After all, I knew scientifically that Mafi was dead; and given the limitations of my knowledge and environment at that time, I had exhausted my personal resources in trying to revive him.

I continued to pray, a second and third time. Guilt and doubt dominated my feelings. Although I begged Heavenly Father to restore Mafi's heartbeat, I was too aware medically that he was actually dead.

My efforts "to do something" were based largely on the fear that I had caused his death. For some reason also I resisted asking help from the two surgeons. Perhaps I feared they would stop their repair work. Perhaps I felt Mafi's problem was beyond us all.

As I prayed again and again, I had the sensation that Mafi's life depended on the genuine sincerity of my prayer and the quality of my belief—that this crisis was to test my faith, almost on the eve of my going to the temple. I prayed again, perhaps the tenth time. Eighteen minutes had passed since Mafi's heart had stopped beating. I asked more fervently, reasoning with the Lord and promising total consecration of my life to him if he would revive the man who had died because of something I had done.

After each prayer I would check the transfusion bottle. There was no movement of the fluid into his body. The flow of blood suddenly became for me the outward sign by which I would know whether Mafi was going to live or not. I bowed my head again and prayed with a fervor and intimacy unmatched in previous prayers. I prayed until I knew absolutely that when I opened my eyes the I.V. would be flowing and Mafi would be alive. As I spoke to the Lord I suppressed every fragment of doubt, as if any wavering of faith on my part would be the end of Mafi. I prayed this time until I knew that, when I opened my eyes, the I.V. would be dripping and Mafi's heart would begin beating. And, miraculously, it was so.

I put my stethoscope to Mafi's chest again and listened. At first, I heard nothing. Then, like some tiny dot of sound far away, there was a faint heartbeat. Was it my own pounding heart in my ears? I listened on, yearning for life to be manifested in Mafi's chest. Then ever so faintly and gently it came, quietly throbbing, ever so gently pounding, until gradually it was a full powerful beat. Mafi's heart resumed beating after twenty-five minutes of complete inactivity. My whole body was atingle. I was overwhelmed with joy and awe and barely restrained myself from crying out the good news to the other two doctors.

Later, however, I did tell them, as well as the nurse who had first observed that Mafi's heart had stopped beating.

The next morning when I made my rounds to the different wards, Mafi was very much alive, alert and articulate, talking animatedly to his wife, who was sitting on the edge of her husband's bed.

Mafi was released to his home after a week and a half in the hospital. His recovery from the surgery was complete and his mind was as keen as ever.

46

Mōleni Tanginoa Fonua

RETURNING GOOD FOR EVIL

Mōleni Tanginoa Fonua serves as president of the Ha'apai Stake and is known throughout the Ha'apai Group as a person of generosity and integrity. He holds the elected position of pule fakavahe (district officer) in the government. His speaking and leadership skills have been important to both the Church and the community at large. The following excerpt from his oral history shows the wisdom of returning good for evil. The humorous twist to the story reveals a sense of good-natured irony which is so much a part of the Tongan nature.

Just after Tonga Toutai Pāletu'a was appointed mission president in 1974, he came to Ha'apai to preside over a conference of the Church. I was district president at the time. After the conference, my counselor, Folau Moehau, and I took the president with all his luggage to the inter-island ferry, the *Olovaha*.

We boarded the *Olovaha* and stowed the president's luggage in his cabin. While we were performing this task and making the president comfortable, we suddenly felt the boat moving. I scurried up on deck and begged a crewman to please ask the captain to return and let us off. I mentioned I was the president of the Ha'apai District for the Church.

I heard the conversation between this crewman and his captain: "The president of what church?" asked the captain.

"The president of the Mormon Church," answered the crewman.

"Order those two men to swim for it then. This vessel is not returning to shore."

I felt desperate and begged the officer to ask the captain a second time to wait and signal a launch from shore to come and get us. We got the same answer.

The *Olovaha* had already pulled out into deep water. We either jumped overboard or sailed with the *Olovaha*, not to return for a whole week. The real problem was that poor Folau Moehau could hardly swim a lick. Yet we really could not leave our duties in Haʻapai.

So we jumped overboard to make our way as best we could. Once in the water I immediately reached for Folau to help him. To my surprise, Folau said that he was just fine, that he was standing on a rock and didn't need help.

Now we were many yards from shore in water dark and deep. I know that area very well. There was no rock or coral head there. But Folau *felt* that he was standing on a rock. He did not struggle at all. Miraculously he had no trouble keeping his head above water even though he was not swimming. Soon a little outboard came and took us rejoicing back to shore.

During the days following, we felt very grateful for the Lord's mercy, especially in behalf of Folau. In this spirit of gratitude, when the *Olovaha* called again at Pangai, Folau and I decided to do a favor for the captain. We prepared for him a formal presentation of food with all the trimmings, a presentation worthy of a high dignitary.

When we presented ourselves with the food, we thanked the captain for commanding us to leave his boat by jumping overboard. Otherwise we would not have had this miraculous experience which has increased our understanding of Heavenly Father's love and power.

47

Tēvita Ka'ili

WHEN THE SPIRIT MOVES

Tēvita Ka'ili has been an influential leader in the Church in Tonga since the late 1960s. A graduate of the Church College of Hawaii, he was among the first bishops called in Tonga. He has served as a stake president and as regional representative of the Quorum of the Twelve. His employment has included teaching, translation, and school administration. He is presently the Regional Director of Temporal Affairs in the Presiding Bishop's Area Office. He and his wife, Lakalaka Mālohifo'ou Ka'ili, have seven children.

When I stood to speak before the huge congregation of Saints in the Nuku'alofa South Stake conference in February 1983, my eyes fell on one person sitting in the middle of the front row, 'Isileli Fa'oliu. 'Isileli and I had been acquainted for many years. He drove a taxi and often took me and Lakalaka to our work at Liahona. Today he was my guest, a man of a different church, who had declined many invitations to come to our home and hear the missionaries. His wife Nūnia had been baptized in the Church three weeks previously.

I had intended to say something by way of greeting to our nonmember guests; but as I gripped the pulpit, I suddenly felt a powerful direction from the Holy Spirit to declare the truthfulness of the gospel and to invite 'Isileli directly to join the Church. This I did with all the fervor that I really felt. Suddenly, in the middle of my talk, 'Isileli leaped to his feet and stated in a loud voice, "Ka'ili, I believe the Church. I know it is true. I want to be baptized as soon as possible."

The congregation was stunned by this unusual outburst in a conference session; but after the meeting, many of them gathered to witness the baptism of 'Isileli Fa'oliu. I had the privilege of taking him into the water to perform this sacred ordinance.

During the baptismal service 'Isileli spoke to the group assembled and told this interesting story:

"My wife came home last night and informed me Tēvita Ka'ili had extended a personal invitation to me to be his guest at the Sunday session of the conference. I was grateful for the attention from an old acquaintance, but I said to myself, 'If I am supposed to attend this Mormon conference, then nothing will distract me, no calls, no friends coming over, no extended family obligations.'

"Well, the next morning no such distractions occurred. There were no excuses to decline the invitation. As I was preparing to attend the conference meeting my heart was strangely affected; and in my mind, I decided that if Tēvita Ka'ili were to look me straight in the eye and tell me this was the true Church, I would accept the invitation to be baptized, for I have been warned enough.

"You can imagine the profound feelings I had when Tēvita stood at the pulpit, singled me out of the whole congregation, declared his testimony, and asked me to be baptized. I was overwhelmed by so much joy, I could not contain my emotions. I simply jumped up and said, 'Yes, I will accept baptism.' "

It was an unforgettable moment in our lives for which afterwards, on bended knee, Lakalaka and I thanked our Heavenly Father.

48

Pita Foliaki Hopoate

"I WILL BE
ON YOUR RIGHT HAND
AND ON YOUR LEFT"
Doctrine & Covenants 84:88

Pita Hopoate has been a prominent Church leader in Tonga since the mid-1970s. A bishop, stake president, mission president, and president of the Missionary Training Center in Tonga, Brother Hopoate has influenced for good thousands of lives and the growth of the Church. He attended Liahona High School and graduated from BYU–Hawaii in 1973. He and his wife, Lani Alconcel Hopoate, have eight children.

My grandfather, Viliami Hopoate, was a stalwart in the Wesleyan Church, having been an honor student (*maamaloa*) at Nafualu College and later a minister in that church for several years. His ministry took him to many places in Tonga as well as to the Solomon Islands. Viliami passed away when he was still relatively young, and Grandmother and her two small children (one of them my father, Makamāpele Hopoate) returned to live with her parents who had decided to move from Kolovai to Fuaʻamotu. There she met and married Sione Maʻu Tomasi.

Sione Maʻu Tomasi's neighbor in Fuaʻamotu was Sione Nau. Together they joined The Church of Jesus Christ of Latter-day Saints, the result of missionary activity generated from the Mormon school in Makeke.

Thus the Church had its beginnings in Fuaʻamotu in our family residence called ʻAhononou. The first chapel, a large Tongan house or hut, was actually built on my father's land allotment. Here I grew up in the middle of a small but very active LDS congregation.

Twice my parents went on missions for the Church to other villages, including two years of service in 'Eua (1950–52). My favorite earliest recollections are of associating with the Caucasian missionaries from Makeke or Liahona, who always came to our home. In my youthful mind, I imagined them as having come from heaven. They made such a powerful impression on me that I longed for the day when I, too, would be a missionary.

I was not a bright child in school. My scores out of primary school were so low that no college [high school] would accept me, so I had to repeat my last year of primary school. When I failed the exam the second year, my educational future looked very bleak indeed. Father told me if I really desired to attend Liahona, he would petition the principal, Kenneth P. Lindsay, to admit me as an exception.

I remember well that interview with Brother Lindsay who spoke fluent Tongan. My father explained to him that no other school in Tonga would accept me because I had twice failed the government exam. Brother Lindsay turned to me and asked just one question. "My boy, do you really want to learn?"

I said, "Yes, I want to learn."

To which he replied, "That's good enough. As far as this school is concerned, your desire to learn qualifies you for entrance."

My success at Liahona seemed always a miraculous thing to me, a mystery, except for the fact that I fasted every Wednesday and prayed earnestly for help. My greatest education was achieved through Church service, especially as a missionary. The very month, November 1966, I graduated from Liahona High School, I received my call to serve in the Tonga Mission and was sent to Tungua, in the western cluster (*Lulunga*) of the islands of Ha'apai.

Two things about me made my call to these tiny islands an extra challenge. First, I was a very weak sailor; and second, I could not swim. Captained by Kouli Tautua'ā and maintained by Fakatou Vaitai, the Church vessel *Faifekau* prepared to embark from Fāua. I started vomiting from seasickness before we even got underway. By the time we reached Malinoa island just out from Tongatapu, I heard Fakatou Vaitai say, "We'd better take him back. He won't survive the trip to Ha'apai. He's vomiting too much. He needs to be assigned to Tongatapu."

I couldn't bear the thought of returning and told them so. Sick as I was, I insisted we continue on. When we arrived in Pangai, I was very weak and hungry. I'll never forget dragging myself to the home of Taisia, wife of Sione Saafi, who had prepared some sweet dumplings (*tōpai*) for the arriving missionaries. We all huddled in her kitchen watching the pot of dumplings as they cooked.

When they were done, she sent a child to buy some sugar to sweeten them. By then I was so famished, I felt I could not wait for the sweetening. I begged Taisia to bring my portion so I could eat then and there. Kindly she brought the plain flour dumplings on a plate. I blessed the food and began to eat. To my surprise it was sweet to my taste, so much so that when the little boy arrived with the sugar, I insisted the *tōpai* was already sweet. Tasting it herself, Taisia was astonished that without sugar the dumplings were already sweetened for the missionaries. I have often referred to this episode as evidence of how the Lord sweetens even the roughest of experiences and how he works miracles to take care of his servants.

The seven months I served in Tungua and the surrounding islands in Western Ha'apai were the most critical in the development of my faith, my character, and my relationship with Heavenly Father. Not only was I weak in the stomach traveling by sea, I was also, as I said, a nonswimmer. Much of our travel was by outrigger canoe and other tiny vessels. I was constantly aware that if we ever sank (not an uncommon occurrence for small craft in these islands), it would be the end of me. Daily prayers became a life-and-death matter as I pleaded for safety on the ocean. My prayers of gratitude were also earnest and frequent. Thus, what was a deficiency in my preparation for tiny island living became a principal source of a spiritual strength which has blessed my life ever since.

Missionary work in the late sixties in the western isles of Ha'apai was difficult at best. The distance, the dangers of the ocean, and the fragile testimonies of only a few members did not promise a strong membership for the future. But the Lord has his way of strengthening through dreams and visions those who are to lay the foundation for the growth of the Church.

One night in 1967 on the island of Ha'afeva, I went to bed very hungry and perhaps a bit overwhelmed by the hardships of missionary work in these islands. I slept and dreamed a dream which made a powerful impression on me. I saw myself sitting on the beach of Ha'afeva village looking out on the ocean which was suddenly full of small boats of every variety and shape. They were vessels full of members of the Church, coming from the different islands of Lulunga to Haʻafeva. I was amazed to see fathers and mothers whose children were dressed in the green uniforms of our own Church schools. The boats landed on the beach, and the Saints walked up and into large, beautiful Church buildings.

Awakening from this "unlikely" dream, I walked down to the shore early the next morning. Sitting on a beached outrigger canoe, I looked out on the very ocean I had seen the night before. Again in my mind's eye, I envisioned the little armada of boats full of Saints from the various islands coming to Haʻafeva with children dressed in green Church school uniforms.

However impossible it seemed at this time that such an "invasion" of Saints and school children could ever occur, I did in fact witness the fulfillment of that singular dream fifteen years later when, as mission president, I went to Haʻafeva to dedicate a new chapel there. The Church had established a middle school on Haʻafeva for the children of the Lulunga islands and I stood on the beach and greeted the Saints arriving in boats from ʻOʻua, Tungua, Matuku, Nomuka, and Kotu, bringing their uniformed children to enroll them in school and to attend conference. These were the Saints I saw in my dream-vision back in 1967.

As a mission president, I marveled again and again how the Lord sustained his servants no matter what dangers they were exposed to. Even when disaster struck, there was always the attendant softening of feelings and opening of doors to the gospel message in places which were inaccessible to the missionaries before. When the *Fetuʻumoana* sank in the stretch of ocean between Haʻafeva and Lofanga, several members of the Church drowned including Elder Hanipale Kinikini and Mele Mafileʻo, wife of Solomone Mafileʻo. Some children of married missionaries also died in this tragic accident.

This event generated a genuine pity for those who were lost and an admiration for our missionaries who risk their lives to serve missions without salary for the Lord Jesus Christ. People seemed more willing to listen to our message. We had their attention and their hearts. Our missionaries worked harder, feeling that they had to be worthy of the sacrifices of those missionaries who had perished.

The same softening effect occurred when Hurricane Isaac devastated many of the islands in Tongatapu and in Haʻapai in 1982. As it destroyed houses and material goods, it also humbled hearts. The doors that were closed to our missionaries before were now torn off literally by the hurricane, crushed, and discarded. Many families became destitute, living on the cement foundation slabs where their houses had once stood. The Church gave enormous amounts of assistance to the members and to others, and our missionaries were like angels of mercy to the public at large. Both convert baptisms and activity among the members increased dramatically.

Our own family experienced the wrath of Hurricane Isaac. When our sea wall collapsed under pounding waves, the mission home was inundated by ocean water which destroyed the interior of the house. The concrete water tank in the garage became the refuge for our family and several missionaries, since it was somewhat elevated and protected by the main house from the buffeting of the waves. Crowded on the top of the tank, we were surrounded by water which rushed by us with the force of a mighty river and kept rising higher. There would have been no escape for us if the water had risen just a few more inches.

But Heavenly Father was close to us that night as we put our lives into his hands. He answered our prayers and we were preserved as were many others.

Perhaps my most harrowing and most spiritual experience as mission president was in the crash of a tiny five-passenger plane at Fua'amotu airport. As a young boy I would often climb the coconut trees on our plantation and watch aircraft land and take off on the grass airfield nearby. Perched atop these exceedingly tall trees, I had long thoughts about someday travelling by air to far places. One of the far places in my mind was Niuatoputapu.

In April of 1983 I was invited by Grant Spencer, pilot for Tonga Airways, to be a passenger on a first flight to Niuatoputapu. As the mission president I had flown many times on this little plane and was particularly anxious to get to Niuatoputapu. What a treat it would be to take Lani along as well and to hold conference with the Saints and missionaries in Niuatoputapu!

Lani was absolutely delighted at the prospect, so I secured two of the five seats for us. As the day of the flight approached, she was more and more excited to go to a place she had never been before.

The day before our flight, I began to resist the idea of Lani accompanying me. I had no particular reason really. We were expecting a baby (our son, Howard Hunter Hopoate), but Lani was healthy and feeling fine. It was just that I did not have a good feeling about her going along. Lani was puzzled when I explained my feelings and told her that I wanted her to stay home, but she did not dispute my decision or complain. I took my counselor, Sione Schaumkel, instead. It was a providential decision.

We boarded the plane with three other passengers, Paula Vivili, Dr. Tauhelangi Kefu, and a woman from the U.S. Peace Corps. President Schaumkel and I were assigned the two rear seats, Paula Vivili and the Peace Corps lady were in front of us, and Dr. Kefu sat by the pilot in the cockpit.

After a cramped three hours in the air, we were delighted to see Niuatoputapu appear on the horizon. But our joy was brief, since the pilot seemed to be having trouble with something under the steering mechanism. We flew over the little Niuatoputapu airport at a considerable altitude, circled around the neighboring island of Tafahi, and came back to the airport at the same altitude. The pilot made no effort to land the plane. We then realized we were flying away from the island, apparently on our way back.

By now we all began to feel uneasy and a bit afraid. Our fear increased when the pilot announced there was an emergency and he had to jettison all excess fuel by taking the plane up, turning off the engine, releasing the fuel as the plane went into a dive, starting up the engine, pulling out of the dive, and continuing to Tongatapu. The execution of this maneuver left us breathless and somewhat shaken. When Vavaʻu came into view, one of the passengers begged the pilot to land there. But Vavaʻu was not equipped well for emergency landings.

No one talked much as we proceeded on our way. As for me, I asked myself that most serious question, "Am I ready to meet my Heavenly Father?" During these moments I saw my life before me from the beginning. However, in my reflections I also felt a definite sensation of peace which dispelled all my fear or anxiety. So profound was the assurance of our safety, I said to President Schaumkel, "Be comforted. Nothing serious will happen to us." This was a great comfort indeed since we were in the back seats in the tail section of the plane, farthest from the door. We would be last to escape in a crash.

We flew low around the Fuaʻamotu airport, so the people in the control tower could confirm what we feared about our predicament. The front wheel could not be lowered to landing position. Below, we could see the fire engines, the ambulance, policemen, soldiers from the

Defence Force, and multitudes of people crowding onto the field, all of which told us we were in big trouble.

We made our final turn and descended to the small grassy field from the direction of Tatakamotonga, the back wheels touching firmly down onto the grass. As the pilot carefully brought the nose of the aircraft down, I shouted to President Schaumkel: "Lean forward and duck!"

We both bent forward at the same time with our heads against the seats in front of us. In the very instant the nose touched the grass, the plane somersaulted and crashed violently upside down, wheels in the air, and skidded forward, tail section first. The screeching of metal and the cries of the passengers filled the plane. President Schaumkel and I remained conscious throughout.

As the plane came to rest, I noticed that the window on President Schaumkel's side, about the size of a car window, had popped out. It was the work, I feel, of angels. Given the twisted condition of the plane this small window provided us the perfect escape hatch. Unbuckling our seat belts, we scrambled out in a matter of seconds.

Our escape was accomplished on the side facing the tall elephant grass at the edge of the field, the side opposite from the onrush of the crowd. Thus none of the people really saw us exit from the plane, still in our clean white shirts and ties. The rescuers were struggling to open the one and only door to the little plane, which was jammed shut. Had there been a fire, perhaps none of the others would have survived at all.

As the rescuers worked to free our fellow passengers, we made our way to the hospital vehicles that had come for us. Again, no one seemed to pay us any attention. When we climbed up into the back of the emergency vehicle, the attending nurse told us to clear out–that this vehicle was for the passengers in the crash. Saying nothing, we quietly got out, walked around, and climbed into the front seat. There we watched the rescue and contemplated, with much gratitude, our miraculous escape.

In due time, the front door was opened and each of the passengers and the pilot removed. Four were injured and poor Paula Vivili was dead.

With the removal of the final passenger we heard the cry "Two more passengers!" They were looking for President Schaumkel and me. I finally said to the nurse who had ordered us out of the ambulance: "Tell the rescuers the two passengers they are looking for are sitting right here."

The nurse whirled around and looked at us: "Were you on this flight?" she asked.

"Yes," I said. "That's why we got into the ambulance in the first place."

Chagrined and embarrassed, she came up and kissed our cheeks in the typical Tongan greeting, then ran out to tell the soldiers and the other rescuers we were already safe and sound.

The people were profoundly moved by the discovery that we had "mysteriously" escaped unhurt, unnoticed, and unruffled. Well-wishers surrounded us immediately, people of all ranks including cabinet ministers. They kissed us and fussed over us, asking the question that we were asked continuously thereafter for weeks: "How could it be that you should have survived without injury?" Official investigators from New Zealand were amazed that the tail section we sat in had not broken off upon impact.

The response, at least by the Tongans, was that we were saved by Heavenly Father. The disaster became another open door to preaching the gospel, a testimony to us and the people of the divinity of the work we do. Those who serve Heavenly Father are honored by him and are guarded by his angels.

49

Tēvita Pōme'e

BROUGHT FORTH
BY PRAYER AND FASTING

Tēvita Pōme'e from Hōfoa, Tonga, has been a bishop of Hōfoa Ward and a high councilor in the Nuku'alofa North Stake. His story illustrates how many fine converts were faithful leaders in other churches before joining The Church of Jesus Christ of Latter-day Saints.

My baptism into The Church of Jesus Christ of Latter-day Saints on February 17, 1981, was due largely to the prayers and fasting of the Mormon branch president, Folau Moehau, and the congregation of the Saints in Hōfoa. Unbeknown to any of us, Folau had only a few months to live. I had not heard a missionary discussion, read the Book of Mormon, or received any real understanding of the Church. But I could not resist the power and the warmth of the Spirit I felt when this wonderful man came to my home one morning at four o'clock and invited me to join the Church.

I was born in Hōfoa, October 2, 1933. My mother, a devout Wesleyan, taught me to believe in God and took me to church. Out of primary school, I attended Liahona High School. It was the year the Mormon school was moved from Makeke to Liahona. Although my teachers liked me because I was energetic and enthusiastic, my stay at Liahona lasted only a few months. Because my father disliked the Church, he removed me from Liahona, and sent me to the Wesleyan boys' college in Toloa. That didn't last long either and I dropped out of school completely.

My ability to sing and lead music was my passport in society. I decided to attend the Tonga Free Church where I soon became a choir director and a lay preacher. After I married in 1953, I became one of the stalwarts of that church, representing our congregation at the annual conferences. The respect and honor of this position were important to me. I participated directly in the formulation of the laws that governed that church.

After three years as conference representative, I finally received the coveted position of *faifekau* or minister. Our poor congregation, however, was not deemed large enough, or active enough, to have its own full-time minister. We were still accountable to the Kolomotu'a minister and congregation. Our chapel was also very small.

Thus, I had two major objectives: to get Hōfoa recognized as its own district worthy to have its own minister, and to build a decent permanent chapel. I gave my all to these projects.

The major source of income for the chapel was my net fishing (*uloa*), the old Tongan way. Today's fishing brought in money to buy materials for tomorrow's work. Fish, sell, buy materials, work on the building, day in and day out. The joy was that the fishing was always terrific. We caught enormous amounts of fish whether we netted in 'Atatā or in the eastern district of Tongatapu, all for the chapel. When the chapel was finally dedicated, we were also able to build a house for the minister, the position I was appointed to.

Since joining The Church of Jesus Christ of Latter-day Saints I have often felt that my testimony of the true gospel and my being led to join the true Church were partly God's reward to me for my diligence in the Tonga Free Church.

I marvel now at the Mormon branch president's method. He was determined to be my friend, to get close to me even though we both presided over congregations in different churches. He followed me around but never harassed or challenged me. Occasionally he would send me a gift or increase the size of my church donation with a present of money. In such cases, I would always give him a pig or something in return so I would never be obligated to him. This is the Tongan way.

The night Folau Moehau came to my home with the Hōfoa Saints I was a bit out of patience. At that time, several of our children had been baptized into the Mormon Church, including our oldest, Tautalanoa, who was actually teaching in Liahona. But the Mormon Church was not for me. In fact, I resented it. More than that, I was very comfortable in the Tonga Free Church. After all I was considered a somebody there, known for my singing, fishing, church building, and my community service as the Hōfoa town officer.

But I could not help feeling drawn to Folau. He was my friend. His consistent kindness to me and the family had already made a deep impression on me. I felt consternation when he asked me right out to be baptized, to join the Church. I tried to escape this straight forward approach by appealing to my wife. "What do you think, honey?"

Her response was only: "I'm not part of that decision. Leave me out of it!"

I gave him an awkward but final *no*! There would be no baptism. Little did I realize, however, that Folau Moehau and his little flock would leave my home and begin with prayer another fast for me. In fact, I don't think they slept that night at all. At four o'clock the next morning, after a night of prayer, Folau again appeared on our doorstep with the same invitation for me to be baptized. At that moment, I felt a profound warmth, a burning sensation in my soul that this was right and that I must join the Church.

Although I understood little of the doctrine of the Church, I knew in my heart it was true. The next day, Saturday, would be my baptismal day. My poor wife was beside herself with grief. The whole village was amazed, and the typical gossip ran its course. An urgent request to come and stop me was even sent to the president of our church. But I never had second thoughts about the rightness of what I was doing, even when on Sunday I walked past my old congregation and strolled all the way to the Mormon chapel. My wife softened and was baptized a few weeks later.

The gossip and the ridicule directed at me never became persecution, but some of my extended family expressed their outrage at my baptism in interesting ways. My maternal uncle, for example, said, "If Jesus himself came and called through the village for everyone to gather at the Mormon chapel, for that was his only true Church, I would open my door and yell, 'Jesus, I'll just die right here where I am.' "

In retrospect the urgency with which Folau Moehau built our friendship and invited me to be baptized may have been part of a premonition he had that he would soon pass away. Hōfoa Branch was about to become a ward. A ward would need leaders who were natives of the village. Shortly after my baptism, Folau Moehau transferred to Pangai, Ha'apai, to teach in the Church school there. In September 1981 we heard that Folau Moehau had suddenly passed away. The Hōfoa Ward was organized on July 7, 1982, and I was called to be a counselor to the new bishop, Sione Schaumkel. On October 9, 1983, Bishop Schaumkel was called to the stake presidency, and I was sustained as the bishop of Hōfoa Ward only thirty months after I had been baptized. I served as bishop for seven years and am now on the Nukuʻalofa North Stake High Council.

50

Muli Lisala

"BEHOLD YOUR LITTLE ONES"
3 Nephi 17:23

Taken from the oral history of Muli Lisala and from my own journal as mission president, this record of the experiences of Muli Lisala and Litiana Ngaluafe Lisala accentuates the sacrifice and faith of young couple missionaries who are called to preside over branches of the Church in the islands of Tonga. Muli and Litiana presently live in Mataika, Vava'u.

Muli Lisala

I was born in Mataika, Vava'u, on December 28, 1957, and married Litiana June 29, 1979. We first really became interested in the Church when two missionaries befriended us after Hurricane Isaac hit our island in March of 1982. We had lost our little house in the wind and were somewhat stunned by our sudden poverty. Even our extended family did not seem as concerned about us as the two Mormon elders in our village.

Through their influence, we became active members of the Church with a strong desire to go to the temple. One of our first responsibilities from our branch president was to care for the full-time missionaries in our village, keep them in food, wash their clothes, etc. We loved this assignment very much. Indeed, our association with the missionaries engendered a desire in us to serve a full-time mission ourselves.

Our call came on September 4, 1985, to serve in Ha'apai, first in the village of Pukotala and then on the island of Lofanga where I labored for three years as a missionary and branch president. Two full-time single elders stayed with us most of the time.

Litiana was pregnant when we arrived in Lofanga, and we were somewhat nervous about being stationed on this rather remote island. But when her time came, I took her by boat to the hospital in Pangai where she gave birth to a healthy baby boy.

The second pregnancy was not so easy. Litiana was ill a lot and very big. Indeed, the rigor of tiny island living, far from medical help, especially when the ocean was rough, took its toll. But we were sustained by the faith that despite our poverty, away from family and friends, we were doing the Lord's work, and that our little sacrifices would be rewarded with the health and strength of our little ones.

When Litiana went into labor the second time, the weather was so bad any effort to get to the hospital in Pangai was out of the question. The winds were strong and the seas heavy. Worse, there was no nurse or midwife in Lofanga at the time. I would have to be the midwife and my wife would simply have to tell me what to do.

I made up her little bed and called Elder 'Uhila Faiva and Elder Dean Huhane to help me administer to Litiana. Even in the extremity of her pain, I was amazed to see how much courage and faith in the priesthood she had. After all, we were on the Lord's errand. What joy we felt when a baby boy was born; and we wrapped him in wide strips of cloth, actually pieces of Litiana's old dresses which she had cut up for that purpose. Our joy was mingled with shock when we suddenly discovered that Litiana was still in labor. In a few minutes, a twin girl was born. We named her Kalolaine and the boy Sikāhema.

Our neighbors knew about the delivery only when they heard the cries of the twins. We were the center of attention for a while, but we were always anxious about the fact we had very little, even though we received a generous care package from the mission home. Litiana could not produce enough milk for the babies. Cleanliness and sanitation were at constant risk, especially when the weather was foul and the village muddy. To keep the herds of pigs from destroying the root crops on this minuscule island, a fence around the village keeps the animals within the village itself. This practice increases the sanitation problem.

Although the babies were generally healthy, boils suddenly popped up all over little Kalolaine's head. A neighbor lady saw them and offered a Tongan home remedy, but it did not help. We were much alarmed at the swiftness with which the infection filled little Kalolaine's body. By the time we were able to get her to Pangai by boat on March 1, 1988, Kalolaine's face had swelled until her features had virtually disappeared and her right shoulder and arm had tripled in size. We had already administered to her but we felt panic now, during the long wait for the doctor.

When the doctor finally came, X-rayed and examined Kalolaine, he set about to drain off this very aggressive infection, making incisions under her eye, on her back, below her armpit, and on her arm. And then for many weeks we stayed in the Pangai hospital as the doctors tried to eradicate the infection. Kalolaine suffered terribly and her condition progressively deteriorated. She had to be held constantly. Elders and sisters stationed in Ha'apai came regularly to relieve Litiana and me. Elder Sioeli Veamatahau donated blood. In the meantime, I was trying to take care of our other children in and around the hospital.

Eric Shumway

The Lisala baby's condition was exceedingly grave. We held a mission-wide fast for her and kept a daily check on her progress. The parents, especially the mother, were worn out with heartache and care. The daily phone calls to us from Pangai were depressing: "We have lost hope." "The death pall has settled." "It is now just a matter of time." We were tense with anxiety and grief.

One night Elder Lisala called weeping and saying that the baby was in such distress he did not believe she would survive the night. He suggested perhaps we should just "release" her to the Lord and stop praying and fasting for her recovery. He mentioned the funeral plans they were making and asked permission to take Kalolaine's body back to his home in Vava'u. Elder Lisala hastened to make it clear he was willing to bury her in Lofanga and continue their service as missionaries there, if I so wished.

After several minutes of conversation, I felt impressed to tell him to give another priesthood blessing to Kalolaine, that the Lord would put into his mind the words to promise Kalolaine, a promise that he would honor.

I hung up the phone and went back to the bedroom and knelt before the Lord to plead again for Kalolaine's life. As I began my prayer the words came into my mind, quietly and irresistibly: *"Vakai, na'a oku si'isi'i ho'o tui"* ("Take care, lest your own faith be insufficient"). With all my heart I prayed the Lord's blessing on this little one.

The next morning we rejoiced over the news that Kalolaine had miraculously survived the night and showed signs of significant improvement. On April 15 I visited the Lisala family in Pangai. Kalolaine was still puffy but able to smile when I held her. Brother Lisala said, "President, she was not merely rescued from the edge of the pit, but from the pit itself."

Still Kalolaine did not recover completely. The doctors in Ha'apai said she could be released to go home, but her right arm was paralyzed and a slight fever lingered. Her face showed signs of more swelling. The family wondered if they should take her to a folk healer or medicine man. I resisted that suggestion.

Early Thursday morning April 28, 1988, the Lord revealed what should be done. I saw little Kalolaine in a vivid dream being held in the arms of an LDS doctor, Sālesi Havili, who worked at Vaiola Hospital on Tongatapu. There was the unmistakable impression that we must bring the baby to Dr. Havili. I remembered also in the dream that I had photographs of Kalolaine taken by missionaries at the peak of her sickness. I got up immediately, found the photos, and drove to Dr. Havili's residence in Liahona. When he looked at the pictures he said: "Yes, I can treat her."

The Lisala family came to Tongatapu the next day; and through the patient attention and care of this good doctor, Kalolaine recovered completely.

Muli Lisala

I know that our daughter was saved by the power of faith and the holy priesthood, and the fastings and prayers of so many people. The whole experience taught us perfectly that *nothing* is impossible in the Lord. Our faith and testimony are forever strengthened.

51

Melino Kinikini

OUT OF THE MOUTHS OF LITTLE CHILDREN

Born and reared in 'Uiha, Ha'apai, Melino Kinikini is presently first counselor in the Ha'apai Stake presidency. President Kinikini and his wife, Meleseini Manisela Kinikini, are the parents of twelve children. Known for his prowess at sea, he has been a strength to the Church in the small islands of Ha'apai, including those of the western cluster, Lulunga.

On August 27, 1988, the stake president, Mdeni Fonua asked me to sail to Lulunga and conduct branch conferences in the islands of 'O'ua and Matuku. I was delighted to represent him in these islands and decided to take my wife with me and our six little ones who were not in school. It would be an opportunity for them to learn about other islands and people and to prepare for the time when they would serve the Lord in other lands.

We started out in our small sixteen-foot craft to go the thirty or so miles from 'Uiha to 'O'ua. It was a windy day and the ocean was choppy. As we passed by the island of Uonuku, around three in the afternoon, suddenly the boat stopped moving. The outboard engine began to race, but the propeller was no longer moving.

Without power the boat was instantly at the mercy of the waves, and before long we were adrift in the open sea. Struggling with the engine, I could hear the children's muffled sobs. I tried to comfort them with words of encouragement, but my expressions were not very convincing. "President, please won't you pray for us!" came a tiny voice from the children huddled in the bottom of the boat. It was our little son, our seventh child. So preoccupied was I with the mechanics of repair, I ignored the plea. That same plea came several times in the three hours that we drifted. At six o'clock I was completely baffled and beginning to feel a chill of fear come over me. Giving up on the engine, I asked the children to join together for a special devotional and prayer.

Although the waves pounded around and over us, the children seemed comforted by my willingness to leave off tinkering with the engine and hold a family prayer meeting. Meleseini led us in singing "Come, Come Ye Saints." As I sang the words of this sacred hymn with my children, I received an immediate lift to my confidence.

This act of devotion as a family freed my mind from the troubling, even horrible, possibilities of our being adrift in heavy seas without food or water. Without a doubt now, I knew we would make shore, for we were indeed on the Lord's errand. Hope and courage replaced fear among the children.

The moment we concluded our prayer, my mind was clear as to what I should do. With a piece of rope I was able to make an ingenious temporary repair, sufficient for us to get underway, although we moved very slowly. We arrived in 'O'ua at 10 P.M. We held the appropriate meetings the next day in 'O'ua, then headed for Matuku under the same temporary repair. When that gave way, we were already prepared from 'O'ua to do with a makeshift sail which my little children held in place.

We made it to Matuku at the agreed-upon time and held a wonderful conference with the Saints there, even though some of them, when they saw our sailing apparatus, wondered how we ever made it. The conference completed we were able to get proper help to get us home to 'Uiha.

The Lord loves and protects those who serve him faithfully. I am so grateful to him and to a stake president from whom I have learned much about sacrifice in the service of the Lord. Especially I am grateful for the voice of the Lord which often comes out of the mouths of little children.

52

Sione 'Oleli Piutau Tupou

"THE HEART OF THE CHILDREN"
Malachi 4:6

Sione 'Oleli Piutau Tupou is a high priest in the Malapo Ward, Vainī Stake. He is currently serving as a stake missionary.

    I grew up in the Church. My parents, Samuela and 'Amelia Puli, were deeply devoted to the gospel. While I was growing up we traveled to church from Malapo to Mu'a (three miles) in our one-horse cart every Sunday and on week days to Primary. They were true stalwarts. I attended the Mormon primary school in Matavaimo'ui and four years in Makeke (1928–32). Father passed away in 1932, and I dropped out of school to care for the family. In 1938, when Mother and my little sister were killed in a whirlwind (*'ahiohio*), I lost my anchor in the Church. I strayed from the Church, staying away for over forty-six years, attending the local Wesleyan congregation, becoming a regular preacher, donating money, and giving banquets for church dignitaries. No one really remembered that I was a baptized member of The Church of Jesus Christ of Latter-day Saints.

    One day, I believe in the month of August, 1984, I heard the announcement that an anti-Mormon film was going to be shown in Malapo village. I was shocked that a church which did so much good would be publicly attacked. On the appointed day and hour, I sat in the community kava club watching people queue up to see the film. I felt disgusted and depressed, even angry, but I kept my feelings to myself. I was very upset.

As I sat in this depression, I suddenly felt the presence of my father and mother who had been dead these many years. It was as if they were alive again. I broke down, unable to control my tears. I wept so much my fellow club members were alarmed, asking if I were ill. I simply said no. I stood up and made my way home without saying another word to them.

That night was miserable for me. I could not sleep. I kept thinking about Mom and Dad and seeing them in my mind. The next morning was worse, and I knew I had to get divine help if I were to escape the darkness that surrounded me.

I started a twenty-four-hour fast in which I begged Heavenly Father to help me, to tell me what I must do. When I broke my fast, I felt an indescribable relief and joy. Heavenly Father had impressed my heart with both the admonition and the courage to return to his church, my church, the church of my father and mother.

All of this happened on Thursday and Friday. On Sunday I dressed in my best and walked to the LDS chapel. The Saints were as surprised to see me as my former church members were bitter to watch me go. I heard some say, "Now there goes a ridiculous fool." But in fact, the personal slights and criticism were short-lived. I have not missed a Church meeting and have since been to the temple. My sweet wife, an invalid after suffering a paralytic stroke, gave a nod of approval when I told her I wanted to return to The Church of Jesus Christ of Latter-day Saints.

So many blessings have come to my family since my "reconversion." I have often considered how ironic it was that it should take an anti-Mormon film to jar me into serious reflection about the Church, to feel the closeness of my deceased parents, and to seek the witness of the truth through fasting and prayer.

53

Tēvita Taimani

HE WILL PROTECT
HIS SERVANTS

Tēvita Taimani was a zone leader for many months in Lulunga, the western cluster of tiny islands in the Haʻapai Group. As zone leader he was responsible for the health, morale, and the safety of sixteen to twenty missionaries spread out over eight islands.

Negotiating vast stretches of frequently treacherous ocean in an eighteen-foot boat requires sound judgment, skill, and much faith. Although a mission president always has a nagging concern about the safety of the Lulunga missionaries, in fact, this area has always been a spiritual training ground for the young men and women who serve in the Tonga Nukuʻalofa Mission.

On November 24, 1986, my companion and I set out in a borrowed boat, owned by Leni Fituafe and powered by a fifteen-horsepower Mariner outboard motor, to visit the missionaries in the surrounding islands in Lulunga. Our own boat, the *Moroni*, was in need of repair. The ocean was bad on this day; and by the time we got to the island of Matuku, it was treacherous. Waves crashed over the narrow reef opening which small craft pass through to harbor. Perhaps we should have just returned to Haʻafeva, but I felt an urgency to see the two missionaries stationed on this little island.

I told my companion, Elder Falakiko Lavaka, to put down the anchor and stay with the boat outside the reef, while I swam in to check on our missionaries. The anchor secured, I jumped in, caught a wave, and swam to shore.

Wading ashore, I was informed of a very sick person who needed to be rushed to the hospital in Ha'afeva. I agreed to take the patient but wondered how to get her aboard. We decided to chance the heavy surf and bring the boat through the reef opening. I motioned to Elder Lavaka to come in, which he tried to do. It was a tricky maneuver. Unfortunately, the engine stalled right at a critical moment and the boat was at the mercy of the heavy breakers. Instantly it was lifted by a wave and slammed down hard on the reef, very nearly capsizing. Several of our things spilled out into the ocean. Unbeknownst to us the gas tank had also tumbled over board, pulling with it the connecting hose to the engine. In the panic that followed, many hands righted the boat, put the patient aboard, and with great effort got us back out to deeper water. I can hardly believe that when I started the engine I did not notice the missing gas tank and hose. But start it did and I turned our bow toward Ha'afeva. It was late evening.

The ocean became more ugly and threatening as we made our way through the channel and around to the Ha'afeva anchorage nearly two miles away. The fifteen-horsepower engine struggled in the massive waves but sputtered once. Had it died we would have been in a disastrous situation, especially with our sick patient. Either we would have drifted into the open sea or been dashed to pieces on a reef.

Only when we were safely anchored in Ha'afeva and began gathering our things to go ashore did I discover that the gas tank was not in the boat and that we had come from Matuku in rough water without any gasoline feeding our tiny outboard engine.

The next morning, November 25th, we went back to Matuku to search for the lost gas tank. There it was, hose and all, in the sandy shallow water, somewhat dented from tumbling in the waves, but still intact and nearly full of gasoline.

I have experienced what I consider many miracles in the course of my mission in these far-away islands. This is one example of how we have been protected as we serve the Lord.

54

Sifa 'Auka Lātū & Feleti Kusitafu Havea

"CRY UNTO HIM
OVER THE CROPS
OF YOUR FIELDS"
Alma 34:24

The following story of faith and prayer came in letters by Elders Sifa 'Auka Lātū and Feleti Kusitafu Havea to their mission president, January 8, 1989. Their experience here is typical of that of thousands of Tongan missionaries over the years, who must work to survive as well as preach the gospel.

On October 30, 1988, we went with Elder Suiti Pupu to the bush to plant the sweet potato cuttings we had received from the mission office to improve our small garden plantation. It was hot and dry. There had been little rain in over two months. To make matters worse, the cuttings, coming from Tongatapu by boat, were shriveled and brown. No doubt they had been exposed to the sun and salt spray. The leaves of many of the cuttings had fallen off altogether. The zone leader who distributed the seed-plants (*pulopula*) had told us they would not survive, but we were eager to plant them anyway.

Our garden in Lofanga is surrounded by the plantations of several long-time residents of the island. When these men, all experienced gardeners, saw us preparing the dry soil and planting the dry stems of shriveled sweet potato cuttings, they made fun of us. One man said we were wasting our time and that we could have saved ourselves much effort had we just asked the opinion of those who were expert in farming this particular soil.

Perhaps we did indeed look very foolish to them. But Elder Lātū answered their mockery with a good-natured response, "We are planting now because it's going to rain tonight on the garden of the servants of the Lord."

At this the men hooted their derision and said, *"Mālie tama hoʻo ʻai faifekau!"* ("How marvelous, boy, that you should mention your ministerial position!")

They had a good laugh. But when we got through planting, we blessed our little garden. That evening we cried again to the Lord to send rain, even though the sky was clear with no sign of moisture, only stars from horizon to horizon. Several times we woke up and prayed.

In the middle of the night, the rain came. It rained heavily until the next morning. We embraced each other and ran to see Elder Pupu, the branch president. When we shook hands with him he said, "The rain came because of your prayer of faith. Never doubt the power within you!"

Our sweet potato patch is alive and well even to this day. Every plant survived.

55

Viliami Fisi'iahi

"THE PRAYER THAT IS MADE IN THIS PLACE"
2 Chronicles 7:15

Viliami Fisi'iahi, presently first counselor in the Nuku'alofa East Stake presidency, suffered from elephantiasis of the scrotum. This painful and humiliating disease had caused a gigantic swelling, the tissues of which were hard and fibrous. For Brother Fisi'iahi the process of healing was as much a quest for faith and a fuller relationship with his Heavenly Father as it was the miraculous disappearance of a grotesque disease which used to plague many inhabitants in mosquito-infested tropical islands.

In humility and praise, I want to tell you how I was miraculously healed from a most painful and maiming disease. In May of 1989, when my sickness had reached its extremity, Elder Joseph Wirthlin of the Council of the Twelve gave me a blessing and promised among other things that I would recover "according to my faith."

Much comforted by this blessing, I flew to Hawaii for medical examinations and treatment. Stake President 'Alifeliti (Alfred) Malupō met me at the airport and took me to the hospital for tests and X-rays. I was very fearful and a bit overwhelmed by the testing procedures and modern medical equipment. After a series of tests and at least four examinations, I sensed that my condition was more critical than I had thought, perhaps hopeless. The doctors seemed baffled about how to treat me. They said my problem was inoperable.

I had come to Hawaii believing that medical science in America must have a surgical technique to solve my problem and remove my misery. Now my prospects were zero. Nevertheless, I continued in prayer and fasting. There were whole nights I could not sleep, so I just prayed. My affliction brought me close to the Lord. I kept rehearsing in my mind the apostle's blessing, keeping before me the image of those who stood in the circle with Elder Wirthlin. In addition, I decided I would spend as much time as possible attending the Hawaii Temple. Kingi Mosaia Langi invited me to stay with his family in Laie; and from there I went to the temple daily.

As I attended the temple, I pondered the Old Testament passages in which the Lord promises mighty miracles and healings to those in Israel who seek him faithfully in his holy temple. In fact, I couldn't get these scriptural words out of my mind. They were an obsession to me and prompted me to attend the temple despite my affliction:

> I have heard thy prayer and have chosen this place to myself for an house of sacrifice.
> If I shut up heaven that there be no rain . . . or if I send pestilence among my people;
> If my people, which are called by my name, shall humble themselves, and pray, and seek my face, and turn from their wicked ways; then will I hear from heaven, and will forgive their sin, and will heal their land.
> Now mine eyes shall be open, and mine ears attent unto the prayer that is made in this place.
> For now have I chosen and sanctified this house, that my name may be there for ever: and mine eyes and mine heart shall be there perpetually.
> (2 Chronicles 7:12–16)

On August 31, 1989, after attending a temple session, I stayed in the celestial room and cried again unto Heavenly Father to heal me, to make me an example and testimony of his power to the four corners of the earth. I told him that for two full months now I had been in Hawaii for medical help and not the slightest decrease in the monstrous swelling had occurred. Alone in this sacred place, I reminded him of the blessing bestowed upon me by his apostle, Elder Wirthlin. Asking his pardon if my request was presumptuous, I even begged Heavenly Father for a visitation from the persons whose work I had performed that day. Perhaps they had a blessing for me. At any rate, as I walked from the temple to Kingi's home I had a profound sense that a heavenly visitor would come to me.

Back in my room at the Kingi Langi home I knelt by my bed and pleaded again for a blessing at the hands of some heavenly messenger.

After my prayers, I lay down to sleep when who should appear to me, handsome and young-looking, but my own father, Fisi'iahi, and two other men. My father had been dead many years.

"Why are you sleeping in this place of hardship?" he asked. "I have known of your suffering."

"I came to Hawaii to be treated for my disease," I replied, "but there is no improvement."

The three men approached me and knelt at the head of my bed. My father spoke and said, "Go to sleep and we will bless you."

I was so amazed by what was happening that I was not aware when I went to sleep. I did not hear the words of my father's blessing; but when I awoke the next morning, I felt light on my feet and vigorous. And when I beheld my lower parts I discovered my affliction had disappeared. There was no ugly swelling. My body was perfectly normal. Instantly I fell on my knees in gratitude and poured out my thanksgiving to Heavenly Father for this miracle in my life. As I prayed, it occurred to me that this happiest of moments was not the result of my prayers alone but also because of the faith of many people who loved me.

I know for myself the gospel is true and promise to live it more perfectly. I know also the real power of "knocking," of "seeking" and "asking," of crying continually unto the Lord. Finally, I know that the skill of man, no matter how clever, will fade, but the power of the priesthood will continue on forever. In the name of Jesus Christ, Amen.

Note by Eric B. Shumway: On Sunday, September 3, 1989, President Fisi'iahi came to our home in Laie at about 6:30 A.M. to tell me about his miraculous recovery. Pointing to a two-quart plastic bottle of cooking oil on our kitchen counter, he said his swelling was much larger than the jar. However, the morning after his remarkable experience with his father, the bloated, fibrous tissue had drastically reduced in size. In tears of joy and before I could stop him, President Fisi'iahi parted his lavalava to show me the evidence of the miracle and I rejoiced with him. A few days later I told President Fisi'iahi's experience to our own family doctor. He commented on the difficulty of treating such advanced elephantiasis and said that only divine intervention could have caused such a sudden and miraculous recovery.

56

'Alofanga Moli

"HE RAN TO MEET HIM AND EMBRACED HIM"
Genesis 33:4

'Alofanga ('Alo) Moli, a counselor in the Neiafu North Stake presidency, has served both a labor mission and a proselyting mission for the Church. His missionary service extended to Tafahi, Niuatoputapu, and to 'Eua. An exceptional gardener, 'Alo supervised the Church Welfare Farm in 'Eua. He and his wife 'Ana have fourteen children. 'Alofanga's story is typical of many uneducated young men who converted to the Church early in life and learned the principles of great leadership by personal study and continued selfless service in the Church.

I was born on February 8, 1939, in the village of Holonga, Vava'u. Both of my parents were strong Wesleyans, having been brought up in that church since their birth. My mother had been a soloist in her church choir for several years preceding her death in 1951. My first real introduction to the LDS Church came when I attended Liahona High School on Tongatapu. Unfortunately my stay there lasted only a few months because of a serious illness which forced me to return home to Vava'u. For two years this mysterious illness plagued my life. By 1956 I was so acutely ill I thought I was going to die. Nothing prescribed by the folk healers or the doctors helped me. During the worst part of my illness, a Mormon missionary serving as a school teacher in the nearby village of Ha'alaufuli stopped by. He had certain medical skills and gave me some medication which brought me a relief I had not felt for two years. The next morning, the missionary returned and spoke with my father. He said he had another form of medication much better than the one he had given me the day before. Of course, the medication he was referring to was the gospel of Jesus Christ and his testimony of its truthfulness.

From that time forth, I began to develop a fondness for the programs of the Mormon Church. I began to think about becoming a member. Unfortunately, the day of my baptism was also the day of an annual celebration in the Wesleyan Church. I knew my father was preparing food for invited guests to celebrate the occasion. When 'Osikā Wolfgramm, the branch president, came by to take me to my baptism, my father said, "I do not want you to be baptized! Why are you doing this on this special day?"

I answered, "Because I believe I have found the true church."

I'll never forget his enlightened response to my testimony, "Son, if indeed it is the true church, I will one day follow you in knowing the truth. If however, it is not true, you will find out and return to the church of your birth."

As I departed from my home that day to enter the waters of baptism, I knew in my heart I was doing the will of my Heavenly Father in joining his true church.

Shortly after my baptism, I was called as a construction missionary to work on the new LDS chapel in Ha'alaufuli. On the very day I began working, I suddenly became very ill. My father told me to give up my new calling or my previous chronic illness would return. I had a terrible pain in my head and my vision was blurred.

Although I felt desperate, I had the presence of mind to ask my father to find two Mormon elders to come and bless me. He went straight out and located two priesthood holders who came and administered to me. They promised me in that blessing that if I remained steadfast and diligent in the building of the kingdom, I would never again become ill. From that point on I have never again experienced any other illness. This dramatic blessing was also the beginning of my father's faith in the truthfulness and healing power of the gospel of Jesus Christ.

I continued my work as a building missionary, moving from one construction site to another in Vava'u. While I was laboring in the village of Tu'anuku, I heard the amazing news that my father was getting baptized. I was astounded by this report, especially sinceI had not really discussed the gospel in depth with him since my baptism.

The Sunday of his baptism he stood before the congregation of Saints and expressed his testimony. He related what he had told me on the day I was baptized – that if this were not the true church, I would return to my father's faith; however, if this were indeed the true church, he would learn of it and would one day join me.

During that year, the rest of my brothers and sisters were also baptized members of the Church. My father's prophecy had indeed proven true.

Father's baptism caused a stir in our village and in the communities round about. It little mattered to him, however, because of the profound feeling he had for the Church. His only concern was the attitude of his brother, Makaneti, whom he had been closest to all his life and with whom he had never argued. Their sweet brotherly relationship was well known throughout the village.

Now Makaneti was the driver of the Wesleyan truck which carried worshippers to special meetings or conferences in other villages. On the Sunday morning of my father's baptism, Makaneti took a load of school girls to their homes for the Sabbath. Coming back to our village, he encountered my father walking along the side of the narrow road. As the truck approached, it suddenly swerved and bore down on my father. Father had to leap frantically into the brush off the road to avoid being hit. The truck sped on.

My poor father was shocked by this behavior, for surely his brother had seen him. Had he not jumped out of the way of the truck he certainly would have been killed.

Disturbed and hurt by Makaneti's behavior, Father pondered what had happened and what could cause such a change to a brother's love. Later, when Makaneti started out again in the truck to pick up the school girls, my father once again stood by the road side, saying in his heart, "If my brother hates me this much for my belief, I will let him run over me as I stand here. I'll not budge an inch to save my life."

This time, however, as the truck approached, it gradually slowed down and came to a complete stop by my father. Makaneti opened the door and jumped out of the truck. He embraced my father, kissed him, and begged his forgiveness. Weeping, he said, "In all my life, I have never felt a bad feeling toward you until I heard that you had been baptized a Mormon. But now those feelings are gone."

Since the day I joined the Church, my life has been enriched with blessings from the Lord. Together with my wife and children, we spent many fruitful years in missionary work. Our greatest blessing occurred in 1974 when we were finally able to travel as a family to New Zealand and be sealed for time and eternity in the temple there.

We had spent much of our married life up to that time serving on a mission for the Church. We had been frugal with the little money we had and always kept an excellent garden. It was not because of our own resources, however, that we were able to attend the temple. It was because of the unexpected generosity of those who sacrificed much to go to the temple themselves and were still sacrificing to help others. Different members of the Church came to me privately and offered to pay for the fare of one of our children. We will not ever forget those precious weeks at the New Zealand Temple or the kindness of others that made it possible for us to be there.

Thus we have been blessed. And though I am but a farmer on a tiny Pacific island, I stand before the world as a witness of truth in The Church of Jesus Christ of Latter-day Saints. When I think of Christ's departure from his apostles, I can imagine their loneliness, their feelings of weakness and fear. But when the gift of the Holy Spirit came upon them they became so strong, so self-assured in the truth of Christ and his gospel that nothing made them waver--not persecution, not hatred, hunger, nor even death. That same Spirit I have felt in my heart and I know Christ is real. Fear and death mean nothing to me. My only desire is to serve Jesus with all my heart.

APPENDIX

Early Priesthood Leaders in Tonga

Sē Saulala invited the LDS missionaries to establish the Church in Haʻalaufuli in 1908, the first official branch of the Church in Tonga. (Courtesy M. Vernon Coombs family)

Sione Tuʻikolongahau, early convert (1908) and missionary, helped establish the Church in Haʻalaufuli, Vavaʻu, and composed many Church hymns. In 1917 he went to Haʻapai with Elders Newell J. Cutler and J. K. Rallison to establish the Church again in those islands. His hymns " ʻOku ʻi ai ʻi Maama ni ʻae Siasi Moʻoni" ("There Is One True Church in the World"), set to the tune of "In Our Lovely Deseret" and " ʻOku Fafangu Mai ʻa e Ongoongolelei" ("The Gospel's Awakening") are rousing testimonials of the Restoration.

Siosifa Naeata from Haʻalaufuli, Vavaʻu, was probably the first Tongan to receive the Melchizidek Priesthood, 1915. He became a mighty missionary and Church leader in Vavaʻu. (Courtesy M. Vernon Coombs family).

Siosaia Mataele invited LDS missionaries to establish the Church in Foʻui, Tongatapu, in 1910. A man of means and influence, he greatly facilitated the work of the early missionaries. A shrewd businessman, Siosaia was also a people's representative in Parliament for many years. He composed several favorite hymns for the Church, including "Monū Ka Ko Ha Monū Ne Tō" ("How Blessed the Gift Bestowed"). (Courtesy Sio Tuʻilatai Mataele)

Kitione Maile, an early convert, established the Church in Nukunuku in 1911. He served as president of Nukunuku Branch and as a proselyting missionary. Gregarious and fun-loving, Kitione was as famous for his humorous orations and hilarious pantomimes as he was for his spiritual energy and serious preaching. He could spark a crowd anywhere and, before he joined the Church, was a favorite "clown" of King Tupou II. Kitione was a successful Church leader, despite the fact that he could neither read nor write. (Courtesy Emile C. Dunn family)

Filimone Tupou Muʻamohōleva established the Church in Muʻa in 1912. He served as president of Muʻa Branch and as a proselyting missionary. For his testimony of the restored gospel and his love of the Church, Filimone gave up much, including a respected ministerial position in the Wesleyan church and, finally, his wife, who refused to have anything to do with the Church. Filimone helped secure land for the Church from the estate of Tungī Mailefihi. (Courtsy Meliame A. ʻUnga)

Metuisela Tuaʻone established the Church in Fāhefa in 1917. Before his conversion, he was a Wesleyan minister. He held fast to the faith, in spite of persecution from village people. A powerful speaker and preacher, he converted many and started a school in Fāhefa where he was branch president for many years. (Courtesy M. Vernon Coombs family)

Sālesi Vānisi established and nurtured the Church and a school in Nakolo, Tongatapu, and was Nakolo Branch president for many years. (Courtesy M. Vernon Coombs collection)

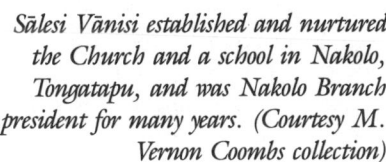

Sione Ma'u Tomasi (left) and Mele Ma'u Tomasi, a faithful couple who established the Church in Fua'amotu, Tongatapu, in the early 1920s. Sione was branch president for many years. Fua'amotu was a favorite spot for Makeke missionaries because of Sione's and Mele's hospitality. (Courtesy Ralph Olson)

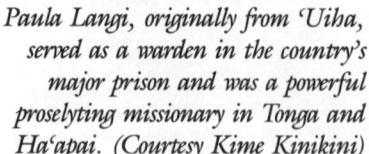

Paula Langi, originally from 'Uiha, served as a warden in the country's major prison and was a powerful proselyting missionary in Tonga and Ha'apai. (Courtesy Kime Kinikini)

Short in stature but mighty in faith and testimony, Militoni Fonua helped establish the Church in Houma, Tongatapu, where he enthusiastically supported the Church, even when discouraged missionaries recommended closing the branch. His family of thirteen children became the anchor of the Church in Houma, which now has two wards. (Courtesy M. Vernon Coombs family)

Tupou Kapetaua, an early convert to the Church in Pangai, Ha'apai, donated the site of Pangai's chapel. He and his wife, Sisi, were "parents" to the fledgling Church in Ha'apai, especially to the missionaries, local and foreign. (Courtesy M. Vernon Coombs family)

Tēvita Pita Pauni, long-time Church and civic leader in Ha'alaufuli, Vava'u; also served as Vava'u District president and as Ha'alaufuli town officer. Educated in the Church schools in Vava'u, he played in the Church band as a youth, survived the flu epidemic of 1918, taught at Makeke, and served several missions. (Courtesy M. Vernon Coombs family)

Paula Malupō served several missions, was president of 'Otea and Vainī branches, was three times a counselor in the East District presidency, was Sunday School district president, and is currently high priest group leader and temple ordinance worker at the Hawaii Temple. His son, 'Alifeleti, is president of Waipahu Stake in Hawaii. (Courtesy M. Vernon Coombs family).

Sione Tuita Vehikite was educated in the Maori Agricultural College in New Zealand, taught at Makeke and Liahona, and assisted in translating the Doctrine and Covenants and Pearl of Great Price into Tongan. He organized the first band at Makeke. (Courtesy M. Vernon Coombs family)

Sioeli Kauvaka Sika, a native of Niuatoputapu, settled in Feletoa, Vava'u, where he established the Church and was branch president for twenty-three years. He was also, in 1937, the first LDS missionary sent to Niuatoputapu. (Courtesy Siola'ā Kauvaka)

Lisiate Talanoa Maile, son of pioneer Kitione Maile, served a mission to Vava'u and Ha'apai, as president of Nukunuku Branch, as president of Tongatapu District, as a Church school board member, and as counselor to two mission presidents, Evon Huntsman and D'Monte Coombs. (Courtesy M. Vernon Coombs family)

Nafetalai 'Alusa was converted before 1920 and served as a missionary and branch president in many places. A master builder of traditional Tongan houses, he built the queen's house at the Polynesian Cultural Center in 1963. Nafetalai was also a respected matāpule *(Mala'efo'ou) of Queen Sālote. (Courtesy M. Vernon Coombs family)*

Index

Note: The U.S. system of alphabetization has been used. For example, words containing a glottal (') are alphabetized according to the letter following the glottal, and *ng* combinations are alphabetized between *nf* and *nh*. Note also that royal persons are indexed under their titles, i.e., King . . . , Queen . . . , Duke . . . , etc.

Key to Abbreviations

Tpu:	Tongatapu	Ntt:	Niuatoputapu
Hp:	Ha'apai	Nf:	Niuafo'ou
Vv:	Vava'u	'Eua:	'Eua

A

Aaronic Priesthood, xiii, 6, 168
Adams, Luella, xiii
Adams, Thomas, xiii, 36
Afā (Tpu), xxxi
Afatasi, 46
Afeaki, Viliami (Bill), 32
Afu, Seini Lola, **201**
Ahivao, Lesieli, **40**
'Aho, Tēvita Kilisimasi, 210
'Ahome'e, 111
'Ahononou, 274
Ake, Malakai, 268
'Alatini, Helu, **199**
Alatini, Tunai, **136**
Alatini, Vakapuna, 17, 19, **136**
Albrecht, Keith, xxvii
Aleamotua, 259
'Alipate, xiii
'Alusa, Nafetalai, xx, xxiv, **313**
'Amasio, 'Atonio, 169
Amos, Richard, 3
Anderson, Brent, xxxiii
Anderson, Edward O., xx
Angilau, Noma, **138**
Angilau, Siu Tu'ifua, **201**
'Anitoni, 238
Aoniu, 185
Apia Samoa Temple, 215
apostolic blessing, xi–xii
'Asilusi, Simaima, **69**
'Atatā, 283
'Atele (Tpu), 195, 210
Auckland, New Zealand, 175
Auckland Second Ward, 98
Auhangamea channel (Hp), 163, 164, 168, 169

B

Baker, Shirley, 3, 4, 5, 153
Ballif, Ariel S., 96
Ballif, Arta, 96
Banks, Douglas, 18, **135**
Batty, M. Walter, 36
Beehive girls, xviii, 77
Beisinger, George, 98
Blake, Bevan, xx
blessings by General Authorities, xi, 91–92, 108, 192–193, 298–300. *See also* gift of tongues, missionaries, priesthood blessings, prayer.
Bloomfield, Lilieta, 212
Bloomfield, Pesi, 212
Bohn, Murry L., 36
Bohn, Charlotte M., 36
Book of Mormon, xviii, xix, 6, 103, 104, 214, 224
Boy Scouts, xviii, xxv; World Jamboree, 212
Brigham Young University–Hawaii campus, xxxv, 184, 190, 240, 241, **250**, 257, 274. *See also* Church College of Hawaii.
Brigham Young University, Provo, 174, 257
British High Commission, 4, 5
Britsch, R. Lanier, xxxiv, 2, 23, 173
Brown, Mele Fakatou, 65
building missionaries, xx, xxii, xxiii, xxiv, xxv, 178–180, 211, 221, 223–225, 257, 302
Butler, Alva, xii, 5, 7
Butler, Carol, xxx
Butler, David, **199**
Butler, Melvin, xxx, xxxi

C

Cahoon, Ada Layne, xvi, 12, 73–78
Cahoon, Jay A., xvi, 73–78
Canada, xv
Cargill, David, 3
Carter, Austin A., xvi, 84
Catholic Church, 4, 51, 61
Charles (missionary), 58
Charles, Ezzard, 174, 175
Chase, Lance, xxxiv
Childs, C. Raymond, xvii
Christensen, James P., xxii, xxvii, xxviii, 31, **207**
Christensen, Metta Heder, xxvii, **207**
Christianity, 1–7, 259
Christiansen, ElRay L., xxvii
Church College of Hawaii, xxiv, 15, 62, 188, 140, 190, 223, 237, 245, 272. *See also* BYU–Hawaii.
Church College of New Zealand, 98
Church News, 18
Church of Jesus Christ of Latter-day Saints, The, 1, 5, 7, 8, 114, 115, 121, 122, 125, 147, 216, 221, 243, 264, 270, 283, 292, 302; area conference, xxx, xxviii; growth of, 15, 23, 30; history of in Tonga, xiii–xxxii. *See also* names of individual units.
Church of Tonga, 59, 147, 148
Church schools, xii, xiii, xiv, xxiii, xxvi, xxviii, xxix, 6, 7, 48, 49, 52, 53, 76, 101, 125, 181–183, 190, 237, 277, 292, 311. *See also* Makeke School and Liahona School.
Church Social Services, 257
Clark, DaCosta, xvi
Clark, Reuben, xv, **41**
Cloward, Mark, xxvii
Cockle, Don, 175
"Come, Come, Ye Saints," 291
conversion experiences, 58–59, 82–83, 90–92, 106–108, 113–115, 118–123, 147–148, 181–183, 216–217, 259–261, 264–266, 272–273, 282–285, 292–293, 301–304. *See also* fasting,

Index

missionaries, prayers, priesthood blessings, visions and dreams.
convert baptisms, xviii, xxx, xxxi, xxxii, 23, 30, 214–215
Cook, Owen, xxiii
Coombs, D'Monte, xxi, xxii, xxxiv, 31, 136, 145–146, 151, 152, 154, 166, 174, 212, 313
Coombs, Joan Winegar, xxi, 14, 145–146
Coombs, LaVera Wilcox, xv, xxiii, 31, **39, 40, 41**, 145, **202**
Coombs, M. Vernon, xv, xvi, xxiii, xxiv, xxxv, 17, 20, 23, 24, 29, 31, **39, 41**, 75, 77, 131, 145, 188, 218, 223, 312
Cottle, Joseph Archie, xxii, xxvi, 172
Cowley, Matthew, xx, 91
Cross, William, 3
Cullimore, James, xxvii
cultural shock, 17, 19, 76
Cutler, Floy B., xvi, xvii
Cutler, Newell J. (Misi Sēmisi), xvi, xvii, 307

D

Dalton, Lela Jesperson, xxv, 11, 131, 165–166, **201**
Dalton, Patrick, xxii, xxiv, xxv, xxvi, xxviii, xxxii, 31, 165, 212, 213
Davis, Ebbie L., xxviii
Department of Education, 211, 212
Dolo, Gideon, xxiii
Dowdle, Jack W., xxii
drought, xviii, xix, 116, 212–213, 296–297
Duke of Edinburgh, xxi
Dunn, Emile C., xv, xvii, xviii, xx, 31, 38, **41**, 86, 96, 97, 101, 102–105, 116, 125, 142, 147, 211, 212, 308
Dunn, Evelyn Hyde, xvii, xviii, 142
Durham, Alfred, xiii
Durham, Margaret, xiii

E

Eia, 172
'Esau, Sione, xvii
'Eteaki, Siale, **132**
'Eteaki, Vehitau, **132**
'Eua, xviii, xix, 22, 66, 127, 141, 148, 215, 221, 275, 301
'Eueiki, xxiv
'Evakihakau, 'Alo, 183, 195
evil spirits, 187

F

Fā, Fangapulotu, 142
Fā, Uai, **136**, 142, 161
Fa'anunu, Lolohea Pupungatoa, xvi
Fa'aoso, Sulieti Ula, **69**
Facer, W. O., xiv, 17, 31, 52
Fāhefa (Tpu), xvi, xxvii, 113, 142, 211, 309
faith, 8–9, 11, 12
– and bereavement, 61
– and conversion, 107, 113–114, 119, 120, 147, 182–183
– and obedience, 116–117, 150–154, 169, 190, 191
– and protection, 125–126, 155–157, 168, 171–172
– and sacrifice, 11–12, 81, 86, 87, 109, 116, 143, 170–172, 178–180, 188, 190
– and testimony, 99, 103, 123
– to be healed, 13, 22, 23, 59, 86, 99, 119–120, 146
– to heal, 54, 88, 98, 109, 110, 146
Faiva, 'Uhila, 287
Faivaola, 25, 26
Fakafanua, 24
Fakahua, Lupeni, 209
Fakalata, Sinisā, xix
Fakataha, Viliami (Vili), 59, 217, 219, 260
Fakatou, Heleine, xix, **65**, 85, 114, 125

Index

Fakatou, Rodney S., xxv
Fakatou, Samuela, xx, xxi, xvi, xvii, xviii, xix, 31, **65**, 83, 84, 85, 114, 122, 125, 127
Fakatou, Seluvaia Mafi, 82
Fakatou, Teleita, 13, 82–84
Fakavā, Sione, **204**
fale, **68, 132, 207**
Fale-'a-liku, 107
Falehau (Ntt), 233
Faleloa (Hp), xviii, xxvii, 12, 125, 147, **208**, 210, 211,
Fale'one Prison, 158
Falevai (Vv), xxi, xxx, 11, 189
famine, xix
Fangale'ounga (Hp), 91
Fanga'uta (Tpu), xiv, 10
Fangupō Hola, 210
Fa'oliu, 'Isileli, 272, 273
Fa'oliu, Nūnia, 272
Fasi, 'Alisi, **69**
Fasi, Silika, **69**
fasting: *See also* conversion, prayer, priesthood blessings, visions and dreams.
  – as principle, 20, 213, 215, 244–245
  – Church-wide in Tonga, 213–214
  – for healing, 22, 28, 98, 99, 119–120, 224–225, 263, 288–289
  – for inspiration, 85, 100, 190–191
  – for repeal of Passport Act, xv, 90
  – for increased faith, 121, 210–211, 233–234, 264, 275, 282–283, 293, 298–300
Fatafehi, Taufa, 110
Fatafehi, Vika, 109
Fatai (Tpu), xxvii, 22, 151, 152, 211, 212
Fatani, Siosaia, xvi
Fāua, 275
Faust, James E., xi
Favini, 172
Fehi, Sili, xvi
Fehoko, 'Isileli, xviii
Fehoko, 'Ofa Simote, **69**, 143, 211
Fehoko, Simote, **136,** 143, 211

Fehoko, Vāvasa, xx
Fei, 172
Feinga, Hāunga, 229–232
Feinga, Sela, 12, 229–232
Feinga, Sione, **257**
Felemea (Hp), 113, 162, 163, 222
Feletoa (Vv), xxxii, 53, 54, 312
Fetu'u, Selu Vili, **69,** 161, 211
Fetu'u, Viliami (Vili), **136,** 161, 211
Fetu'u'aho, 52
Fetu'u'aho, Mele, **69**
Fetu'umoana, xxix, 277
Fie'eiki, Filimone, **258**
Fie'eiki, Lesieli, **202**
Fie'eiki, Simote, 183
Fielakepa, 24
Fifita, Liahona Taufa, **201**
Fifita, Mele Laukau, 113
Fifita, Moeaki, **208**
Fifita, Samuela Lelei, 113
Fiji, xix, xxiii, xxix, 99, 107, 166, 267
Fiji Mission, xxiii, xxvii, xxviii
Filipe, Fine, 211
Filipe, Sione, xvi, xx, 125, 211
Fine [surname not known], **40**
Fineanganofo, Falaetau Mahu'inga, 243
Fineanganofo, Mahu'inga, **249**
Fineanganofo, Sione, Jr., **249**
Fineanganofo, Sione Moala, xxx, 243–245, **249, 258**
First Presidency, 104, 145, 215
Fisher, Orrin, xvi
Fisi, Tu'ivakanō, xx, **132**
Fisi'iahi, Viliami, 298–300
Fituafe, Leni, 294
Fletch, Carol P., 2
Fletcher, Floyd C., xviii, 97, 103
Flynn, Reuben M., xx
Foini, 172
Folaha (Tpu), xix
Folau, 'Asi Lolohea, xxiv, xxvii, **202**
Folau, Noa, **202**

Index

Folau, Senitila, **204**
Folau, Vili Pele, xxviii, 228, **252**
Fonua, Kaati, **132**
Fonua, Kalake, **132**
Fonua, Lilika, **132**
Fonua, Lupeni, **132**
Fonua, Maka, **132**
Fonua, Mele, **132**
Fonua, Militoni, **132**, **311**
Fonua, Mōleni Tanginoa, xxxi, 14, **136**, **208**, 270–271, 290
Fonua, Nikolasi, 210
Fonua, Nola, **132**
Fonua, Piuela, **132**
Fonua, Pōsesi, 93
Fonua, Saia, 233, 234
Fonua, Sinipata, 189
Fonua, Taina, 210
Fonua, Teiko, **132**, 210
Fonua, Tilini, **132**
Fonua, Tohi, 13
foreign LDS missionaries. *See* missionaries.
Fotua (Hp), xxvii
Fotuhaʻa (Hp), 153, 229, 230
Foʻui (Tpu), xiv, xvi, 48, 49, 58, 60, 62, 80, 87, 184, 308
Free Church of Tonga, 4, 5, 6, 53, 83, 106, 124, 209, 243, 283
French, Adele, **199**
Friendly Islands, 155
Fuaʻamotu (Tpu), xvi, xxiii, 51, 150, 151, 152, 153, 274, 278, 310
Fuaʻamoto airport (Tpu), 279–281
Fuahelotu, 23
Fulivai, ʻIki Tupou, xiv
Fulivai, Levaitai, **40**
Fūnaki, Kesaia, 209
Fūnaki, Kolo, 141, 142
Fungavaka, ʻOtiti, 189
Fungavaka, Tohuʻia, **200**

G

Garfield, Reed, **199**
Gerber, Tisinā Wolfgramm, 66, 87–89
Germany, 95
Giles, Ellen, **36**
Giles, Emma, **36**
Giles, Fatamafi, 36
Giles, George, **36**
Giles, James E., **36**
Giles, Louisa, **36**
Giles, Rachel, **36**
gifts of the spirit, 13–14, 43; of healing, 13, 14, 22–23, 46; of tongues, 2, 13, 19–20, 43–46, 101–102, 145. *See also* prayer, blessings by General Authorities, missionaries.
Glines, Alden, xvi
Goo, Charles, Sr., 241
Gowing, Lionel, xxi
Grant, Heber J., 73, 77, 103
Gribble, Cecil F., 210
Groberg, Jean Sabin, xxvi, 155
Groberg, John H., xxii, xxvi, xxvii, xxix, 18, 31, 155–157, 161, 213, 214, 222, **258**

H

Haʻafeva (Hp), xxix, 124, 229, 230, 235, 264, 277, 294, 295
Haʻakame (Tpu), xiv, xvi, 256
Haʻakame Ward, xxvii
Haʻakio (Vv), xxix, 147, 199
Haʻakupu (Niue), 171
Haʻalalo (Tpu), xxxi
Haʻalaufia, Kupu, **202**
Haʻalaufuli (Hp), 257, 302
Haʻalaufuli (Vv), xiv, xvi, xvii, xviii, xxii, 9, 51, 52, 76, 85, 102, 160, 185, 187, 189, 213, 242, 257, 301, 302, 307

Ha'amonga, **253**
Hā'ano (Hp), xvi, 193, 211
Ha'apai, 6, 131, 135, 136, 208, 215, 255
Ha'apai Group, 152, 193, 229, 270, 294
Ha'apai Tonga Stake, xxx, xxxi, 208, 270, 290
Ha'apulou (Tpu), 18
Ha'atafu (Tpu), 142
Ha'ateiho (Tpu), xxx, 115
Ha'atua ('Eua), xxviii
Hafoka, Pesi, 210
Hafoka, Silivenusi, 264, 265
Halaloto (Tpu), xviii, xx
Hall, Sally, xxxiv
Handy, Duane, **199**
Hansen, Reuben L., **39, 41**
Hansen, Thomas, xxi
Hardy, Rufus K., xviii, 103
Harmon, Dean, **199**
Harmon, Rondo, xxv
Harris Devere, xxx
Harris, James William, xxviii, xxix, 175
Harris, Norman, **204, 258**
Harris, Percy, **204**
Harris, Tupou, **204**
Haskell, Lynn E., xxvii
Hatch, Arson, xxvii
Hā'ungatau, Sione, **136**
Havea, Feleti Kusitafu, 296–297
Havealeta, 235
Haveluloto (Tpu), xi, xxvii, 214
Haveluloto Ward, xxvii
Havili, Nomani, **136**
Havili, Sālesi Falefo'ou, 12, 163, 263, 267–269, 289
Havili, Selu, 267
Havili, Sione Moala, 163
Hawaii Temple, 237, 299, 312
Helquist, Boyd, 16, 23, 24, **202**
Helu, 'Iteni, **258**
Hemaloto, Taupeavai Mapa, 71

Henderson, Clarence, xv, **41**
Hiatt, Duane, xxiii
Hifofua, 152
Higbee, Edwin, **199**
Hihifo (Hp), xxi, 153
Hihifo, (Ntt), 51
Hikutamole, 52
Hinckley, Gordon B., xxx
Hoatatau, 'Aisake, xxii
Hōfoa (Tpu), xxiv, 211, 217, 218, 237, 282, 283, 284, 285
Hōfoa Ward, 282, 284, 285
Hoi (Tpu), xxxi
Hola, Siosaia, xx
Holdaway, Harold, xvi
Holonga (Vv), xxx, 301
Hopoate, Howard Hunter, 278
Hopoate, Lani Alconcel, 274, 278
Hopoate, Lātū, **138**
Hopoate, Makamāpele (Māpeli), **138**, 274
Hopoate, Mele Māpeli, **138**
Hopoate, Pita Foliaki xxviii, xxix, xxx, xxxi, xxxii, 9, 31, **258**, 274–281
Hopoate, Seleti, xxix
Hopoate, Viliami, 274
Houma ('Eua), 148
Houma (Tpu), xiv, xvi, xxvi, 87, **132**, 185, 210, **311**
Hu'akau, Sione, 209
Huhane, Dean, 287
Hunga (Vv), xxix, 151
Hunter, Howard W., xxvii
Hunter, William P., xiii, 36
Huntsman, Evon W., xiv, xix, xx, xxi, xxxiv, 31, 104, 313
Huntsman, Martha, xix
hurricanes, xvii, xxii, xxiv, xxx, 75, 143, 158, **199–201**, 226, 227, 228
Hurricane Isaac, **254**, 277, 278, 286
hymns, 148–149, 214, 291, 307, 308

Index

I

Ika, 'Asaeli, **256, 258**
Ika, Selu, **256**
Ikakoula, Fauniteni, xx
Iketau, Nola, **204**
Iketau, Sioeli, xxxi, **204**
'Iloa, Fūnaki Sione, 235
'Iloa, Samuela, xxx, 8, 235–236, **258**
'Iloa, Sela, 235
'Iloa, Silivia, 235–236
influenza, xv, xvii, 53, 96
'Iongi, Musie, **204**
'Iongi, Sēmisi, **204**
'Iongi, Sione, **204**
'Iongi, Tofua, 235

J

Jaynes (missionary), 44, 45, 46
Jensen, Christian, 49
Jensen, Maurice, xvi
Jensen, Verda Nelson, xxxiv, 43
Jerusalem Center, 100
Jesus Christ, events in life of, 113, 218, 304; name of, 227–228; dream of, 142
Jets, 66, 82
Johannson, Albin ('Alipini), 93–94
Johannson, Feleti, 92–93
Johnson, Bea, 37
Jones, Albert S., 36
Josephs, Lillie, xiv
Josephs, Malia, xiv

K

Kahuku Second Ward (Hawaii), 79
Kaifoto, Sione, 87
Ka'ili, Lakalaka Mālohifo'ou, 255, 272
Ka'ili, Tēvita, xxvii, xxviii, xxx, xxxii, xxxiii, 70, **252**, 258, 272–273
Kalaniuvalu, 24, 212
Kanokupolu (Tpu), 142
Kao, 163
Kapa (Vv), 189
Kapetaua, Melesisi, **69**
Kapetaua, Tupou, **311**
Kaufusi, Ma'ake Mafi, **136**
Kaumatule, Heu'ifanga, **204**
Kaumatule, Veuki, xxxi, **204, 258**
Kauvaka, Sioeli, xviii, **312**
Kauvaka, Siola'ā, **312**
kava, 24–28, **39,** 110, 238, 292
Kavafau, Fifita, **69**
Kavapalu, Tautua'ā, 263
Kefu, Tauhelangi, 279
Kimball, Spencer W., xxviii, xxix, xxx, 192, 213, 215, **250, 251,** 262
King George Tupou I, xiii, 2, 3, 4
King George Tupou II, xiv, xv, 49, 308
King Taufa'ahau Tupou IV, **x,** xi, xxvi, xxx, xxxi, xxxiii, 24, **131,** 213, **250, 251**
Kinghorn, James, xiii
Kinikini, Hanipale, xxix, 277
Kinikini, Kime, 67, 310
Kinikini, Le'o Langi, **67, 69,** 106–112
Kinikini, Meleseini Manisela, 290–291
Kinikini, Melino, 290–291
Kinikini, 'Ofa Vakena, **204**
Kinikini, Sione Takapautolo, **199**
Kinikini, Taniela, 106
Kinikini, Tēvita Muli, 9, 10, 14, 22, **67,** 106–112, **202,** 217, 219
Kinikini, Susana 'Auhangamea Pō'uha, 108
Kinikini, Vaiokema, **204**
Kioa, Filipe, 90–92
Kioa, Folau, xxxiii
Kioa, Mele Līvai, **134**
Kioa, Sālote, 235
Kioa, Sela Kava, 14, 90
Kioa, Viliami Sovea, xxi, xxii, xxvi, xxvii, 26, 31, 101, 122, **134,** 178, **199,** 212, 223

Kitekeiʻaho, Tēvita, xxiv
Kīvalu, Kelikupa, **204, 256, 258**
Kīvalu, Manu Mahuʻinga, **204, 256**
Knowlton, Franklin R., xxii, 178
Ko e Taʻu e Teau ("One Hundred Years"), 103
Koka Sione, 27
Kolikoli, 172
Kolo, Heamasi, **136**
Kolo, ʻInoke, xxv
Koloa, 212
Koloa (Vv), xiv, xvi, 52, 95, 109, 110, 185
Kolomotuʻa (Tpu), xxviii, 53, 216, 259
Kolonga (Tpu), xxiii, 24, 26, 51
Kolovai (Tpu), 274
Komatsu, Adney Y., **251**
Konaʻī, Piliote, 147, 210
Konaʻī, Tangivale, 147
Konaʻī, Uiketolu, 210
Kongaika, ʻIsileli, xxxi, xxxiii, 9, 158–159
Kongaika, Luʻisa Palauni, 12, **69,** 141–144, 158–159, 160, **255**
Kongaika, Mele, 211
Kongaika, Sioeli, **136**
Kongaika, Sione, 211
Kongaika, Viliami (Vili), **136,** 141–144, 158–159, 160, **255**
Kongaika, Viliami F., **255**
Kotu (Hp), 277
Koulo (Hp), 193, 194

L

Laaʻiafi, Kēlepi Ikatauʻimoana, **136,** 153, 161, **204,** 210, 211
labor missionaries. *See* building missionaries.
Laie Hawaii North Stake, 79
Laie Hawaii Stake, 257
lakalaka, 21, 67
Lakepa (Tpu), xxx

Lane, Rex, 174, 175
Langi, ʻAkesa, **204**
Langi, ʻAna Tuʻifeleʻunga, 160, 162
Langi, Kingi Mosaia, 299, 300
Langi, Mosese, xxvii, xxviii, xxix, xxxi, 151, 153, 154, **204**
Langi, Paula, xvi, 58, 106, 113, **310**
Langi, Pauline, **199**
Langi, Saia, 114, 160, 162
Langi, Sione ʻIufoni, 136, 210
Langi, Taniela, 162–164
Langi, Taukolo, 160–161, 162–164
Langi, Temalisi, 162
Langi, Timote, xvi
Langi, Uinise Tuaʻone, xxxiv
Langston (missionary), xv
Lao, Sāteki, **138**
Laomakeʻi, Katalina, **201**
Lasson, Carol Jensen, xxxiv, 43
Latai, Nukuʻalofa, 192, 219, 265
Lātū, Helen Kaleialoha Kaneakua, 264–265
Lātū, Kahealani, 265
Lātū, Kalatiola, 54, 55
Lātū, Maamaloa, **136**
Lātū, Sifa ʻAuka, 296–297
Lātū, Sione Tuʻalau, xxvii, xxviii, xxix, xxxii, 31, 195, 235, **252, 258,** 264–266
Lātū, Vai Iloamanu, 73, 145
Lātūkefu, Sione, 2
Lavaka, Falakiko, 294, 295
Lavaka, 127
Lavaka, Mele, **69,** 211
Lavaka, Tēvita, 211
Lavaki, Stella, **204**
Lave, Kitione, 172, 173, 175, 176
Lavengatonga (Tpu), xxxi
Lavulo, Fīnau Malakai, **69**
Lavulo, Māhanga, **136**
Lavulo, Paula Tuʻiʻonetoa, **136**
Lavulo, Tovi, 183

Index

Law, Reuben D., 15
Leavitt, Lawrence, **41**, 75–76
Leavitt, Mary Ann, **41**, 75–76
Lee, Victor, xvii
Leimātuʻa (Vv), xxiii, 97, 186
Lever Brothers, 96
Liahona School, xx, xxi, xxiii, xxv, xxviii, xxx, xxxii, 12, 17, 20, 21, 68, 81, 82, 101, 127, 134, 143, 147, 169, 178, 181, 182, 188, 199, 206, 212, 222, 240, 243, 244, 274, 275, 312
Liahona Ward, xxvii
Lifuka (Hp), xvi, xxi
Likiliki, ʻAisake, 211
Likiliki, Tēvita, **208**
Lindholm, Sherman, xxviii
Lindsay, Kenneth Powell, xxiv, xxv, xxxiv, **199**, 275
Lisala, Kalolaine, 287, 288, 289
Lisala, Litiana Ngaluafe, 286–289
Lisala, Muli, 9, 14, 286–289
Lisala, Sikāhema, 287
Lofanga (Hp), xxix, 286, 288, 296
Lolohea, Fīpē Tonga, **134**
Longden, John, xxiv, 20, 21
Longden, LaRue C., xxiv
Longolongo (Tpu), xxx
Longomapu (Vv), 236
Losa, 46
Lotofoa (Hp), xxix
Lotulelei, Sefanaia, **204**
Luani, 24
Lulunga (Hp), 208, 235, 275, 277, 290, 294
Lund, Anthon H., 44
Lutui, Edith, 223
Lutui, Mele, **256**
Lutui, Mele Kafoʻatu, 223
Lutui, Mele Tafuna, 221–225
Lutui, Samisoni, 223
Lutui, Seisela, 225
Lutui, Tevisi, xiii
Lutui, Vaikalafi, xxviii, xxix, xxxi, 221–225, **256**, **258**
Lutui, Whitikei, 223

M

Maʻafu, Same, **204**
Maʻafu, Sione, **204**
Maʻake, Sione, **204**
Maʻake, Tiu, **204**
Maʻasi, ʻAlisi, 187
Maʻasi, Kalisi, 187
Maea, 218
Mafi, Filimone, **202**
Mafi, Kalisi, **202**
Mafi, Maʻake, 211
Mafi, Mele, **202**
Mafi, Seini, **69**, 211
Mafi, Taufuʻi, **202**
Mafi, Tēvita, **202**
Mafi, Tuʻipulotu, 27, **202**
Mafileʻo, Mele, xxix, 277
Mafileʻo, Solomone, 277
Mahuʻinga, Mele, 194, 210
Mahuʻinga, ʻŌnita, 192, 194
Mahuʻinga, Tēvita, 192, 194, 195, 210
Mahuʻinga, Tēvita Folau, xxvii, xxviii, 12, 14, 192–195
Maile, Kitione, 9, 13, 31, 57, 113, **308**, 313
Maile, Lisiate Talanoa, xvi, xx, xxiv, 31, 58, 152, **313**
Maile, Lose Feleti, 57
Maile, Mele, 148
Maile, Pī Feleti, 9, 57–59
Maile, Sēmisi, 148
Maile, Sione Vailiki, 148
Maile, Siosaia, xvii
Maile, Tēvita, xvii
Maile, Vaisa, 58
Mailefihi, Tungī (consort), 28, 309
Makaafi, Lātū, 14, 210, 211, **136**

Makaafi, Moala, 210
Makamaile, 75
Makave (Vv), 185
Makeke (Tpu), xxx, 51, 185, 195
Makeke School, xvi, xvii, xviii, xix, xx, 14, **65**, 77, 79, 83, 93, 97, 101, 141, 167, 181, 185, 221, 274, 275, 282, 292, 312
Makeke School Board, xvii
Makogai, Fiji, 97
Mākoni, Viliami, **258**
Malapo (Tpu), xix, xxx, 292
Malapo Ward, 292
Malekamu, Tupou ʻAhofaiva, 210, 211
Malinoa, 275
Mālohifoʻou, ʻAna Toki, 12, 18, 226–228, **255**
Mālohifoʻou, Tonga Pōteki, xxiv, 12, 13, 226, **255**
Malupō, 24, 106, 107
Malupō, ʻAlifeleti (Alfred), **257**, 298, 312
Malupō, Lesieli, xix
Malupō, Paula, xix, 31, **312**
Malupō, Selita Valu, 106
Manisela, Filisone, xvi
Manti Temple, 99
Manwaring, Enoch LaVell, 178–180, 212
Maori Agricultural College, 65, 83, 96, 312
Mapa, Penisimani (Peni) Lātūsela, xix, xxiv, xxvi, xxvii, 151
Mapa, Tēvita, xviii, xix, xxvii, **71**, 102
Mapa, Tuavavaʻu Mataele, **201**
Mapa, Uatahausi, xxvii, **135**
Māsila, Havea, 13
Masilamea (Tpu), xxiv
Masiu, ʻAlisi Pahulu, **204**
Masiu, Simote Fehoko. *See* Fehoko, Simote.
Mataele, ʻElenoa Mē, 60–62, 184
Mataele, ʻInoke, xx, **67**, 114, 210
Mataele, Lolohea, 60
Mataele, Maʻasi, **207**
Mataele, Maile, xxii, xxiii, xxiv, 31, 37, 48, **202**
Mataele, Sio Tuʻilatai, 308
Mataele, Sione Lolo Manaʻia, 60–62
Mataele, Siosaia, xiv, xxiii, 28, **37**, 60, 140, **308**
Matahau (Tpu), xxii, 147, 185, 244
Mataika (Vv), xiv, xvi, xxxii, 244, 286
Matangiake Ward, xxvii
Matavaimoui, Nukuʻalofa (Tpu), xv, 71, 79, 210, 211, 292
Matelau, Tuiʻone, xxiv
Matoka, 53
Matua, Pauliasi Fua, **38**
Matuku (Hp), 211, 277, 290, 294, 295
Maʻu, Sione. *See* Tomasi, Sione Maʻu.
Maʻufanga (Tpu), xiv, 48, 58
Maʻukavaongo, ʻIlaise, 221
Maxim, Joey, 174
May, Stirling Ivie, xv, **39**, 52
McBride, Don C., 49
McKay, David O., xxii, xxiii, xv, 11, 15, **38**, 103, **131**, 165, 192
McKay, Emma Ray Riggs, **131**
McKay, Heber J., xiv, 52
McMurray, Lynn, xxxiii
Meister, Don, 175
Melchizedek Priesthood, xv, 6, 13, 14, 54, 86, 88, 93, 108, 109, 110, 111–112, 119, 182, 184, 211, 227, 228, 307
Mendenhall, Wendell B., xxii, xxiii
Merrill, Olonzo, xiii, 6, **35**
Methodist Church. *See* Wesleyan Church.
Miller, Scott, 107
Misi Sēmisi. *See* Cutler, Newell J.
Missionary Training Center, xxi, xxxi, xxxii, 78, 249, 274
missionaries, LDS. *See also* conversion experiences, fasting, gift of tongues, gift of translation, persecution, prayer, priesthood blessings, testimony, Tongan missionaries.
– aid by non-members, 8–11, 189–190, 235–236

Index

- answers to prayers, 296–297
- culture shock, 16–21, 73–78
- foreign missionaries, xiii, xvii, xviii, xx, 5, 7, 9, 10, 13, 21, 48, 58, 73, 107, 109, 158, 259, 275
- guidance and protection, 155–157, 167–172, 233–234, 270–271, 279–281, 294–295
- obedience and sacrifice of, 11–12, 150–154, 184–191
- persecution, 124–127, 236
- perseverence of, 60–62, 73–78, 116–117, 229–232
- preaching, 21–22, 147–148
- service of, 57–59, 60–62, 173–177

Mitchell, Brother, 98
Moala, Ma'ata Hafoka, **204**
Moala, Senili, 263
Moehau, Folau, 14, **249**, 270, 271, 282, 283, 284
Moffat, Riley, xxxiv
Mokofisi, Malakai, 212
Mōleni, Siaosi, **258**
Mōleni, Sione, xix
Moli, 'Alofanga, 301–304
Moli, 'Ana, 301
Moli, Makaneti, 303
Monson, Thomas S., xxvi, xxvii, 213
"Monū Ka Ko Ha Monū Ne Tō" ("How Blessed the Gift Bestowed"), 308
Mormon Church. *See* Church of Jesus Christ of Latter-day Saints.
Mormon exclusion law. *See* Passport Act, 1922.
Moroni, 294
Mortensen, Ronald, **199**
Morton, Ermel J., xviii, xxi, xxii, xxvi, xxxiv, 2, 31, 65, **68**, 70, 71, 101–105, 132, 212
Morton, Lena, xxi
Motu'apuaka, 28, 61
Motu'apuaka, Hola Mataele, 28, 29, 61–62
Motuliki, Sēmisi, 259, 260
Moulton, James Egan, 3, 103
Mo'unga'one (Hp), 211

Mu'a (Nf), 118, 125
Mu'a (Tpu), xiii, xiv, xvi, 4, 6, 292, 309
Mu'a chapels, 72, **138**
Mu'amohōleva, Filimone Tupou, **138**, **309**
Mu'amohōleva, Tavake, **138**
Murdock, David, **200**
Muti, Ma'ake, **258**
Muti, Meleseini, 169
Muti, Mosese Lui, xx, xxvi, xxvii, 8, 11, 14, 31, 150, 167–172, 174, 176, 210
Muti, Penisimani, xxix, xxxi, **258**
Muti, Salavia, 11, 167–172, 174, **201**
Muti, Sini, 172
Mutual Improvement Association, xvii, 134

N

Naeata, 'Akanesi Hikilā, 184, 190
Naeata, Fakaola, 188
Naeata, Lenisi Vea, 240
Naeata, Ma'ata, 242
Naeata, Mosese, xxx, 11, 14, 184–191, 212, **258**
Naeata, 'Ofa, 186, 187, 188, 189
Naeata, Sālome Wolfgramm, 85
Naeata, Siosifa, 31, 85, 184, **307**
Naeata, Tomasi, 185, 190
Naeata, Tonu, 14, 51, 240–242
Naeata, Vika, 186
Naeata, Viliami, 185, 186, 187, 188
Nafualu College, 274
Nakolo (Tpu), xvii, 79, 80, 194, 309
Nāpa'a, 151
National Championship Rugby team, 190
Nau, Manase, xxiv, 11, 84, 150–154, **200, 202, 207**
Nau, Mele, 84
Nau, Salina, 11, 150–154
Nau, Sione, 151, 274
Nau, Takilisi, 151

Navutoka (Tpu), xxviii
Neiafu (Vv), xiv, xvi, xviii, xxiii, xxx, **70**, 75, 85, 102, 227, 267
Neiafu Vavaʻu Tonga North Stake, xxix, xxxi, 240, 242, 301
Neiafu Vavaʻu Tonga Stake, xxviii, xxix, xxxii, 56
Neilsen, Vaughn, 244
Nelson, John Alexander, Jr., 13, 14, 43–47
Nelson, Vera Wilcox, 43
Nelson, Robert, xvii
New Zealand, xviii, 97, 166, 223
New Zealand Temple, xxiii, 12, 61, 95, 97, 143, 172, 174, 177, 193, **204**, 261, 262, 304
Ngatuvai, Moli, xxvii
Ngāʻunoho (Vv), xx, 185
Nielsen, Emma, **199**
Niko, Tēvita, xvi
Niu, 167
Niu, Maile, xxvi
Niu, Poasi, 6
Niuafoʻou (Tin Can Island), xiv, xix, 66, 118, 121, 122, 125, 127, 141
Niuatoputapu, xiv, xviii, 23, 60, 61, 62, 131, 185, 233, 234, 278, 279
Niue, xxii, xxiv, xxvi, 11, 166, 170, 171, 174
Niukapu, 25
Niumate plantation, xxiv
Niumeitolu, Siaosi, 194
Niumui, 52
Niupalau, Sitani, 209
Niuʻui (Hp), 168
Nomuka (Hp), xiii, xxix, 211, 277
Nuapapu (Vv), xxix
Nuku, 24, 25, 26
Nukuʻalofa (Tpu), x, xiii, xv, xvi, xxii, xxiii, xxiv, xxvii, xxviii, xxix, xxx, xxxi, xxxii, xxxiii, xxxv, 1, 10, 12, 16, 17, 23, 30, 37, 52, 53, 71, 74, 80, 96, 102, 115, 117, 141, 151, 158, 165, 181, 182, 184, 192, 216, 219, 233, 235, 238, 243, 249, 250, 252, 253, 259, 262, 264, 272, 282, 285, 294, 298
Nukuʻalofa Tonga East Stake, xxvii, xxviii, xxix, xxxi, 252, 298
Nukuʻalofa Tonga Eighth Ward, 259, 262
Nukuʻalofa Tonga Liahona Stake, xxix, xxx, 183, 256
Nukuʻalofa Tonga North Stake, xxx, 243, 249, 282, 285
Nukuʻalofa Tonga Second Ward, xxvii
Nukuʻalofa Tonga South Stake, xxvii, xxviii, xxix, xxxi, 233, 272
Nukuʻalofa Tonga Temple, xxii, xxix, xxx, xxxi, 12, **132**, 165–166, 195, 215, **249, 250, 251, 252, 253**, 262
Nukuʻalofa Tonga Third Ward, 216
Nukuʻalofa Tonga Stake, xxvii, xxviii, xxxi, 181, 250
Nukuʻalofa Tonga West Stake, xxvii, xxviii, xxix, xxxi
Nukuʻalofa Tonga Vainī Stake, xxx, 235, 292
Nukuʻalofa Ward, xxvii, 243
Nukuleka (Tpu), xxi, xxxi
Nukunuku (Tpu), xiv, xvi, xxi, xxiii, xxxi, 48, 49, 51, 57, 58, 308
Nukunuku Branch, 308

O

Oborn, Clermont A., xv, **39**
ʻOfa, ʻAmelia, 82
ʻOhonua (ʻEua), xxxi, 147, 149
ʻOkoa, Fifita, 209
" ʻOku Fafangu Mai ʻa e Ongoongolelei" ("The Gospel's Awakening"), 307
" ʻOku ʻi ai ʻi Maama ni ʻae Siasi Moʻoni" ("There Is One True Church in the World"), 307
ʻŌkusi, Luʻisa Haʻakeli, 124
ʻOlive, Kaulave, xxvii
ʻOlive, Sēmisi Moʻunga, **138**
ʻOlive, Sione, **132, 138**

Index

'Olive, Ta Tapenisi, **138**
Olovaha, 270
Olsen, O. Wilford, xv, **41**
Olson (missionary), xiv
Olson, Ralph, xxii, xxiv, 13, 68, 310
Oriana, 262
Ormond (missionary), xiv
'Otea (Vv), xvi, xxiii, 24, 44, 52, 95, 99, 116, 189
'Otuafi, Fe'ofa'aki, **204**
'Otuafi, Nola Lātū, **204**
'Otualea (Vv), 96, 185, 187
'O'ua (Hp), xxix, 235, 277, 290
Overstreet, Nedra, xxxiv

P

Pacific Board of Education, xxiii
Packer, Boyd K., 215
Pago Pago, 43
Pakalani, Kepueli, **258**
Palauni, 'Alisi, 125
Palauni, Kalanite, **136**
Palauni, Lu'isa. See Kongaika, Lu'isa Palauni.
Palauni, Siaosi, xviii, **136**, 211
Palauni, Soko Siaosi, **69**, 211
Palei, 217
Palelei, Peauafi, 122
Pāletu'a, Lu'isa Hēhea Kona'ī, 209, 211, **249**
Pāletu'a, Milika Mafi, 209
Pāletu'a, Tonga Toutai, xviii, xxvii, xxx, xxxi, xxxii, 12, 14, 31, 178, **199**, 209-215, 249, **258**
Pāletu'a, Viliami, 109
Pangai (Hp), xiii, xxii, xxiii, 59, 111, 124, 141, 143, 153, 162, 185, 209, 271, 287
Pangaimotu (Vv), xxx
Paongo, Saia, 233-234
Papeete Tahiti Temple, 215

Parkin, Lewis B., xv, **41**
Parkinson, Reed, xvi
Pasi, Sione, **136**
Pasi, Sione Filipe, **136**
Pasi, Taniela, xxvii
Pasi, Viliami (Vili), xx, xxvi, xxviii, xxxi, **199**, 209, 210, 243, **258**
Pāsoni, Kami, xxiii
Passport Act, 1922, xv, 17, 73, 90
Paula, Sione, xiii
Pauni, Sione, xxi
Pauni, Tēvita Pita, xvi, xvii, xviii, 31, 51-54, 85, 86, **311**
Pea and Ha'ateiho Ward, xxvii
Penrose, Charles W., xxi, 44
persecution, 4, 6, 27, 124-127, 216-220
Petersen, Mark E., xxv
Phillips, Walter J., xv, **41**
Pickeral, Glen, 207
Pīkula, Pauliasi, xvii
pioneers, 43-47, 48-50, 305-313. *See also* prayer, missionaries.
Pipiena, Sangata, 51
Polynesian Cultural Center, 67, 95, 99, 140, **207**, 313
Polynesians, 22, 99
Pōme'e, Tautalanoa, 283
Pōme'e, Tēvita, 8, 282-285
Pope, Albert, xxvii, **199**, 240-241
Pō'uha, Sione, **202**
Pō'uha, Susana 'Auhangamea. See Kinikini, Susana 'Auhangamea Pō'uha.
Pratt (missionary), 52
prayer, 78, 79-81, 82-84, 136, 163, 164, 213, 214, 276. *See also* blessings by General Authorities, conversion, fasting, gift of tongues, missionaries, priesthood blessings, visions and dreams.
– for food, 233-234, 235-236
– for guidance, 237-239
– for healing, 287-289, 298-300
– for protection 162-164, 290-291
– for rain, 212-213, 296-297
– for restoration of life, 267-269

Presiding Bishopric Area Office, 264, 272
priesthood blessings. *See also* conversion, blessing by General Authorities, prayer, fasting and prayer, missionaries, visions and dreams.
– for controlling nature, 84, 226–228
– for restoration of health, 46–47, 53–54, 85–86, 87–89, 97, 145–146, 216–217, 237–239, 262–263, 286–289, 298–300
– for restoration of life, 22–23, 59, 93–94, 98, 111–112, 194–195, 109–111, 119–121, 241–242, 224–225
Primary, xiv, 52, 70, 131, 134, 181, 255
Princess Sālote-Pilolevu, xxxiii
Privy Council, 104
Proctor, Mervin, xvii
Pukotala (Hp), 286
Pule, Siosifa Tuʻiketei, xviii, xxii, xxiv, 31, **70**, 101, 102, 245
Pule, Sūlia Tuʻiketei, xix, **70, 201,** 210
Puli, ʻAmelia, 292
Puli, Samuela, 292
Pulotu, Ane Lupe Tuione, **69,** 211
Pulotu, Finehika Palauni, **201**
Pulotu, Kākolosi Tuiʻone, 200, 206, 208, **249,** 250, 251, 252, 254, 256, **258**
Pulotu, Sela, **69**
Pulotu, Taani, 151
Pulotu, Taufa Tuiʻone, **136,** 161, 193, 210, 211
Pulu, Tēvita, **136**
Pulu, Tupou, xxvi, 140
Pupu, Suiti, 296
Puta, Teu, 189
Pututau, Filiiku, 126, **204**
Pututau, ʻOfisi, xxv

Q

Queen Elizabeth II, xxvii, xxi
Queen Halaevalu Mataʻaho, x, xii, xxxiii

Queen Sālote Mafileʻo Pilolevu Tupou III, xix, xv, xviii, xxi, 25, 104, 124 134, 201
Queen Sālote College, 216

R

Rabone, Stephen, 3
Rallison, J. K., 39, 307
Rasmussen, Althen, xv, **41**
Relief Society, xiv, xvii, xix, **40, 69,** 70, 77, 92, 110, 131, **134,** 144, 145, 181, **201,** 216, 249, 255, 256
Richards, LeGrand, xxi, xxvii
Richards, Stephen L, 145
Robinson, George W., xv
Romney, Marion G., xxiii, 180, 192–193, 215

S

Saʻafi, Sione, **204,** 276
Saʻafi, Taisia, **204,** 276
Saile, Malekamu Kēlepi, 211
Sainehā High School, xxix, 51, 240
Sākisi, Sione, **138**
Sālote. *See* Queen Sālote Mafileʻo Pilolevu
Salt Lake City North Mission, 263
Salt Lake Temple, 226
Samoa, xvii, 51, 166
Samoan Mission, xiii, xiv, xix, xxvi, 7, 14, 43, 44, 46
Sandwich Islands, 102
Sanft, Faʻalupenga, xx
Sanft, Siale, 84
Sāpoi, 25
Sāteki, ʻAisea Pīkula, **258**
Sātua, 220
Satuala, ʻAla, **69**
Saulala, Sē, xiv, **307**
Schaumkel, Sione, **258,** 279, 280, 285

Index

Schwendiman, Fred W., **204**
Schwendiman, Lillian A., **204**
Seely, George, xiv
Sēkona, Fine, 87
Sēkona, Makeleta, 87
Sēkona, Nanasi Fine, 140
seminary, xxiv, xxv, xxix
Sēmisi, Misi. *See* Cutler, Newell J.
Senituli, Manuoso, **138**
Sevelio, Father, 51, 52
Shumway, Carolyn Merrill, xxxi, xxxiv, 30
Shumway, Eric B., xi, xxxi, 9–10, 16–32, 199, 201, **202**, 219, 228, 288, 300
Sifahenga, 172
Sika, Kāsimia, xviii
Sika, Sēmisi, xviii
Sika, Sioeli. *See* Kauvaka, Sioeli.
Sika, Sione, xxvii
Sika, Viliami, xxvii, xxviii, xxix
Sikalu, Soana Lātū, 235
Sikalu, Tēvita, 264
Simote, 'Ofa. *See* Fehoko, 'Ofa Simote.
Simpson, Robert L., xxx
Siola'ā, Sione, 209
Siosefa, 52
Sisifā, Mele, 6
Sīsilia, 217
Sitela, 172
Skinner, Duane, **199**
Smith, George Albert, xviii, **71**, 103, 108, 172, 179, 180
Smith, Jenny, xv
Smith, Joseph, 45, 46, 67, 106, 121, 125, 147, 149, 215, 218
Smith, Joseph F., 44, 102
Smith, Robert, xiv
Smith, Willard L., xv, 90
Smoot, Brigham, xiii, 5, 7
Solomon Islands, 274
Sonntag, Philip T., xxx
Sopu (Tpu), xxvii

Sorenson, Harvey G., xvi, **41**
Soukop, Kalo Mataele, 62, 140
South Pacific Area Presidency, xxx
Spencer, Franklin, 94
Spencer, Grant, 278
Spendlove, Elaine, 35
spiritual gifts. *See* gifts of the spirit.
Stapley, Delbert L., xxv
Stone, David, xxii
Stone, Fred W., xxii, xxiii, **131**, 162, 169, 170, 180, 192
Stone, Sylvia, xxii, xxiii
Stubbs, Verl, xvii
Suli, 153
Suluka, Fīnau, 117
Suva Branch, xix
Suva, Fiji, xxiii
Sydney Australia Temple, 215

T

Ta'anea (Vv), xxvii, 9
Tāfahi (Ntt), 301
Tāfisi, Sela, 12, 13, 216–220
Tāfisi, Sifa, 216–220
Tāfisi, Viliami, 219
Tafuna, 'Olotomu, 211
Tafuna, Tēvita Fīnau, xviii, **136**, 161, 209, 211
Tafuna, Vāvasa, 221
Taimani, Alaimaluloa, **201**
Taimani, Kale'anga, **138**
Taimani, Mauloa, **138**
Taimani, Tēvita (of Mu'a), **138**
Taimani, Tēvita (of Lulunga), 294–295
Taimani, Tokilupe, **138**
Talafo'ou (Tpu), xxviii, 211
Talai, Palu, **69**
Talakai, Siaosi Loiti, xix, xx, xxiv, **202**
Talakai, Sulieti Laa'iafi, **69**
Talanoa, Mele, **204**

Talanoa, Pōsesi, 237
Talanoa, Sione, **204**
Tali ʻEva, 260
Talihau (Vv), xxxi, 189
Talikavili, 52
Talikavili, Lupe, 53
Talivakaola, Feʻao, xxxii
Tangi, Viliami, 268
Tangitau, Vaea, xx
Tangitau, Vuki, xxix
Tanita, 172
Tanner, Nathan E., 215
Tapa, Sione, 61
Tapu, ʻAmelia, **69**
Tapuhia, 52
Tatafa, 107, 111, 168
Tatafu, Viliami, 227
Tatakamotonga (Tpu), 195, 280
Tau, Lītani Vili, 164
Tau, Tēvita Fatogia, 49
Taufa, Sione, xvi
Taufa, Tēvita, 245
Taufaʻahau. *See* King George Tupou I.
Taufaʻahau. *See* King Taufaʻahau Tupou IV.
Taufuʻi, 218
Tauia, 172
Taukolo, Kisione, 237
Taumoepeau, Mateʻi, 210
Taumoepeau, Sēmisi, xxi, 101, **199**
Tausinga, 116
Tautuaʻā, Kouli, 193, 275
Tavake, Seini, **138**
Tavake, Tītali, 61
Tavalu, Peni, **136**, 161
Tāvutu, Vaikato, 69, 178–180
Taylor, Henry D., xxvii
Teacher Training College, 210
Teʻekiu (Tpu), xxvii
Tefisi (Vv), xvi, xxix, 48, **200–201**
temple experiences, 143–144, 165–166, 173–177, 192–195, 259–262, 298–300. *See also* individual temples by name, and missionaries, prayer, priesthood blessings, testimony, visions and dreams.
Tenney, William, **138**
testimony, 5–9, 19–20, 29–32, 46, 99–100, 103, 122–123, 168–169, 221–225, 259–263, 301–304
Teutau, Lupe, 210
Tew, Earl, 94
Thomas, John, 3
Tin Can Island. *See* Niuafoʻou.
tithing, 77, 79–80, 245, 224, 245, 261
Toa, 164
Toʻangutu, Meleana, **69**
Tofoa (Tpu), xxxi
Tofua, 16, 75, 97, 170
Toitau, Malia Tuiono, **138**
Toki, Laukau, 22, 23
Toki, Sāmiu, 22, 23
Tokomololo (Tpu), xxvi, xxvii
Tokomololo Ward, xxvii
Tola, 244
Toliai, Henelē, 49
Toloa, 282
Tolutaʻu, Talikavili, **208**
Tomasi, Mele Maʻu, **310**
Tomasi, Sione Maʻu, 16, 274, **310**
Tōnē, Seini, **40**
Tonga College, 125, 209, 210
Tonga Defence Force, 280
Tonga, Fīpē, **204**
Tonga, Manase, 209
Tonga Mission/Tonga Nukuʻalofa Mission, xiv, xxiii, xxv, xxvii, xxviii, 16, 31, 44, 174, 249, 256, 264, 294
Tonga, Motulalo, 87, **202**
Tonga, Peni, **132**
Tonga, Sela Pulu, xix, 119, 125, 126, **134**, **204**
Tonga, Sēmisi Nukumovahaʻi (Vahaʻi), xix, xxxi, 31, 101, 119–121, 124–127, **134**, **199**, **204**, **258**
Tonga, Tēvita, 124
Tonga, Timani, **258**

Index

Tongaleleka (Hp), 59

Tongamamaʻo (ʻEua), xx, xxviii, 221

Tongamamaʻo (Nf), 126

Tongan missionaries, xxix, xxx, 9, 11, 21, 30, 32, 59, 148, 158, 165, 169, 189, **206,** 296

Tongan Saints, 11, 12, 14, 15, 18, 21, 26, 30, 31, 43, **71,** 102, 173, 215; women, 12, 60, 77, 82–84, 141, 142, **201, 206,** 210–211

Tongaʻonevai, Taliaʻuli, **258**

Tongatapu, 215, 256

Toutai, Piliote, 25

Toutai, Sālesi, xvi

Tovo, Fatai, **204**

translations, of Book of Mormon, xviii, xix, 102–105; of Doctrine and Covenants, xxii, xxiv, 24, 312; of pamphlets, xxi; of Pearl of Great Price, xxii, xxiv, 312

Trueblood, Mary, **199**

Tuʻanekivale (Vv), xx

Tuʻanuku (Vv), xxiii, 48, 109, 236, 302

Tuaʻone, Epalahame Kumā, xvii, xxii, 113–117

Tuaʻone, Kalisi, 116

Tuaʻone, Lilevai, 67, 113–117

Tuaʻone, Metuisela, 113, **309**

Tuaʻone, Sūnia, 116

Tuaʻone, Viliami, 116

Tuavao, Kēlepi, xxiv

Tufui, 209

Tuʻi Kanokupolu, 3, 4

Tuiʻāfitu, 24

Tuiaki, ʻIsileli Lolo, xxix, xxxi, 14, **136,** 147–149, **258**

Tuʻiʻāsoa, ʻAtonio, xix, xx, xxii, xxvii, 101, **199**

Tuʻifua, ʻUluʻamū, xxix, xxxi, **258**

Tuʻihalangingie, ʻAisake, **202**

Tuʻihalangingie, Leni, 12, 14, 259–263

Tuʻihalangingie, Losaline, 259

Tuʻihalangingie, Nanisi Hafoka, 259, 261–262

Tuʻihalangingie, Siosaia Lātū, 259, 261–262

Tuʻihalangingie, Taina, 261–263

Tuʻikolongahau, Sione, **307**

Tuʻikolovatu, Senivia, 13, 181–183

Tuʻikolovatu, ʻUiha, xxxi, 181–183, **250, 258**

Tuʻileʻila, Lanipaka, **136**

Tuʻileʻila, Tema, **69**

Tuiolo, 172

Tuiono, Malakai Lomu, 209

Tuita, 24. *See also* Princess Sālote-Pilolevu.

Tuita, Maʻulupekotofa (consort), xxxiii

Tuʻivai, Simeni, xxxi, **258**

Tuʻivakanō, 24, 49, 50, 57

Tukikava-ʻi-Falelahi, Mele Lea-ʻa e-Maka, 97

Tukuafu, 164

Tukuafu, Irene Clare Holmes, 237–239

Tukuafu, Losimani Mafi, **202**

Tukuafu, Salelei, **202**

Tukuafu, Tomasi, 237–239

Tungī. *See* King George Tupou IV.

Tungua (Hp), xxxi, 235, 275, 276, 277

Tupou, Filimone, xvi

Tupou I. *See* King George Tupou I.

Tupou II. *See* King George Tupou II.

Tupou III. *See* Queen Sālote Mafileʻo Pilolevu Tupou III.

Tupou IV. *See* King Taufaʻahau Tupou IV.

Tupou, Manukia, 190

Tupou, Mele, 49

Tupou, Sione ʻOleli Piutau, 292–293

Tupou, Siosaia, xxi

Turner, Nathaniel, 3

Tyler, Arlene, **138**

Tyler, V. Lynn, xxxiii, xxxiv, 35, 138, **199, 204**

typhoid fever, xv, xvii, 114, 222

Tyson, Jean, **199**

U

'Uasikē, Suliasi, **258**
Uasila'ā, Ana, 53
Uasila'ā, Pelepetua, 53
Uasila'ā, Samisoni, xxix, xxxii, 53, 56, **258**
Uasila'ā, Talitaufa Vaha, 55–56
Uasila'ā, Viliami, 53, 54
Uata, 'Uliti, xxvi, xxvii
Uhi, Sēmisi, 263
'Uiha (Hp), xvi, xxiii, 10, 58, 106, 108, 114, 163, 164, 167, 168, 178, 221, 222, 290, 291, 310
'Uluaki'ahoia, Mafua, xxi
'Ulu'ave, 'Emeline, 121, 122
'Ulu'ave, Pita Seti, 119
'Ulu'ave, Sailosi, 122
'Ulu'ave, Sālome, 12, 13, **66**, 118–123
'Ulu'ave, Solomone, **66**, 118–123, 126
'Ulufonua, Sione, xvii
'Ulukālala, 24
'Ulukālala, Fīnau, 3
'Unga, Malakai Manu, xxiv, 21
'Unga, Meliame A., 309
United States, xv; Peace Corps, 16, 26, 279; soldiers, xviii, xix, 86, 87
Uoleva (Hp), 163, 168, 169
Uonuku (Hp), 290
'Utui (Vv), 185
'Utungake (Vv), xxix, 52
'Uvea, 51

V

Vaea, xxv, 24
Vaenoka, Lesitelo, **136**
Vaha'i, 24
Vainī (Tpu), xxiii, 102, 229, 257, 312
Vaiola Hospital (Tpu), 267, 289
Vaipapālangi, 76
Vaipoa (Ntt), xviii
Vaitai, Fakatou, xxii, xxiv, xxvi, 212, 275
Vaitai, Fanongonongo, xxx, xxxi, **258**
Vaitai, Kaliopasi, 82
Vaitai, 'Ofa, 84
Vaivela (Nf), 121
Vaka, Taipe, **258**
Vakalahi, Paula, 263
Vakaloa, Mafi, 267
Valahulu, Sione Fine, xvi
Vānisi, Meleane Siu, 79
Vānisi, Sālesi, xvii, 79–81, **309**
Vānisi, Similati, 79
Vānisi, Sione, 97
Vānisi, Vavalo, 79
Vaotu'u (Tpu), xxiv, xxvii
Vava'u, xiii, xiv, xv, xvi, xvii, xviii, xx, xxi, xxii, xxiii, xxiv, xxviii, xxix, xxxi, xxxii, xxxiii, 3, 9–10, 11, 12, 13, 14, 21, 24, 40, 51, 52, 53, 54, 55, 56, 58, 59, 70, 75, 77, 84, 85, 95, 96, 97, 99, 102, 109, 110, 111, 116, 147, 150, 151, 166, 171, 184, 185, 187, 188, 189, **199**, 200, **201**, 212–213, 215, 227, 236, 240, 241, 244, 255, 257, 267, 279, 286, 288, 307, 311, 312
Vava'u North Stake, 51
Vave, Tēvita, 142
Vea, Meleseini, **131**
Vea, Meleseini 'Ilo'ilo, **69**
Vea, Misitana, xvi, xvii, xx, xxii, xxiv, 31, **131, 199,** 212
Vea, Sione, xxi, **136,** 161
Vea, Teisa Mataele, 184
Vea, Tupou, 161
Veamatahau, Sioeli, 288
Ve'ehala, 24
Vehikite, 24
Vehikite, 'Ilisa, 87
Vehikite, Lesieli Tuita, **69**
Vehikite, Puli Tau, xvi
Vehikite, Samu, 87, 219
Vehikite, Sione Tuita, xvii, xix, xxii, **312**
Veitongo (Tpu), 57, 147, 221

Index

Vete, Hale, xxiv, **202**, 260
Vī, Peter, 3
Vīmahi, 'Alikisānita, xxvii, **199**
Vīmahi, 'Inoke, **136**
Vīmahi, Sione T., 212
visions and dreams, 19, 141–143, 178–180, 192–194, 218–220, 264–266, 276–277, 286–289, 298–300. *See also* conversion experiences, fasting, gift of tongues, missionaries, prayer.
Vivili, Paula, 279, 280
Vuki, Sione, 61

W

Wade, Alton, xxxiv, 190
Wainui, 5
Waipahu Stake (Hawaii), 257, 312
Watkin, James, 3
Webb, William, 3
Welker, James R., xiv
Wesleyan Church (Methodist), 3, 4, 28, 44, 91, 118, 119, 136, 210, 216, 243, 259, 264, 265, 274, 282, 292, 301, 302; missionaries, 1–7
West (missionary), 52
West, Thomas, 2, 3
Westover, Richard, **258**
Westoway (missionary), 52
White, Barbara, xxvi
White, Orson Hyde, xxvi, xxvii
Wiberg, Reuben M., xv, xvii, **39, 41,** 167
Winn, Frank, xiv, 31, 48, 58, 60
Wirthlin, Joseph B., 9, 298, 299
Wiser, C. C., 49, 58
Wishart, Alexander, xxi
Wolfgramm, 'Ana, 85
Wolfgramm, Charles (Siale) 'Ataongo, xvii, xxv, 14, 95–100

Wolfgramm, Ella, 84
Wolfgramm, Emil, xxv, 98
Wolfgramm, Emil Otto Fredrick, 95–96
Wolfgramm, Hāmani, xxxi, 212, 242
Wolfgramm, Hena Langi, 97–98
Wolfgramm, Herman, xvi
Wolfgramm, 'Iohani, 14, **66,** 82–89
Wolfgramm, Lataheanga, 95–96
Wolfgramm, Lili Taufa, **201**
Wolfgramm, Ma'ata, xvii, **40**
Wolfgramm, Mā'ele, **40**
Wolfgramm, Malina, 85
Wolfgramm, Meletoto Mu'a, 96–97
Wolfgramm, 'Osikā, 302
Wolfgramm, Otto, 97–98
Wolfgramm, Rudi (Luti), xx, 181, 182
Wolfgramm, Sālome **40**
Wolfgramm, Sālote, **66,** 82–89
Wolfgramm, Tisinā. *See* Gerber, Tisinā Wolfgramm.
Wolfgramm, Verna Davis, 99
Wolfgramm, Vuna, xviii
Wood, A. Harold, 2, 15
Woodworth, Charles "Chuck", xxii, xxviii, 171, 172, 173–177, **199**
Woodworth, Marsha, xxviii, **199**
Woolley, Mark, 52
World War I, 95
World War II, xviii, 86, 109, 210
Wright (missionary), xiv
Wright, W. Brent, 103, 104

Y

Year of the Lamanites, 214
Young, Huldah Parker, xxvi
Young, S. Dilworth, xxvi

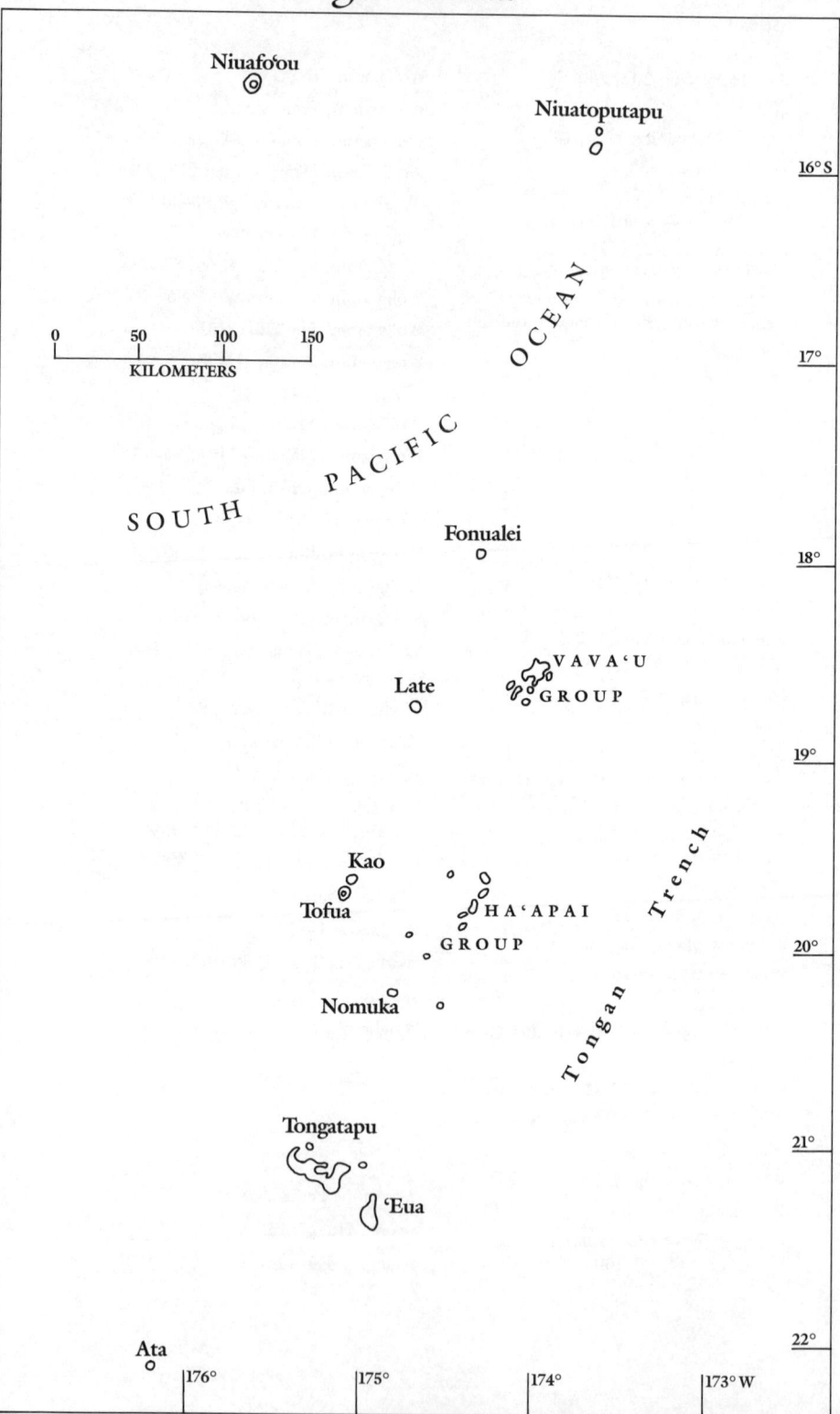

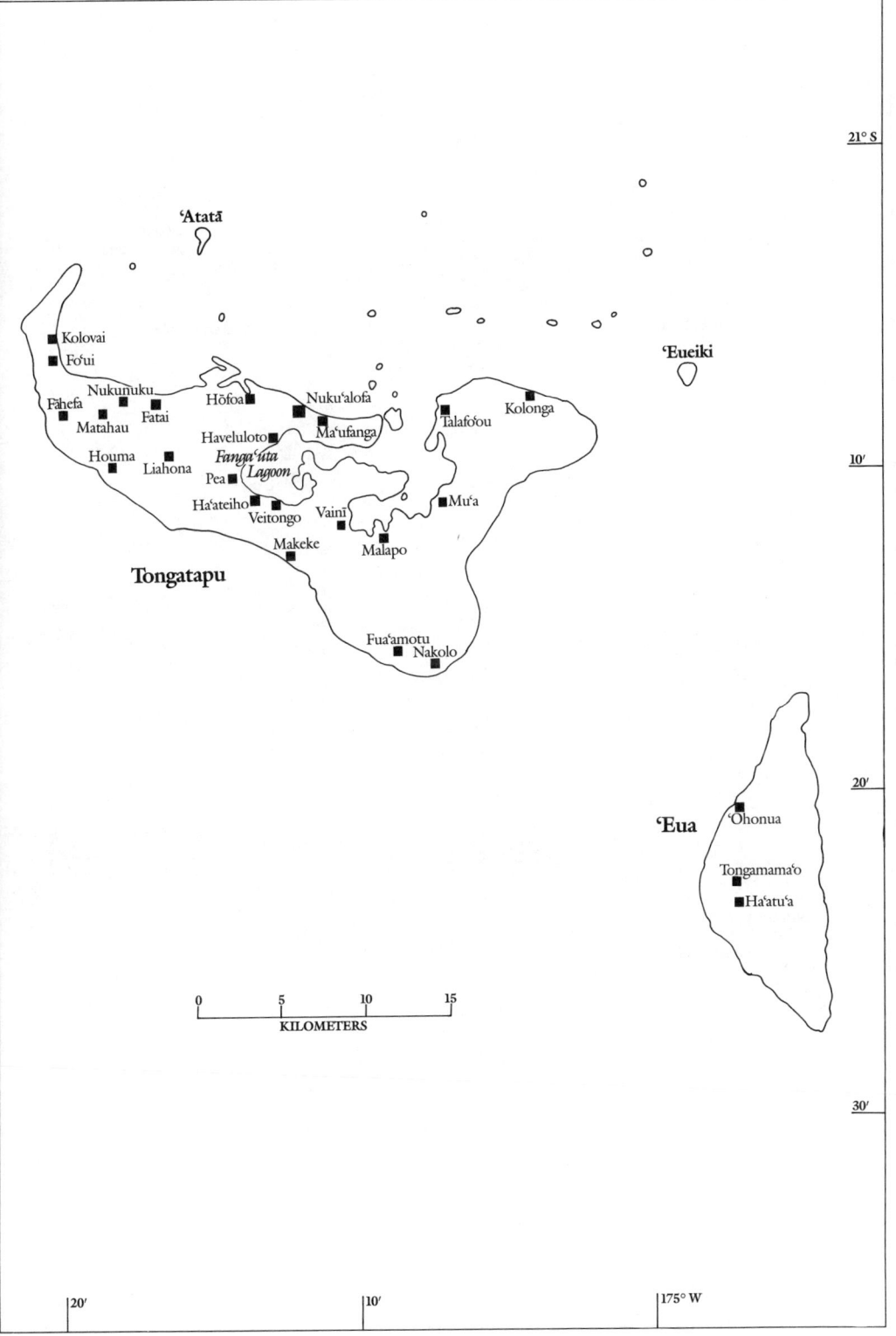

Ha'apai Group

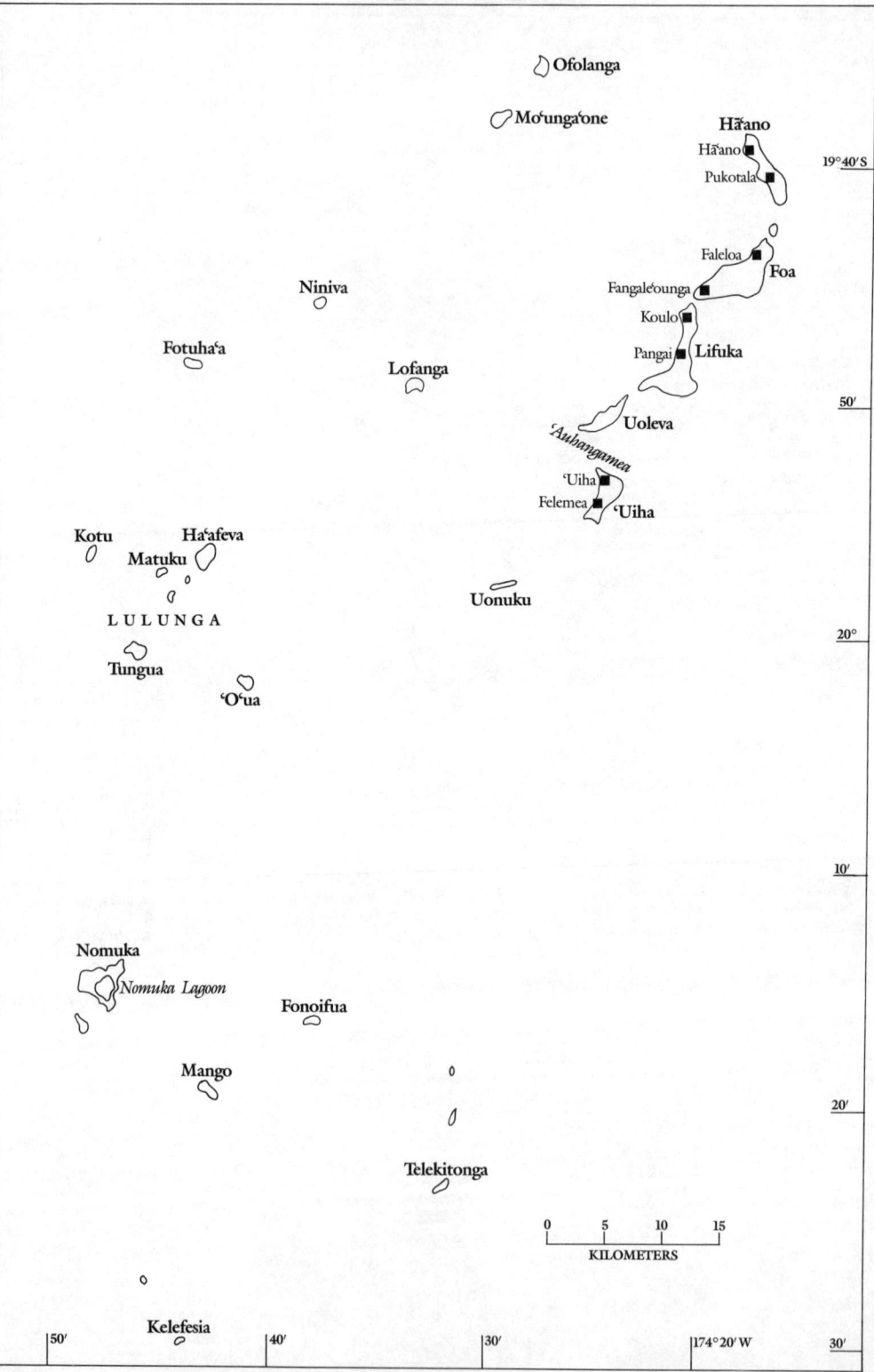

Niuafoʻou

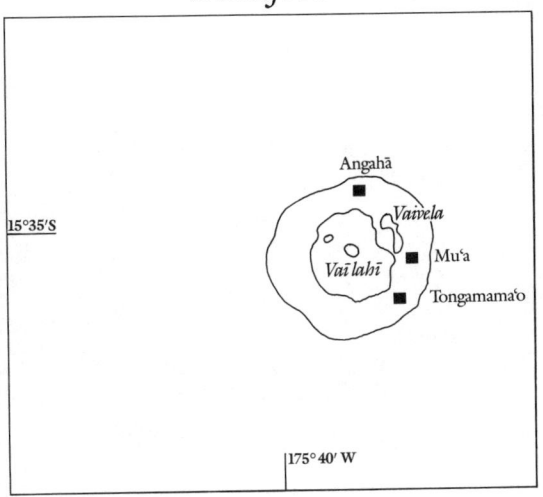

Niuatoputapu

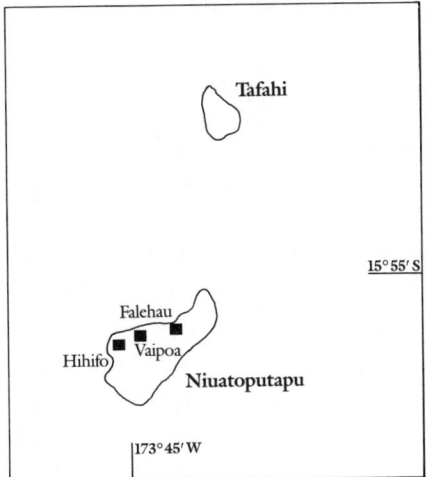

Vavaʻu Group

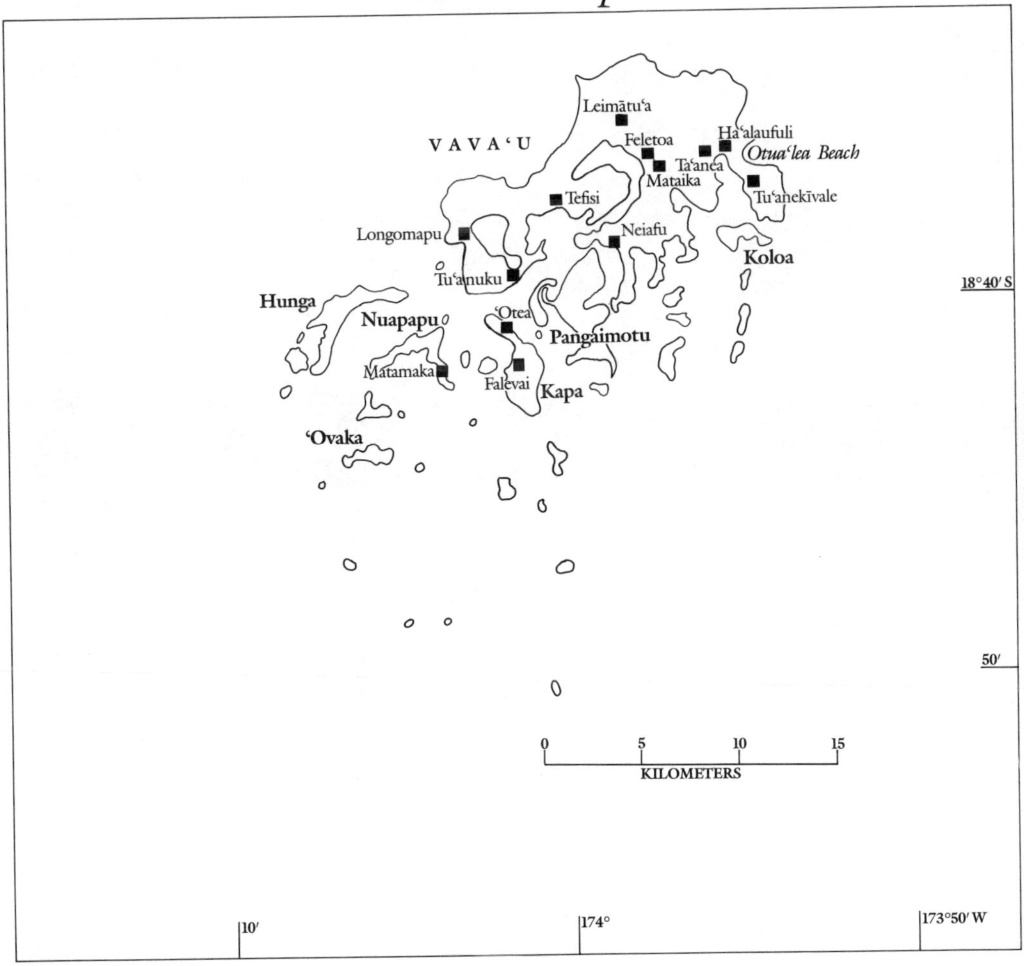

About the Author

Eric B. Shumway, president of Brigham Young University–Hawaii Campus, has an interest in Tonga that began with his experiences there as a young missionary more than thirty-five years ago. His love for the Tongan people, his expertise at their language, and his immersion in their culture earned him the chiefly title of *Faivaola* (One Whose Talents Produce Success). A native of St. Johns, Arizona, he earned B.A. and M.A. degrees in English from Brigham Young University (1964, 1966), and taught English at the Church College of Hawaii (1966–69). Taking a six-months leave from the college in 1967–68, he served as a language training coordinator and Tongan linguist for the United States Peace Corps.

After receiving his Ph.D. in 1973 from the University of Virginia (his dissertation was on the love poems of Robert Browning), he returned to BYU–Hawaii where he taught a wide range of English courses and courses in Tongan. From his interest in language emerged his *Intensive Course in Tongan* (rev. ed. 1988 by The Institute for Polynesian Studies, BYU–Hawaii), a text of 750 pages that Princess Sālote-Pilolevu Tuita praised in a warm foreword, adding, "Eric B. Shumway is the only papālangi I know that speaks Tongan so perfectly that even Tongans are baffled."

In 1976, Shumway chaired the convocation committee for the bestowal of an honorary degree upon the King of Tonga. After serving as a bishop, on the high council, and as stake president in Hawaii, he was called with his wife, Carolyn, and four of their seven children to Tonga to preside over the mission in 1986–89. He currently serves as high councilor in the Laie Hawaii stake.